Learning to Read and Write in the Multilingual Family

MIX
Paper from
responsible sources
FSC® C018575

PARENTS' AND TEACHERS' GUIDES
Series Editor: Colin Baker, Bangor University, UK

This series provides immediate advice and practical help on topics where parents and teachers frequently seek answers. Each book is written by one or more experts in a style that is highly readable, non-technical and comprehensive. No prior knowledge is assumed: a thorough understanding of a topic is promised after reading the appropriate book.

Full details of all the books in this series and of all our other publications can be found on http://www.multilingual-matters.com, or by writing to Multilingual Matters, St Nicholas House, 31–34 High Street, Bristol BS1 2AW, UK.

PARENTS' AND TEACHERS' GUIDES
Series Editor: Colin Baker, Bangor University, UK

Learning to Read and Write in the Multilingual Family

Xiao-lei Wang

MULTILINGUAL MATTERS
Bristol • Buffalo • Toronto

This book is dedicated to my multilingual children, Léandre and Dominique.
You are my inspiration for writing about multilingual topics.

Library of Congress Cataloging in Publication Data
A catalog record for this book is available from the Library of Congress.
Wang, Xiao-Lei
Learning to Read and Write in the Multilingual Family/Xiao-lei Wang.
Parents' and Teachers' Guides: 14
Includes bibliographical references and index.
1. Language acquisition–Parent participation. 2. Multilingualism in children. 3. Native language–Study and teaching. 4. Linguistic minorities–Education. I. Title.
P118.5.W364 2011
372.65′1–dc22 2011000617

British Library Cataloguing in Publication Data
A catalogue entry for this book is available from the British Library.

ISBN-13: 978-1-84769-370-9 (hbk)
ISBN-13: 978-1-84769-369-3 (pbk)

Multilingual Matters
UK: St. Nicholas House, 31–34 High Street, Bristol BS1 2AW, UK.
USA: UTP, 2250 Military Road, Tonawanda, NY 14150, USA.
Canada: UTP, 5201 Dufferin Street, North York, Ontario M3H 5T8, Canada.

The policy of Multilingual Matters/Channel View Publications is to use papers that are natural, renewable and recyclable products, made from wood grown in sustainable forests. In the manufacturing process of our books, and to further support our policy, preference is given to printers that have FSC and PEFC Chain of Custody certification. The FSC and/or PEFC logos will appear on those books where full certification has been granted to the printer concerned.

Typeset by Datapage International Ltd.
Printed and bound in Great Britain by the MPG Books Group Ltd.

Contents

Acknowledgements

Since the publication of my book *Growing Up with Three Languages: Birth to Eleven*, I have received lots of e-mails from parents. Many of them ask questions specifically about multilingual children's reading and writing issues. I have replied to some parents, but not to many others. This book can hopefully make up for those unanswered e-mails. The birth of this book is the direct result of those who wrote to me. Thank you!

Over the years, I have been fortunate enough to meet, in person and online, many parents who are raising multilingual children. The interactions and exchanges between us have helped me greatly in understanding various aspects of multi-lingual childrearing. Some parents I have been in contact with are featured in this book. I want to express my sincere thanks to them for allowing me to share their examples.

I am grateful to many people who have helped me with this book in direct and indirect ways. However, space limit only allows me to mention a few.

I especially want to thank my elder son Léandre for stepping up and offering his moral and editorial support for this book. As a high school freshman then, Léandre exhibited an unusual and unexpected maturity both in his critical and linguistic abilities. Even though time does not allow me to take into consideration all his revision suggestions, I wholeheartedly appreciate his efforts and intelligence. 妈妈真心感谢你的批评和建议! I will, however, incorporate all his brilliant suggestions in my future work.

I would also like to express my gratitude to the reviewer of the book for constructive comments, insightful suggestions and down-to-earth guidance.

I want to show my appreciation to the Pace University Kenan Scholarly Research Committee and School of Education Dean's Scholarship Committee for granting me course release time for this book project, to Sheila Hu of Mortola Library for her timely assistance in locating materials for this book and to my dear husband Philippe for his constant support on all fronts (intellectual, technological and domestic).

Several of my graduate assistants helped with this book project as well. Some of them deserve special mention for their contributions. Thanks go to Jennifer Argenta, June Hedley and Mary Rose Loverso for proofreading the book drafts at different stages and Li Huan and Zhao Jing for helping photocopy many materials needed for the book.

Finally, I would like to thank Multilingual Matters for giving me another opportunity to publish a book with them.

Chapter 1
Introduction

On a recent flight from Seoul to Shanghai, I sat near a 5-year-old Korean girl, Choon-Hee and her mother, Mrs Pak. The mother and daughter were on their way to join the girl's father in China. They planned to settle there because of Mr Pak's job relocation. During the nearly 2-hour plane ride, little Choon-Hee was keenly making drawings and experimenting with different ways of forming Korean *Hangul*[1] letters and *Hanja* (Chinese characters). From time to time, Mrs Pak modelled the details of how to write *Hangul* letters and *Hanja* strokes. The mother and the child seemed to enjoy immensely what they were doing.

Watching the interactions between Mrs Pak and her child, I realised that I was witnessing the little girl's multilingual[2] literacy[3] development in the making. I imagined that with this level of child engagement and with this level of parental support, Choon-Hee would certainly become multiliterate in the years to come.

However, as much as I was impressed with the mother-child enthusiasm and as much as I wanted to be optimistic about the girl's future multiliterate development, I could not help but worry if the child would remain so eager down the road and if the child's multilingual reading and writing skills would be thriving a few years from now. My seemingly pessimistic outlook for this child's future multilingual literacy development may not be entirely baseless. You will probably understand my concern after you read an e-mail that I received from a mother.

Dear Dr. Wang,

I am delighted to read your book *Growing up with Three Languages.*[4] I am grateful that you shared with us your experience in raising trilingual children. Like you, I am also raising a trilingual child in Italian, Dutch and English. My native language is Dutch and my husband's is English. We live in Italy. We have tried to teach our daughter Dutch and English at home because we don't have support in the community where we live. We didn't have problems getting her to speak the languages. When she was little, she was eager to learn to read and write in the two home languages. Now she is in elementary school and we have tremendous difficulties to get her read and write Dutch and English. She is just not interested. Tension has grown because we often nag her about reading Dutch and English books. The other day, she told me angrily why I bothered to request her to read English and Dutch. She said that she was reading Italian in school and that was enough! I don't know what to do. Should

---

I insist that my daughter read and write English and Dutch? This doesn't look like an option right now. Should I ask her to read one of the languages? I don't know any good strategies to involve my child. I am on the verge of giving up. But, I think it would be a pity! Dr. Wang, can you offer some advice?

Sincerely,

Anna[5]

Anna's frustration is not unusual. Many parents who attended my parents' workshops or corresponded with me have substantiated Anna's sentiment based on their experiences of raising multilingual and multiliterate children. Below are some of their challenges and concerns.

Challenges of Developing Multilingual Literacy

Time constraints

It takes a great amount of time for a child to develop reading and writing skills in one language. Needless to say, those children who grow up with more than one language require even more time to develop the skills in multiple languages. It is already difficult for busy parents to cope with the mundane routines of their everyday lives and it is even harder for them to find time to teach their children to read and write their heritage language.[6] Many parents commented that even though they wanted to engage their children in heritage language literacy activities, there was simply no time.

Moreover, there is always a competition between the time needed for heritage language literacy activities and the time needed for other events, such as sports, leisure and regular school assignments. Thus, the time constraint is often the major issue that prevents children from continuing with their heritage language literacy development.

Lack of pedagogical information

Parents who are determined to help their children develop heritage language literacy skills often have two options. First, there are community-based language schools.[7] When they are available and affordable, parents may choose to send their children to these schools. Alternatively, some parents opt to teach their heritage language literacy at home. The issue, however, is that most teachers who teach in the community language schools are parent volunteers[8] (I call them parent teachers). Even though some may be well educated, they have never gone through any teacher preparation programmes. Some of them simply teach by drawing on their recollection of learning to read as children.[9] As a result, many parent teachers may lack the skills necessary to engage their students. Even if some parent teachers had teaching experience in their heritage country, they may not be familiar with the teaching pedagogy in their current country of residence. Therefore, these parent teachers may not be quite aware that their students experience a different kind of world from that of their own.[10] Many parents who teach their children at home face a similar situation.

Hence, while almost all children are ready to learn, not all parent teachers are ready to teach. Consequently, many children grow exasperated and lose their motivation for heritage language learning. The lack of adequate heritage language teaching pedagogical skills of some parent teachers and parents may be one of the reasons why some children do not make progress or continue with their heritage language literacy development. Research has long indicated that teacher qualification is positively related to student achievements[11] and teachers and their teaching methods do matter.[12]

I want to stress that some parent teachers' lack of pedagogical information does not mean that all parent teachers in community language schools do not contribute to children's heritage language learning. Many of them have greatly contributed to children's success in their heritage language development.[13]

Conflicting teaching styles

The teaching styles of many teachers in community heritage language schools and parents are sometimes drastically different from the ones their children are used to. As a result, their teaching styles unintentionally conflict with their children's learning styles and hinder the children's heritage language literacy skill development. The following is a quote from a 10-year-old boy who attended a community Chinese language school in Montreal in Xiao-lan Curdt-Christiansen's study:[14]

> I don't like the Chinese school, it's boring and the characters are too difficult to remember. Plus, there is no action in the class. I feel like sleeping. But my mom says I have to go. I like action. But in the Chinese school, we are not allowed to do anything. We are not allowed to talk or to write except dictations. So all the Chinese I have learned, I forget it all when I come home. In my French school, we are allowed to make up stories, we can talk about our stories in front of the whole class, and the teachers are nice.

This boy's comments pinpoint the obvious differences in teaching styles between his teachers in the community language school and his teachers in his mainstream language school. It is clear that when children are not used to the teaching styles in their community language school or at home, their motivation to learn subsides. I have recently taken my two children out of a local Chinese language school for fearing that they would lose motivation to read and write Chinese because the teaching style there is drastically different from the one in their regular school.

Teaching materials are remote from children's lives

The literacy materials used by community language schools or parents are often textbooks imported from the heritage countries. Frequently, the contents and vocabulary in these textbooks are too remote from children's lives. For instance, a group of teachers in a Canadian community Urdu language school researched some Urdu textbooks and discovered that the reading materials from the heritage regions were full of political undertones and religious dogma too foreign for the children who grew up in Canada to relate to.[15]

A Chinese mother who attended one of my parents' workshops complained that her 12-year-old son refused to learn a poem from the Tang Dynasty.[16] The boy commented that he did not see any point in learning this poem because he had no place to use it. Despite his mother's good reasoning (she argued that it would help him appreciate the beauty of the Chinese language and culture), he remained unconvinced.[17] From his standpoint, the boy may be reasonable. Indeed, why should he learn a poem written hundreds of years ago that is so seemingly unconnected to his life?[18]

Research has shown that it is important how children connect to what they read.[19] As literacy experts Jo-Anne Reid and Barbara Comber rightly point out, children's learning from literacy events is contingent on their being able to make sense of the genre, content and social significance of the task at hand.[20] When the literacy materials are too remote from their reality, children are not motivated to read. In fact, using existing heritage language teaching materials that are not specifically intended for heritage language learners has generally been unsuccessful.[21]

Lack of practical advice books for parents

Despite the fact that there are many parenting advice books on how to raise multilingual children, few specifically address the reading and writing issues of multilingual children. Although some books may touch on these aspects, parents often find them too general and not practical. When parenting advice books occasionally do mention multilingual children's reading and writing, they tend to focus on young children and not on older children. Many parents like Anna (you read her e-mail earlier in this chapter) are desperate to find help in the parenting literature.

Lack of support

Ideally, to facilitate a child's multilingual literacy development, four elements must work together: family, school, community and society. However, children who grow up in a multilingual family rarely receive adequate support from the four milieux. The balance of power often tips heavily towards the mainstream language and literacy development. Few opportunities are offered for children to study their heritage language literacy outside their homes.[22] When school, community and society support for multilingual education is lacking or absent, the responsibility to help children develop multilingual literacy skills falls mostly on parents' shoulders.[23]

Purpose of the Book

The purpose of this book is to help parents explore various ways to make their children's multiliteracy development possible. Drawn on interdisciplinary research in multilingual literacy development as well as experiences of parents who have raised their children with multilingual literacy, this book walks parents through the process of multiliteracy development from infancy to adolescence. It identifies the target skills at each developmental stage and proposes effective strategies that facilitate multiliteracy development in the home environment.

However, I want to stress that this book does not intend to diminish the role of community heritage language schools or school heritage language programmes. I would be very happy to see parents working together with these education entities to promote their children's heritage language literacy development (see Chapter 7). Nevertheless, when many parents are currently left alone to shoulder the challenging task of teaching their children heritage language literacy without adequate school, community or societal support, this book can provide immediate help for them to bring up multilingual children.

This book can be used as a guide for home heritage language literacy teaching or as a supplement for those parents who send their children to heritage language schools. It can also be used as a reference for teachers who teach in community heritage language schools and in school heritage (or foreign) language programmes.

Targeted Child Population

This book focuses on typically developing children who are growing up in multilingual households. It excludes children with cognitive (intellectual) and language learning disabilities for two major reasons. First, within the multilingual child population, there is extraordinary variability with regard to the linguistic, social and cultural environments. It is already a perilous enough undertaking to address this diverse population without delving into the issue of disabilities.

Second and most importantly, the issues related to children with cognitive and language learning disabilities are complicated by the fact that many characteristics of these children cannot be generalised. It would not do these children justice if they were included in this book without enough research evidence to support the home teaching strategies for children with disabilities. However, Appendix A lists some useful references for readers who wish to explore the multilingual literacy development issues on children with cognitive and language disabilities.

Advantages of Teaching Children in the Home Environment

Although teaching children at home alone is not necessarily the most ideal learning environment, when parents cannot find a better solution to fit their needs, it is an option. If the right strategies are employed, there will be positive results associated with home teaching. Research has suggested that children who are home schooled in all the required school subjects tend to perform one grade level higher than their public and private school counterparts and they tend to achieve better educational outcomes. Likewise, research has confirmed that children who are home schooled their entire lives have the highest scholastic achievements.[24] In addition, long-term studies found no apparent social deficiency of home-schooled children.[25]

As of now, little research evidence is available to suggest the absolute advantages of teaching heritage language literacy skills in the home environment. However, studies conducted in different cultural communities have challenged the assumption that school-based literacy is the only legitimate way to engage children with heritage language literacy development.[26] There is evidence to suggest that when parents engage their children in heritage language literacy activities at home, children are likely to make headways in their heritage language literacy development.[27]

Thus, it is reasonable to postulate that children who are taught heritage language literacy skills in the home environment may benefit from the experience for at least the following four reasons.

Parent–child relationship

There is a special relationship between parents and children. The emotional bond established with parents can often motivate children to listen to their parents and learn from them.[28] Moreover, the nature of the parent–child interaction context enables parents to know about their children in ways that many others, including teachers, do not. Parents certainly have unique advantages in reaching their children over others.

In fact, the first literacy learning experience most children encounter is often provided by parents in the home.[29] A growing body of research has shown a close relationship between young children's early home literacy experience, their print knowledge, interest in reading[30] and their later engagement in independent reading.[31] Parental overall responsiveness and support in early literacy is the strongest predictor of children's language and early literacy skill development.[32]

Scheduling, location and content flexibility

Each family can set its own schedule based on their family situations. The spontaneous nature of home literacy activities means that learning can occur in the midst of everyday activities, such as mealtimes, shopping and travelling in the car. These kinds of literacy activities do not present an onerous time burden on even the busiest of parents.[33]

Children and parents can spend time flexibly on different language topics based on children's progress at their own pace. In addition, parents can use a variety of environmental prints,[34] such as food packages, newspapers, advertising flyers, magazines, religious texts, game or toy packages, television programme guides, shopping lists, letters, e-mails or text messages and catalogues, to initiate and carry out heritage language literacy activities.[35] These materials are often directly related to children's lives and tend to be more meaningful to children's learning.

Instruction adapted to individual needs

In the home environment, parents can focus more on children's individual language and literacy learning needs and adjust their teaching pace and method accordingly. Children can benefit from the extra time and learn well when their parents do not have to rush to finish a language-learning task before their children are ready.

Learning centred rather than grade centred

In the home learning environment, children are usually not formally graded or tested on their performance. They also do not have to worry whether they will be promoted to the next grade level if they do not do well. Children can therefore concentrate on the learning activities instead of being stressed with grades or tests.

In addition, parents can help motivate children by providing them with alternative forms of reinforcement or rewards, such as verbal praise or something that is related to children's immediate interests. For instance, my younger son Dominique[36] is a football (soccer) fan and an enthusiastic player. To motivate Dominique to read French (one of his heritage languages), my husband introduced him to online European football news. In doing so, Dominique realised that if he read French online, he would be able to get the European football news faster. Such intrinsic motivation (the internal desire to perform a particular task) tends to be longer lasting[37] than grades.

Given the above-mentioned home teaching advantages, teaching children heritage language literacy skills at home may present an attractive option for many families who wish to help their children develop multilingual literacy skills in addition to other possibilities.[38]

Benefits of Developing Multilingual Literacy

There are many benefits associated with developing and maintaining heritage language and literacy. As the well-known second language researcher Stephen Krashen and his associates pointed out, 'Heritage language development appears to be an excellent investment. For a small effort... the payoffs are enormous'.[39] Some benefits of being multiliterate are discussed below.

Benefits in everyday life and international travel

Knowing how to read and write in more than one language can provide convenience in everyday life as well as international travel. For example, once on a car trip to a conference in Utrecht (the Netherlands) from Neuchâtel (Switzerland), our French rental car displayed a French message on the front screen that the suspension was broken and service was needed immediately. Pressed for time to reach Utrecht that same evening, my husband and I were worried that we would not have time to drive the car to a garage and repair it before the conference. While driving, my husband asked our then 11-year-old son Dominique to read the French vehicle manual and figure out whether the electronic message was really true. After studying the French manual, Dominique concluded that if we restarted the car, the suspension would adjust itself. Dominique's ability to read French was obviously handy. We were able to make our Utrecht conference on time.

Similarly, when 20-year-old Marco from New York travels to his heritage country, Italy (Milan to be specific), he feels at home largely because he is literate in Italian. For example, he can read restaurant menus and find exactly what he wants to eat. He can read local newspapers and find out what's going on in town. He can read advertisements before he goes shopping. Most of all, he can keep in constant touch with his Italian relatives via e-mail communication while he is in New York.[40]

Benefits in academic learning

There is clear evidence that multiliteracy does not pose a major academic disadvantage to the individual. In fact, research shows that there is a very tangible academic payoff for those children who invest in heritage language learning.[41] There are, of course, multilinguals who do poorly in school, but there are more who do well. Research indicates that retention of the heritage language is related to better school success and better grade point average.[42] Children with more than one language have often been shown to outperform monolinguals in many cognitive tasks.[43]

Furthermore, in academic subject areas, children with more than one language have advantages in transferring their concepts from their heritage language to the mainstream language or vice versa.[44] Educators Debra Giambo and Tunde Szecsi gave a good example of this. They stated that understanding in a heritage language of how an electrical circuit functions, for example, is the same understanding in English (school language). When discussing or learning about such concepts in English, a child who is already familiar with the concept in his/her heritage language may only need to learn the new vocabulary to talk about the concept in English.[45]

Benefits in mainstream literacy development

Research shows that literacy in heritage language does not detract from children's mainstream school language literacy development and even supports school literacy development.[46] Frequently, those children who have developed heritage literacy skills progress more in their school literacy skills than those who have not developed heritage literacy skills.[47]

Heritage language literacy knowledge and skills can help children enrich their literacy experience in their mainstream literacy. Children can draw on their cultural and linguistic knowledge from heritage language literacy and use it as a starting point in their mainstream literacy. For example, the young writer of a ghost story can draw on knowledge of ghost stories from Bangladesh, while the writer of poetry can draw on rich imaginary and use of metaphor in Bollywood film songs or ideas from the Buddhist tradition about peace and harmony.[48]

Moreover, the ability obtained in the heritage language reading and writing process can help children participate in mainstream literacy events with a critical lens.[49] For instance, 5-year-old Kanya told her kindergarten classmates that her native Thai language book, *Snow White*, did not use the same words to describe Snow White as the English book.[50] At such a young age, Kanya has already formed emergent analytical (critical) abilities when reading books.

Thus, supporting children's home language and valuing their culture can actually enhance their mainstream literacy development.[51] Additionally, developing the attitude and disposition of a reader through the use of the heritage language can be carried over to the mainstream language.[52] A longitudinal (long-term) study of a 15-year-old boy named Gurdeep, who is bilingual in English and Panjabi, has shown remarkable literacy achievement in both English and his heritage language (Panjabi).[53]

Benefits in oral language development and other language learning

Research suggests that learning to read a language can facilitate the development of oral language proficiency.[54] Learning to read and write a heritage language can help children improve their spoken heritage language. I have noticed that my two children often 'import' the French vocabulary and sentences from their favourite French books to their daily French conversations.

Moreover, research has shown that reading can prevent children's attrition in their home language. For example, a study by Elena Zaretsky and Eva Bar-Shalom indicates that reading in children's home language, Russian, has lessened the degree of deterioration in that language.[55]

Research also suggests that mere oral proficiency in the heritage language might not affect either second or third language learning in a positive way. However, a strong positive effect of heritage language literacy knowledge in learning the third language is certain.[56] The metalinguistic ability (e.g. the ability to notice and analyse different language features) developed in the process of learning more than one literacy will facilitate the learning of additional languages.

Benefits in having access to heritage culture

Reading and writing a heritage language can help children from multi-heritage backgrounds gain access to the wealth of their heritage cultural resources[57] and enable them to examine the world from multiple perspectives. For example, in her social studies class, 14-year-old Adrienne could give a dynamic discussion on the early people of the Aegean by using information she read in her Greek heritage language books.[58]

Higher self-esteem and confidence

There is convincing evidence that children who are proficient in their heritage literacy tend to have higher self-esteem and confidence. For example, a study examining 1500 Chicano college students concluded that heritage language maintenance was not a problem but rather an advantage. Fluency in the heritage language was positively related to self-esteem, more ambitious plans for the future, confidence in achieving goals and the amount of control that subjects felt they had over their lives. All these factors were positively related to grade point average. All the participants in the study had very high competence in English.[59] Another study reported similar results: Mexican-American eighth graders who described themselves as biliterate had higher self-confidence than monoliterates (Spanish or English).[60]

In summary, as multilingual literacy expert, Charmian Kenner, remarked in her book, *Becoming Biliterate*, by helping our children develop multilingual literacy abilities, 'we will help children become accomplished communicators who can draw on a range of different culture experiences. These young people will grow up well equipped to benefit from and contribute to our complex global community'.[61]

Key Features of the Book

Treating parents as active partners

This book treats parents as active rather than passive consumers of information. I try to include you (from here on, I will use 'you' instead of 'parents' to involve you directly in the dialogue) as my partners in exploring heritage language literacy teaching issues through:

- inciting you to build on what you have already been doing;
- inviting you to think about the strategies suggested in the book by providing opportunities for you to practise and reflect on how to incorporate these strategies into your particular circumstance;
- motivating you to become reflective parents by keeping reflective journals so that you can systematically reflect on your teaching practice and adjust the strategies that best suit your children;
- encouraging you to treat the information I have provided as provisional and to search for new information to enrich your experiences.

Moreover, I have moved away from the common practice of parenting advice books to omit the original source of information. I intentionally kept the original references in the endnotes to give you a head start in case you want to purse further on these topics. I also purposefully included some terminologies (with explanations, of course) to help you get familiar with them in case you want to access research literature to learn more about a particular topic of interest.

Furthermore, I promote the idea of 'parent as a researcher',[62] that is, you are encouraged to experiment with your home teaching, reflect on what you do, be an active consumer of research information on multilingual children and find the best way to help your children.

Expanding the traditional definition of literacy

Traditionally, literacy has been regarded mainly as an individual's reading and writing ability.[63] In the past few decades, there has been a growing concern about the limitation and simplicity of this traditional view. This book recognises the changing dimension of literacy and pays attention to the multiple abilities that children need to function as literate people in the modern world. The activities suggested in this book reflect the contemporary understanding of literacy in several ways.

First, this book considers literacy as a social and cultural practice rather than a context-free cognitive achievement.[64] This implies that the beliefs and attitudes of participants (children, parents, other family and community members) and their *habitus*[65] (the lens through which people interpret and relate to the world[66]) play a central role in a child's literacy development process.[67] This also implies that what is considered an appropriate literacy activity is determined by its specific cultural or social context. Therefore, the activities suggested in the book value the different ways that parents and children practise literacy.

Second, this book treats heritage language literacy development and the dominant (mainstream) literacy development as a power relationship.[68] Conscious of this power relationship, the strategies and activities suggested in this book aim to help children negotiate between the different genres, styles and types of texts in the heritage culture and dominant culture by involving them in diverse reading and writing practices that are meaningful to them.[69]

Third, this book endorses the view that literacy includes other domains, such as visual, audio, spatial and behavioural.[70] The activities suggested in the book go beyond the traditional text form by including different communicative practices in children's lives, such as drawings, songs, sports, cartoons, movies, and talking while playing video games. Although these domains are not congruent with the traditional literacy, they nevertheless offer a good opportunity to use the materials and genres that children are familiar with and help them represent meanings in print. For example, research shows that children who play video games have a different way of developing texts. The structure of their stories tends to be recursive rather than follow the traditional story-telling style (beginning and ending).[71]

Moreover, the development of information communication technology has significantly changed the way we communicate[72] as well as the way we read and write. Reading and writing on the internet and through digital modalities require different ways of interacting with texts.[73] When we use the internet and other multimedia, we move away from the narrow, linear, print-only expectations of reading.[74] Today, both monolingual and multilingual children are living in a multimedia and digital world where ideas of reading and writing are carried out differently from the times when their parents were growing up. A *New York Times* article predicts that in a digital future, traditional textbooks could be history. Some educators have already noticed that children today do not engage with textbooks that are finite, linear and rote.[75] Thus, the activities suggested in the book go beyond the traditional paper-based texts,[76] and the attainment of the ability to use multimedia is treated as an integral part of multilingual literacy development.[77]

Finally, this book treats the ability to critique texts as equally essential as the ability to decode them.[78] Many researchers now believe that the ability to analyse texts should be a part of every child's literacy pathway.[79] The critical ability for multilingual children demands even sharper uses of critical lenses because they are crossing more than one cultural and linguistic ground.

In essence, to be literate in today's society means being able to engage in a range of literacy practices, drawing on different sets of skills and processes suited to those particular practices. Not being able to negotiate heightened and diverse literacies will certainly prevent our children from accessing a full array of life choices.[80]

Providing strategies with the support of children's developmental needs

The strategies recommended in this book are divided into several developmental stages: infancy and early childhood (birth to 5 years), middle childhood (6–11 years) and adolescence (12–18 years). In each of these stages, children's distinct learning characteristics are briefly discussed and developmentally sensitive strategies are suggested to help you select heritage language literacy materials and conduct activities.

Situating multiliteracy development in children's everyday lives

Corresponding to the nature of home teaching and learning, many heritage language teaching and learning activities introduced in this book are incorporated in everyday activities, such as surfing the internet, writing letters and notes, shopping and watching television or films.

Emphasising the planning process

Since heritage language literacy development is challenging, this book emphasises the importance of planning and organisation before you put your strategies into practice. Detailed steps and processes are recommended to help you think through what you plan to do to avoid frustration.

Highlighting overt instruction in heritage language literacy learning

Recognising the differences between the learning conditions of heritage language learners and those of children who live in a mainstream language environment, this book values the importance of explicit literacy instruction for heritage language learners (Chapters 5 and 6 in particular). Drawing on research evidence, this book suggests that deliberate instruction on certain linguistic features may be necessary for heritage language literacy development.

In addition, since literacy skills require explicit teaching efforts, some effective school literacy teaching methods are modified and introduced for you to consider in your home literacy teaching.

Including home assessment strategies

Traditionally, little attention has been paid to the assessment and evaluation of literacy learning in the home environment. Assessment means the process of gathering information and evidence on what a child knows and can do. Evaluation is used to describe reflections and judgements made after analysing and interpreting the assessment data collected about children's literacy development.[81] This book recognises that assessment and evaluation form the base for home literacy instructions. It introduces home-suitable assessment methods to help you monitor your children's progress in heritage literacy development.

Valuing parents' practical experiences

Even though most of the information in this book is drawn from the research literature, it also includes parents' voices and experiences in multilingual literacy childrearing practices. Many parents who are raising multilingual and multiliterate children are featured in this book and their home literacy teaching strategies and reflections are shared. It is my belief that parents' day-to-day interactions with their children should be valued and validated. When research findings and parents' experiences differ on certain literacy teaching aspects, they are both put forth for you to consider.

Promoting home and school collaboration

Although the emphasis of this book is on home literacy teaching, it underscores the connection between home and school in heritage language literacy development. Useful strategies are introduced to help you communicate with your children's teachers and find ways to incorporate home literacy learning into your children's school learning and vice versa.

Overview of the Book

This book contains seven chapters including this introductory chapter. The following is an overview of the remaining chapters.

Chapter 2 provides a background for understanding the intricacies involved in the process of developing multilingual literacy. It discusses the definition of multilingual literacy and explores what it means to be multiliterate. It identifies the unique characteristics of multilingual learners and analyses the complex factors that influence multiliteracy development skills. Reflective questions and activities are provided at the end of the chapter to help you digest the information discussed and make connections to your own situation.

The importance of planning and its necessity for successful multilingual literacy development in the home environment are addressed in Chapter 3. By encouraging you to think carefully about various factors that may influence your children's multiliteracy development, you will be better prepared to respond to the possible challenges ahead and minimise frustrations. At the end of the chapter, you will have a chance to engage in activities that will help you link the ideas suggested in the chapter to your own practice.

In Chapter 4, the learning characteristics of children from birth to age 5 are described to inform you of what kinds of parental interaction are most suitable to promote development during this period. The emergent literacy skills, including emergent digital-mediated skills, are identified as the focus. Suggestions are made on how to choose stimulating home language literacy materials, design engaging activities and assess children's progress. At the end of each major section, you will have an opportunity to apply the strategies recommended in this chapter and to reflect on how to incorporate them into your own home teaching.

Chapter 5 addresses the learning characteristics from age 6 to 11. It points out the essential home language literacy skills that children need to develop during this period. The chapter also suggests how to balance school literacy skills with home language literacy skills and provides effective strategies that can help children navigate the demands between regular schoolwork and home language literacy work. It recommends home language literacy materials and activities that can complement children's school experience. Assessment priorities are discussed to help you monitor your children's progress. You will have opportunities to practise the strategies suggested in this chapter and reflect on how to apply them in your home.

The learning characteristics from age 12 to 18 are identified in Chapter 6. It notes the major home language literacy skills that adolescents need to develop. The chapter suggests how to motivate adolescents to continue with their home language literacy development when they are undergoing many changes in their lives and offers effective strategies that facilitate the development of self-motivated multi-lingual literacy learning behaviours. Home language literacy materials and activities are recommended that can foster sustainable interests in furthering multiliteracy development throughout their lives. Assessment methods are suggested to evaluate your children's progress. Reflective questions and examples are included to provide you with a setting to analyse the strategies suggested in the chapter and to reflect on how to use the strategies in your own practice.

Chapter 7 revisits the multilingual home teaching strategies used by the parents featured in this book. Through analysing the strategies and reflections of the featured parents, the key areas of their practices and distinct differences are discussed. It concludes by briefly recapitulating the main points conveyed throughout the book, leaving you with a positive message: Although it is challenging to develop multilingual literacy skills in the home environment, it is possible with strong support, dedication and effective strategies.

Notes and References

1. Hangul is a writing system developed by Sejong the Great in the 15th century. It is now the official script in both South Korea and North Korea.
2. The word 'multilingual' used throughout this book refers to people who know more than one language. Some researchers believe that the term 'multilingual' clearly distinguishes the macrolinguistic level (bilingual or trilingual) from the microlinguistic level (monolingual). See Hoffmann, C. (2001) Toward the description of trilingual competence. *International Journal of Bilingualism* 5 (1), 1–17.
   Also, Marilyn Martin-Jones and Kathryn Jones gave four reasons why it is more accurate to use the term 'multilingual' than 'bilingual'. First, many people have more than two spoken or written languages and language varieties within their communicative repertoire. These include the languages and literacies associated with their cultural inheritance, the regional variety of dialects spoken in their local neighbourhoods and some form of 'standard' language (such as 'standard' English). Second, the term 'multilingual' signals the multiplicity and complexity of the communicative purposes that have come to be associated with different spoken and written languages within a group's repertoire. Third, the term 'multilingual' takes account of the fact that in any linguistic minority household or local group, among speakers of (for example) Welsh, Gujarati or Cantonese, there are multiple paths to the acquisition of the spoken and written languages within the group repertoire and people have varying degrees of expertise in these languages and literacies. Finally, the term 'multilingual' is more useful than the term 'bilingual' because it focuses attention on the multiple ways in which people draw on and combine the codes in their communicative repertoire when they speak and write. See Martin-Jones, M. and Jones, K. (2000) Multilingual literacies. In M. Martin-Jones and K. Jones (eds) *Multilingual Literacies: Reading and Writing Different Worlds* (pp. 1–15). Amsterdam: John Benjamins.
3. The contemporary definition for 'literacy' goes beyond the traditional perspective, which restricted literacy to an ability to read and write at the individual level rather than social level. The contemporary definition of literacy includes a wide range of areas and intersections that relate to understanding and using symbolic systems. See more discussions later in this chapter and in Chapter 2. If you are interested in exploring the contemporary definition of literacy further, please read:
   Gee, J.P. (2007) *Social Linguistics and Literacies: Ideology in Discourse*. London: Routledge.
   Street, B.V. and Lefstein, A. (2007) *Literacy: An Advanced Resource Book*. London: Routledge.
   Pahl, K. and Rowsell, J. (eds) (2005) *Travel Notes from the New Literacy Studies: Instances of Practice*. Clevedon: Multilingual Matters.
   The New London Group (1996) A pedagogy of multiliteracies: Designing social future. *Harvard Educational Review* 66 (1), 60–92.
   Makin, L. and Diaz, C.J. (eds) (2002) *Literacies in Early Childhood: Changing Views, Challenging Practice*. Sydney: MacLennan & Petty.
4. Wang, X-L. (2008) *Growing Up with Three Languages: Birth to Eleven*. Bristol: Multilingual Matters.
5. E-mail communication on 3 February 2009. Consent was obtained from Anna to include her e-mail in this book.
6. There are still on-going debates on the definition of heritage language and heritage language learners among scholars. Some scholars are not content with these terms.

Alternative terms have been suggested in the literature, e.g. allochthonous language, home language, language of origin and immigrant minority language. For details, see Van Deusen-Scholl, N. (2003) Toward a definition of heritage language: Sociopolitical and pedagogical consideration. *Journal of Language, Identity, and Education* 2 (3), 211–230. My working definition of heritage language is 'a language of personal relevance other than the dominant language', which is adopted from Fishman's definition 'a language of personal relevance other than English'. See Van Deusen-Scholl (2003). My working definition of heritage language learners is 'language learners with a heterogeneous ability in their heritage languages either in a spoken or written form'. Some scholars may even include those who are unable to speak their heritage language, but identify with it as a cultural background. See Cho, G., Cho, K-S. and Tse, L. (1997) Why ethnic minorities need to develop their heritage language: The case of Korean Americans. *Language, Culture and Curriculum* 10, 106–112. According to Jim Anderson (2008), 'community languages' is the term commonly used in the UK to describe those languages that are used by minority groups or communities and 'heritage languages' is widely used in North America. See Anderson, J. (2008) Toward an integrated second-language pedagogy for foreign and community/heritage language in multilingual Britain. *Language Learning Journal* 36 (1), 79–89. In this book, I use 'heritage language' and 'home language' interchangeably.

7. Many immigrant communities have established complementary language schools to promote heritage language maintenance. These schools teach the languages and cultures of their community for a few hours after school or at weekends. See Conteh, J., Martin, P. and Robertson, L. (2007) Multilingual learning stories from schools and communities in Britain: Issues and debates. In J. Conteh, P. Martin and L. Robertson (eds) *Multilingual Learning: Stories from Schools and Communities in Britain* (pp. 1–22). Stoke-on-Trent: Trentham Books. Some of these schools also serve religious functions.

8. Chao, T. H. (1997) Chinese heritage community language schools in the United States. Online source from the Center for Applied Linguistics: http://www.cal.org/resources/digest/chao0001.html
    Brecht, R. D. and Ingold, C. W. (2002) Tapping a national resource: Heritage languages in the United States. Online source from the Center for Applied Linguistics: http://www.cal.org/resources/digest/0202brecht.html

9. Ran, A. (2000) Learning to read and write at home: The experience of Chinese families in Britain. In M. Martin-Jones and L. Jones (eds) *Multilingual Literacies: Reading and Writing Different Worlds* (pp. 71–90). Amsterdam: John Benjamins.

10. Cruickshank, K. (2004) Literacy in multilingual contexts: Change in teenagers' reading and writing. *Language and Education* 18 (6), 459–473.

11. This is not to say that all parent teachers in community language schools do not contribute to children's heritage language learning. Some parent teachers play an important role in children's heritage language development. For example, see Chen, Y.G. (2007) Contributing to success: Chinese parents and the community school. In J. Conteh, P. Martin and H. Robertson (eds) *Multilingual Learning: Stories from Schools and Communities in Britain* (pp. 63–85). Stoke-on-Trent: Trentham Books.

12. Darling-Hammond, L. (2000) Teacher quality and student achievement: A review of state policy evidence. *Educational Policy Analysis Archives* 8, 1–48.

13. Chen, Y.G. (2007) Contributing to success: Chinese parents and the community school. In J. Conteh, P. Martin and H. Robertson (eds) *Multilingual Learning: Stories from Schools and Communities in Britain* (pp. 63–85). Stoke-on-Trent: Trentham Books.
    Gregory, E. (2008) *Learning to Read in A New Language*. Los Angeles, CA: Sage.

14. Curdt-Christiansen, X-L. (2006) Teaching and learning Chinese: Heritage language classroom discourse in Montreal. *Language, Culture and Curriculum* 19 (2), 189–207.

15. Naqvi, R. (2008) From peanut butter to Eid… blending perspectives: Teaching Urdu to children in Canada. *Diaspora, Indigenous, and Minority Education* 2, 154–164.
16. The Tang Dynasty was from the period 618 to 907 AD in Chinese history.
17. Wang, X-L. (2009) Ensuring sustained trilingual development through motivation. *The Bilingual Family Newsletter* 26 (1), 1–7.
18. Please note that by providing this example, I do not mean that the heritage concept and ideology are not important to pass on to children. My point is that when children cannot relate to these cultural concepts or ideology, they often tend to lose interests. Please see later chapters for strategies on how to introduce cultural knowledge.
19. Larrotta, C. and Gainer, J. (2008) Text matters: Mexican immigrant parents reading their world. *Promising Practice* Winter issue, 45–48.
20. Reid, J. and Comber, B. (2002) Theoretical perspectives in early literacy education: Implications for practice. In L. Markin and C.J. Diaz (eds) *Literacies in Early Childhood: Changing Views, Challenging Practice* (pp. 15–34). Sydney: MacLennan & Petty.
21. Kagan, O. (2005) In support of a proficiency-based definition of heritage language learners: The case of Russian. *The International Journal of Bilingual Education and Bilingualism* 8 (2 & 3), 213–221.
    Bermel, N. and Kagan, O. (2000) The maintenance of written Russian in heritage speakers. In O. Kagan and B. Rifkin (eds) *Teaching and Learning Slavic Languages and Cultures* (pp. 405–436). Bloomington, IN: Slavica.
22. Kenner, C. and Gregory, E. (2003) Becoming biliterate. In N. Hall, J. Larson and J. March (eds) *Handbook of Early Childhood Literacy* (pp. 178–188). New York: Sage.
23. Li. G-F. (2006) Biliteracy and trilingual practices in the home context: Case studies of Chinese-Canadian children. *Journal of Early Childhood Literacy* 6 (3), 359–385.
    Li, G-F. (2006) What do parents think? Middle-class Chinese immigrant parents' perspectives on literacy learning, homework, and school-home communication. *The School Community Journal* 16 (2), 27–46.
24. Butler, S. (2001) The 'H' word: Home schooling. *Gifted Child Today* 23 (5), 44–50.
25. Webb, J. (1999) *Those Understood Minds: Home-Educated Children Grow Up*. The Educational Heretics Series 102. Nottingham, UK: Educational Heretics Press.
26. Edwards, V. (2009) *Learning to be Literate: Multilingual Perspectives*. Bristol: Multilingual Matters.
    Martin-Jones, M. and Jones, K. (eds) (2000) *Multilingual Literacies: Reading and Writing Different Worlds*. Amsterdam: John Benjamins.
    Kenner, C. (2005) Bilingual families as literacy eco-systems. *Early Years* 25 (2), 283–298.
    Cruickshank, K. (2004) Literacy in multilingual contexts: Change in teenagers' reading and writing. *Language and Education* 18 (6), 459–473.
    Street, B. and Street, J. (1991) The schooling of literacy. In D. Barton and R. Ivanic (eds) *Writing in the Community* (pp. 143–166). London: Sage.
27. Li, G-F. (2002) *"East is East, West is West"?: Home Literacy, Culture, and Schooling*. New York: Peter Lang.
    Wang, X-L. (2008) *Growing Up with Three Languages: Birth to Eleven*. Bristol: Multilingual Matters.
28. Smetana, J.G. (1999) The role of parents in moral development: A social domain analysis. *Journal of Moral Education* 28 (3), 311–321.
29. Strickland, D.S. and Taylor, D. (1989) Family storybook reading: Implications for children, families, and curriculum. In D.S. Strickland and L. Morrow (eds) *Emerging Literacy: Young Children Learn to Read and Write* (pp. 147–159). Newark, DE: International Reading Association.

30. Weigel, D.J., Martin, S.S. and Bennett, K.K. (2006) Contributions of the home literacy environment to preschool-aged children's emergent literacy and language skills. *Early Child Development and Care* 176 (3 & 4), 357–378.
31. Baker, L., Scher, D. and Mackler, K. (1997) Home and family influences on motivation for reading. *Educational Psychologist* 32 (2), 69–82.
32. Roberts, J., Jurgens, J., Burchinal, M. and Graham, F.P. (2005) The role of home Literacy practices in preschool children's language and emergent literacy skills. *Journal of Speech, Language, and Hearing Research* 48, 345–359.
    Weigel, D.J., Martin, S.S. and Bennett, K.K. (2006) Contributions of the home literacy environment to preschool-aged children's emergent literacy and language skills. *Early Child Development and Care* 176 (3 & 4), 357–378.
33. Neumann, M., Hood, M. and Neumann, D.L. (2009) The scaffolding of emergent literacy skills in the home environment: A case study. *Early Childhood Education Journal* 36, 313–319.
34. Kuby, P., Goodstadt-Killoran, I., Aldridge, J. and Kirkland, L. (1999) A review of research on environmental print. *Journal of Instructional Psychology* 26, 173–182.
35. Martello, J. (2002) Many roads through many modes: Becoming literate in early childhood. In L. Makin and C.J. Diaz (eds) *Literacies in Early Childhood: Changing Views, Challenging Practices* (pp. 35–52). Sydney: MacLennan & Petty.
36. Dominique is trilingual in English, French and Chinese. See Wang, X-L. (2008) *Growing Up with Three Languages: Birth to Eleven.* Bristol: Multilingual Matters.
37. Deci, E.L. and Ryan, R.M. (eds) (2002) *Handbooks of Self-Determination Research.* Rochester, NY: University of Rochester Press.
    Wang, X.-L. (2009) Ensuring sustained trilingual development through motivation. *The Bilingual Family Newsletter* 26 (1), 1–7.
38. There may also be some disadvantages associated with teaching children heritage literacy skills in the home environment (such as lack of a language community and requirement for parental self-discipline). However, these can be overcome if alternative plans can be put in place, such as deliberately looking for socialisation with other multilingual families.
39. Krashen, S.D., Tse, L. and McQuillan, J. (1998) *Heritage Language Development.* Culver City, CA: Language Education Associates.
40. Personal communication on 20 March 2007.
41. Barradas, O. (2007) Learning Portuguese: A tale of two worlds. In J. Conteh, P. Martin and L.H. Robertson (eds) *Multilingual Learning: Stories from Schools and Communities in Britain* (pp. 87–102). Stoke-on-Trent: Trentham Books.
42. Garcia, H. (1885) Family and offspring language maintenance and their effects of Chicano colleague students' confidence and grades. In E. Garcia and R. Padilla (eds) *Advances in Bilingual Education Research* (pp. 226–243). Tucson, AZ: University of Arizona Press.
43. Goetz, P.J. (2003) The effects of bilingualism on theory of mind development. *Bilingualism: Language and Cognition* 6 (1), 1–15.
    Thomas, W. and Collier, V. (1997) *School Effectiveness and Language Minority Students.* Washington, DC: National Clearinghouse for Bilingual Education.
44. Cummins, J. (1981) The role of primary language development in promoting educational success for language minority students. In California State Department of Education (ed.) *Schooling and Language Minority Students: A Theoretical Framework* (pp. 3–49). Los Angeles, CA: Evaluation, Dissemination, and Assessment Center, California State University.
45. Giambo, D.A. and Szecsi, T. (2005) Parents can guide children through the world of two languages. *Childhood Education* 81 (3), 164–165.
46. Bialystok, E. (2002) Acquisition of literacy in bilingual children: A framework for research. *Language Learning* 52, 159–199.

Geva, E. and Siegel, L.S. (2000) Orthographic and cognitive factors in the concurrent development of basic reading skills in two languages. *Reading and Writing: An Interdisciplinary Journal* 12, 1–30.

Durgunoglu, A.Y., Nagy, W.E. and Hancin-Bhatt, B.J. (1993) Cross-language transfer of phonological awareness. *Journal of Educational Psychology* 85, 453–465.

47. Riches, C. and Genesee, F. (2006) Literacy: Crosslinguistic and crossmodal issues. In F. Genesee, K. Lindholm-Leary, W.M. Saunders and D. Christian (eds) *Educating Language Learners: A Synthesis of Research Evidence* (pp. 64–108). Cambridge: Cambridge University Press.

48. Data, M. (2000) *Bilinguality and Literacy: Principle and Practice*. London: Continuum.

49. Cazden, C., Cope, B., Fairclough, N., Gee, J. *et al.* (1996) A pedagogy of multiliteracies: Designing social futures. *Harvard Educational Review* 66 (1), 60–92.

50. Example provided by Karen Kinston on 21 May 2003.

51. Fitzgerald, J. (1995) English-as-a second language learners' cognitive reading process: A review of research in the United States. *Review of Educational Research* 65, 145–190.

Wagner, D.A. (1998) Putting second language first: Language and literacy learning in Morocco. In L. Verhoeven and A.Y. Durgunoglu (eds) *Literacy Development in a Multilingual Context* (pp. 169–183). Mahwah, NJ: Lawrence Erlbaum.

52. Giambo, D.A. and Szecsi, T. (2005) Parents can guide children through the world of two languages. *Childhood Education* 81 (3), 164–165.

53. Minns, H. (1993) Three ten year old boys and their reading. In M. Barrs and S. Pidgeon (eds) *Reading the Difference: Gender and Reading in the Primary School* (pp. 60–71). London: Centre for Language in Primary Education.

Minns, H. (1997) Gurdeep and Geeta: The making of two readers and the nature of differences. Paper presented at IEDPE Conference, London, 17 October.

54. Garton, A. and Pratt, C. (1989) *Learning to Be Literate: The Development of Spoken and Written Language*. Oxford: Basil Blackwell.

55. Zaretsky, E. and Bar-Shalom, E.G. (2010) Does reading in shallow L1 orthography slow attrition of language-specific morphological structures? *Clinical Linguistics & Phonetics* 24 (4–5), 401–415.

56. Swain, M., Lapkin, S., Rowen, N. and Hart, D. (1990) The role of mother tongue literacy in third language learning. *Language, Culture and Curriculum* 3 (1) 65–81.

57. Taylor, L.K. (2008) Of mother tongues and other tongues: The stakes of linguistically inclusive pedagogy in minority contexts. *The Canadian Modern Language Review* 65 (1), 89–123.

58. Example provided by Jody Epstein on 1 March 2009.

59. Garcia, H. (1985) Family and offspring language maintenance and their effects of Chicano colleague students' confidence and grades. In E. Garcia and R. Padilla (eds) *Advances in Bilingual Education Research* (pp. 226–243). Tucson, AZ: University of Arizona Press.

Huang, G.G. (1995) Self-reported biliteracy and self-esteem: A study of Mexican-American 8th graders. *Applied Psycholinguistics* 16, 271–291.

60. Huang, G.G. (1995) Self-reported biliteracy and self-esteem: A study of Mexican-American 8th graders. *Applied Psycholinguistics* 16, 271–291.

61. Kenner, C. (2004) *Becoming Biliterate*. Stoke-on-Trent: Trentham Books.

62. I want to thank my colleague Dr. Christine Clayton for proposing this idea.

63. Goody, J. (ed.) (1968) *Literacy in Traditional Societies*. Cambridge: Cambridge University Press.

Olson, D. (1977) From utterance to text: The bias of language in speech and writing. *Harvard Educational Review* 47 (3), 257–281.

Ong, W. (1982) *Orality and Literacy: The Technologising of the World*. London: Methuen.

64. Street, B.V. and Lefstein, A. (2007) *Literacy: An Advanced Resource Book*. London: Routledge.

Street, B. (2000) Literacy events and literacy practices. In M. Martin-Jones and K. Jones (eds) *Multilingual Literacies: Reading and Writing Different Worlds* (pp. 17–35) Amsterdam: John Benjamins.

Diaz, C.J. and Markin, L. (2002) Literacy as social practice. In L. Makin and C.J. Diaz (eds) *Literacies in Early Childhood: Changing Views, Challenging Practices* (pp. 3–14). Sydney: MacLennan & Petty.

Hall, N., Larson, J. and Marsh, J. (2003) *Handbook of Early Childhood Literacy.* New York: Sage.

65. Bourdieu, P. (1991) *Language and Symbolic Power.* Cambridge, MA: Polity Press.
66. Barratt-Pugh, C. (2002) Children as writers. In L. Makin and C.J. Diaz (eds) *Literacies in Early Childhood: Changing Views, Challenging Practices* (pp. 93–116). Sydney: MacLennan & Petty.
67. Diaz, C.J. and Markin, L. (2002) Literacy as social practice. In L. Makin and C.J. Diaz (eds) *Literacies in Early Childhood: Changing Views, Challenging Practices* (pp. 3–14). Sydney: MacLennan & Petty.
68. Hall, N., Larson, J. and Marsh, J. (2003) *Handbook of Early Childhood Literacy.* New York: Sage.
69. Martin-Jones, M. and Jones, K. (eds) (2000) *Multilingual Literacies: Reading and Writing Different Worlds* (pp. 4–5). Amsterdam: John Benjamins.
70. The New London Group (1996) A pedagogy of multiliteracies: Designing social futures. *Harvard Educational Review* 66 (1), 60–92.
71. Pahl, K. (2004) Narrative spaces and multiple identity: Children's textual explorations of console games in home setting. In J. Marsh (ed.) *Popular Culture, New Media and Digital Literacy in Early Childhood* (pp. 126–145). New York: Routledge.
72. Hall, N., Larson, J. and March, J. (2003) *Handbook of Early Childhood Literacy.* New York: Sage.
73. Markin, L. and Groom, S. Literacy transitions. In L. Makin and C.J. Diaz (eds) *Literacies in Early Childhood: Changing Views, Challenging Practices* (pp. 71–91). Sydney: MacLennan & Petty.
74. Hill, S. and Broadhurst, D. (2002) Technoliteracy and the early years. In L. Makin and C.J. Diaz (eds) *Literacies in Early Childhood: Changing Views, Challenging Practices* (pp. 269–287). Sydney: MacLennan & Petty.
75. Lewin, T. (2009) In a digital future, textbooks are history. *New York Times,* 9 August.
76. Chevalier, J.F. (2004) Heritage language literacy: Theory and practice. *Heritage Language Journal* 2 (1), 1–9.
77. Cummins, J. (2006) Identity texts: The imaginative construction of self through multi-literacies pedagogy. In O. García, T. Skutnabb-Kangas and M. Torres-Guzmán (eds) *Imagining Multiliteracy School: Language in Education and Globalization* (pp. 51–68). Clevedon: Multilingual Matters.

Lotherington, H. (2007) From literacy to multiliteracies in ELT. In C. Davison and J. Cummins (eds) *Handbook of English Language Teaching* (pp. 809–823). Berlin: Springer.

78. Stevens, L.P and Bean, T.W. (2007) *Critical Literacy: Context, Research, and Practice in the K-12 Classroom.* Thousand Oaks, CA: Sage.
79. Martello, J. (2002) Many roads through many modes: Becoming literate in early childhood. In L. Makin and C.J. Diaz (eds) *Literacies in Early Childhood: Changing Views, Challenging Practices* (pp. 35–52). Sydney: MacLennan & Petty.

Diaz, C.J., Beecher, B. and Arther, L. (2002) Children's worlds and critical literacy. In L. Makin and C.J. Diaz (eds) *Literacies in Early Childhood: Changing Views, Challenging Practices* (pp. 305–322). Sydney: MacLennan & Petty.

80. Stevens, L.P. and Bean, T. (2007) *Critical Literacy: Contexts, Research, and Practice in the K-12 Classroom.* Thousand Oaks, CA: Sage.
81. Tayler, C. (2000) Monitoring young children's literacy learning. In C. Barrat-Pugh and M. Rohl (eds) *Literacy Learning in the Early Years* (pp. 197–222). Buckingham: Open University Press.

Chapter 2

Understanding the Multilingual Reading and Writing Process

This chapter examines the important aspects involved in the process of becoming readers and writers of more than one language. It discusses the definition of multilingual literacy and explores what it means to be multiliterate. It identifies the unique characteristics of multilingual learners and analyses the complex factors that influence multilingual literacy development. The chapter concludes with a home literacy pedagogical framework that is based on some prominent literacy teaching approaches and ideas. Reflective questions and activities are provided at the end of the chapter to help you think further about the intricacies involved in developing multilingual literacy and become better prepared to respond to the challenges that you may encounter when interacting with your children.

Definition of Multiliteracy

In the last chapter, I indicated that literacy encompasses much more than reading and writing skills and includes a range of other important abilities. In this section, I will build on similar ideas and briefly define the meaning of multilingual literacy.

The New London Group researchers[1] believe that in a rapidly changing world, the definition of literacy needs to shift from the narrow focus on the dominant literacy and culture to a wider focus on different literacies in different cultures and that literacy needs to include the multimodal (multichannel) meaning-making opportunities offered by new communication technologies (such as the internet[2]). Thus, the term 'multiliteracies' is more accurate than the term 'literacy'.[3]

However, literacy expert, Brian Street, cautioned that when thinking about the term 'multiliteracies', one needs to avoid simply lining up a single literacy with a single culture and assuming that multiple 'literacies' are associated with multiple cultures. He pointed out further that although it is important to distinguish the multiple forms of literacy associated with channels such as computer literacy or visual literacy, it is more useful to consider how these channels actually give meaning in the social and cultural practice in using these modes.[4]

Therefore, the important focus in understanding multiliteracy should be on the social practice, that is, how children use literacy to solve real-life problems in a specific cultural context. Emphasising social practice can help us capture how reading and writing are carried out in different cultural communities and see the ways that people use written texts to reflect their values. Focusing on how literacy is used in a particular context can also help us recognise the diversity of reading and writing practices and the different genres, styles and types of texts associated with various activities, domains and social identities.[5]

Grounded in the above-suggested ideas, a working definition of multiliteracy may be: reading or writing that occurs in more than one language (or dialect), via more than one channel, in meaningful social and cultural practices.

There are three key features associated with this working definition of multi-literacy:

- The use of more than one language or dialect (e.g. a child reads or writes in Chinese and English or a child reads or writes in High German and Swiss German dialect[6]).
- The involvement of more than one channel (e.g. a child negotiates meaning through printed texts and multimedia texts).
- The use of more than one language in social and cultural practices (e.g. a child writes letters to his relatives in Arabic and reads his textbooks in French in school).

Who is Multiliterate?

Having briefly explored the definition of multiliteracy (or multiliteracies), let us now look at what it means to be multiliterate. The common misconception of a multiliterate person is that he or she can read and write fluently and equally well in more than one language. Before I address this misconception, it is helpful to examine the following three cases.

Case 1: Oum

A Moroccan woman named Oum Fatima had never been to school and could not read and write or do simple arithmetic on paper. However, she could take letters delivered by the mailman to the appropriate addresses by recognising the scripts in Arabic and French.[7]

Case 2: Mario

Mario was born into a working-class family in Tijuana, Mexico. His parents never read children's books to him. However, they often told him family stories when he was young. He lived in Mexico until age 15 and came to the USA to finish high school. He has lived in San Francisco for nearly 20 years. He speaks both Spanish and English fluently. He can read and write Spanish at 7th grade level. He can read English at 10th grade level and write it at about 8th grade level. His bilingual literacy ability allows him to function sufficiently in his daily necessities, such as exchanging personal e-mails, reading magazines and newspapers, and doing financial transactions and book-keeping for his restaurant business.[8]

Case 3: Philippe

Philippe was born in Switzerland. He spent his early childhood in Paris and Berne, and his middle childhood, adolescence and young adulthood near Neuchâtel (French-speaking Canton of Switzerland). Philippe started his life as a simultaneous bilingual in French and German (Swiss German and High German). His parents spoke exclusively in Swiss German to him at home, and his mother read him many books in High German to make sure that he acquired High German as well. He lived in a French-speaking environment and went to the French school until university level with High German as a mandatory subject. At age 25, Philippe came to the USA as an exchange graduate student and thus, added a third language, English, to his linguistic repertoire. Eventually, he earned a doctoral degree from an American university. Today, he is able to function at a high level in each of his three languages in listening comprehension, speaking, reading comprehension and writing (as evidenced by his university teaching and academic publications), in addition to possessing reading competence in Latin, ancient Greek and biblical Hebrew.[9]

Are any of these three people multiliterate? The answer is that all of them are multiliterate. However, if we put them on the multilingual literacy competency continuum shown below,[10] it is clear that they differ in their multiliterate competence.

Low _____ High
Oum   Mario   Philippe

Oum is at the lower end of the multilingual literacy competency continuum because her multiliterate knowledge is restricted to recognising the different scripts of Arabic and French and she is able to deliver the right letter to the right address. Mario's multilingual literacy proficiency can be placed somewhere at the middle point in the multilingual competency continuum. He can use both languages to manage his everyday needs (e.g. reading newspapers and book-keeping for his business). Philippe's multilingual literacy proficiency can be put at the higher end of the multilingual literacy competency continuum because he can function well in the academic setting with French, English and German in addition to other languages.

In reality, a multiliterate person can rarely read or write equally well in all his or her languages. For example, Mario can read English better than he can write it. Both his English reading and writing are better than his Spanish, even though Spanish is his first language. Philippe reads fluently in three languages, however, his French and English writing at present are a little better than his German writing because he has more opportunities to write in French and English than in German.

It is clear that when defining what it means to be multiliterate, it is not an 'all or nothing matter'.[11] Rather, it is a matter of proficiency degrees at different points on the multilingual competency continuum. Thus, being multiliterate means that an individual can actively use more than one language in reading or writing with different levels of proficiency for a particular purpose in his or her environment.[12] The key elements include:

- actively using more than one language in reading or writing;
- with different proficiency levels;
- for a particular purpose.

The advantage of defining multiliterate abilities in this way is that it helps us look at the multilingual and multiliterate phenomenon in a more realistic and achievable way. Most importantly, this definition focuses on what a person can do with more than one language in his or her everyday life instead of his or her limitations. With this definition in mind, you will feel more encouraged to raise multiliterate children and cherish what they can do in their unique multilingual learning environment.

Factors Influencing Multilingual Literacy Development

Oum, Mario and Philippe's cases show that multilingual literacy development is a complex phenomenon. There are many factors that may contribute to a person's multilingual literacy attainment. Below are some examples.

Parenting

Parental cultural beliefs

Different cultures and socioeconomic groups have different beliefs about how reading and writing should be practised (learned). Reading and writing can mean different things to different people. For example, in North America, educated middle-class parents tend to relate reading in the home environment to enjoyment and fun. However, in some other cultures, reading and writing are believed to be serious work. Multilingual literacy expert, Eve Gregory, shared a telling story about how cultural beliefs can affect a child's literacy behaviour. She described a young boy named Tony who lived in Northampton, UK. Tony's family immigrated to the UK from Hong Kong. His English teacher was surprised and concerned when she observed that Tony only wanted to copy words instead of experimenting with writing them like other children in the class. The teacher failed to understand that

Tony's literacy behaviour was exactly what his family expected of him. Tony's grandparents and parents believed that learning to read and write should follow a clear sequence: First understand the meaning of the word; then learn how to pronounce it correctly; repeat it; memorise it; carefully copy it and use it to make different sentences. Once a child can prove competency in these aspects, he or she will be given a book to read. To have immediate access to books devalues both the book and the principle of hard work. Children must work their way towards knowledge step by step, and the book is a reward for a child's conscientious achievements. A love of books comes after reading is learned and not as a necessary prerequisite to it.[13]

This example suggests that parents' or caregivers' cultural beliefs about reading and writing and the way that they guide their children in literacy activities provide a cultural template[14] for their children to act, which directly influences their children's literacy performance and outcome.

Parental education level and socioeconomic status

Parental educational levels and their socioeconomic status can also influence their children's literacy development.[15] Parents with more years of schooling tend to have children with better literacy skills[16] because educated parents are likely to read more to their children[17] and to ask more decontextualised questions (questions that are not restricted to here and now) during book reading.[18] Research has shown that there is a close relationship between young children's exposure to storybook reading and successful literacy outcome, and the literacy skills established in book-reading interactions at home are a prerequisite for later school literacy achievement.[19] Children who are read to, often develop better vocabulary and cognitive ability than children who are not read to.[20] Children with a large vocabulary size learn to read more easily and tend to enjoy reading.[21] By contrast, parents who are less educated tend not to provide enriched early literacy experience to their young children.[22] For example, research suggests that children whose mothers did not graduate from high school are more likely to have a language delay.[23]

Children from low socioeconomic families tend to have weaker language and literacy skills than children from high socioeconomic families. For example, research indicates that by the age of 3, children in welfare-receiving homes have a vocabulary that is half the size of their more affluent peers.[24]

In the case of multilingual children, when parents are more affluent, they can afford to send their children to language schools or hire language tutors. These children are likely to have more accesses to multilingual materials and have more opportunities to travel to their heritage countries.

Parental availability

Another important factor that can influence children's multilingual literacy development is whether parents spend time talking, reading and writing together with their children. The amount of time that parents or caregivers spend with their children in language and literacy-related activities on a daily basis can affect children's multilingual and multiliteracy outcome.[25] For example, Mrs Cho[26] of Columbus, Ohio, has spent close to two hours a day helping her daughter Jessie with her Korean reading and writing since she was 6 years old. As a result, Jessie, who is now in high school, is doing very well in her Korean reading and writing (you will read more about Mrs Cho's home teaching approach later in this chapter and in Chapters 5 and 7).

Support from siblings, extended family and community

Sibling support as an important factor in a child's multiliteracy development has been largely ignored.[27] When reviewing the literacy practices in different cultural communities, it is evident that in many families, siblings play an important role in helping each other to maintain heritage language literacy.[28] For example, Eve Gregory found in her study that siblings supported each other's language and literacy learning at home through their play routines.[29]

The extended family involvement in children's multilingual literacy development is another important factor (such as grandparents, aunts and uncles). In Washington, DC, 11-year-old Ashley has lived with her Chinese-speaking grandparents from birth. Since she was 5 years old, her grandmother has spent one hour every day helping her read and write in Chinese using a set of published textbooks from the People's Republic of China.[30] By contrast, the parents of Ashley's classmate, Jimmy, work long hours and there are no other family members nearby to provide Chinese language and literacy support for him.[31] Needless to say, Ashley has more of a chance in succeeding with Chinese literacy than Jimmy.

Community support is also crucial in a child's multilingual literacy development. For example, Mrs Kim is actively involved in her Korean community in New Jersey and has a close relationship with many other Korean families. Her 9-year-old daughter Mary goes to Bible study class twice a week in a Korean Baptist church. Mary also attends the Korean language school every Sunday afternoon.[32] By contrast, 9-year-old Amy, who lives in the suburbs of New York, does not have a Korean community around her.[33] The strong community language and literacy support for Mary and the lack of community support for Amy will no doubt influence the Korean language literacy development outcomes of both these two girls.

Opportunities to use languages

A child needs to have ample opportunities to read and write in different languages in different social activities to become multiliterate. For instance, 11-year-old Rehana, who lives in London, has many opportunities to use Gujarati as well as English in most areas of her life: there are Gujarati children in her class at school, she attends a play centre where all the children are Gujarati/English bilinguals, she goes swimming regularly with her friends, many of whom are also Gujarati speakers and she also attends the Madrasa (Madrasah) – religious classes attached to the mosque. Her mother tells stories to her in Gujarati and there are lots of materials in Gujarati and Urdu around the house because her father is actively involved in the running of a centre that caters for the needs of the Gujarati- and Urdu-speaking communities. In addition, both Gujarati and Urdu languages are used regularly for reading and writing.[34] Children like Rehana will likely become multiliterate because they have frequent opportunities to use their heritage languages in their surroundings.

Attitude and value

The general attitude that mainstream culture has towards non-mainstream languages can influence whether children are likely to maintain their heritage language. The mainstream cultural attitude can also influence whether parents want to make the effort to help their children maintain their heritage language. Some languages (such as French) tend to have a prestigious status in some countries and others (such as Urdu) do not. When a language is favoured by a society, children are encouraged to maintain that language. They also tend to have more opportunities to get an education in that language and are likely to become multiliterate. However, when a language is not favoured, the motivation to maintain that language is weak and so are the opportunities to be educated in that language.

Language features and language convergence and divergence

The differences in language structure and writing systems can affect a child's multiliteracy progress. It has been suggested that children tend to acquire literacy abilities faster in languages where spelling is regular or rule bound.[35] As the Australian educator Mary Rohl explained:

> Some alphabetic language systems, such as Finnish and Spanish, have a very close relationship between sounds and letters; the relationship in English is not so close. It is true that there are many words like *cat*, *spring* and *print* that have a complete regular one-to-one correspondence between sounds and letters, but there are many words, such as *yacht*, *debt* and *colonel*, for which the correspondence is not so close ... Another complicating feature of English spelling is the fact there are some words that sound the same as each other but are spelt differently, such as *their*, *there* and *they're*; and other words that are spelt the same but are pronounced differently, such as the word *wind* and in "The wind blew", and "Wind the hose".[36]

Studies confirm that children from a language system in which the correspondences between sounds and symbols are regular (such as Hebrew and German) tend to perform better in tasks related to phonological awareness[37] (conscious awareness of the phonological properties of language, such as the ability to count the number of syllables in a word and to identify rhymes[38]).

Moreover, different orthographic (writing) systems may pose different challenges to learners.[39] For example, it has been estimated that a child learning Chinese must learn to recognise at least 4000 different characters by the time they reach 12 years old. The number of visual forms that the child must master is enormous by comparison with the number of letters that a child reading an alphabetic system must learn.[40]

Furthermore, in some languages, the relationship between sound and symbol is not as transparent as in other languages. Take the Chinese character 猫 (cat) for example, the symbol 猫 does not correspond to the sound [māo]. Whereas, in Finnish, the written symbol 'kissa' (cat) corresponds to its sound.

Some researchers believe that the more characteristics two orthographic systems have in common, the greater or more immediate the potential for transfer of reading skills or strategies[41] (even though other researchers may disagree).[42] In my own trilingual childrearing experience (my children are simultaneous trilinguals in English, French and Chinese),[43] I have noticed that the different orthographic systems do impede and facilitate my children's literacy progress in these languages. My kids tend to have more ease in learning to read and write in French than in Chinese because their mainstream language, English, shares more linguistic features with French than with Chinese.

In addition, some languages or dialects may share the same writing system but have distinct speaking systems, such as Cantonese and Putonghua.[44] It is likely that it is more convenient for children who speak Putonghua to learn to read Chinese with the help of Pinyin[45] or zhu yin fu hao /注音符号[46] than for those who speak Cantonese.

In short, when multilingual children's languages share similar linguistic and orthographic features, cross-language facilitation in reading and writing may occur more conveniently and when children's different language systems are less similar to one another, the task to become multiliterate may be more challenging.

The relationship between oral language and literacy

Research has provided ample evidence to establish the close link between a child's oral language skills and the child's later reading and writing competence. Children with higher levels of oral proficiency and more elaborated vocabulary can read more easily than their less proficient peers.[47] For example, research suggests that the property of spoken words such as stress (in English), syllables (in French) and morae (in Japanese) is closely associated with written language processing.[48]

A child's knowledge established in oral language, such as phonological awareness and phonemic awareness, is closely linked to a child's ability to read. Phonological awareness and phonemic awareness are terms that refer to children's understanding about words and sounds in words. Phonological awareness is broader in scope and includes the ability to separate sentences into words and words into syllables. Phonemic awareness includes the ability to recognise that words are made up of a set of sounds and the ability to manipulate sounds. Phonemic awareness is an oral ability -- the ability to hear that words begin alike, that words rhyme, and that, for example, there are three sounds in the word c-a-t.[49] Research indicates that both phonological awareness and phonemic awareness are highly correlated with success in beginning reading,[50] even in non-alphabetic languages such as Chinese.[51]

The relationship between reading and writing

Reading and writing abilities are strongly correlated. It is likely that children who read well tend to write well,[52] though instruction in one cannot be substituted for the other. However, the relationship between reading and writing is not unidirectional, but bidirectional. Reading does not necessarily have to precede writing. Children can write before they are able to read; progress in either can lead to progress in the other.

Value placed on oracy and literacy

The term 'oracy' was coined by the British researcher and educator Andrew Wilkinson in the 1960s. Oracy means oral language skills. Traditionally, oracy is valued less than literacy. Oracy is characterised as formulaic, conservative and homeostatic and literacy is characterised as abstract, analytic and objective.[53] In fact, oracy and literacy share many common features in terms of how language is used in a specific context. In some cultural communities, many literacy events occur embedded in oral language use and children learn to read and write through heavy reliance on spoken language.[54]

My own studies on American Indian mother–child interactions suggest that some American Indian mothers do not read books to their young children. Instead, they tell their children stories about their family members. Oracy is much more valued by these American Indian mothers than literacy.[55]

Hereditary and individual factors

It is debatable to what extent a child's reading and writing ability is hereditary and to what extent it is environmental. Some scientists, however, found that genetic factors may play a moderate role in a child's literacy development.[56] A genetic predisposition may influence literacy development through its effect on general cognitive abilities, such as information processing speed, memory and attention control.[57] Moreover, a genetic predisposition may lead some young children to be more responsive to books by pointing and vocalising during reading, which encourages their parents to read more to them.[58]

Understanding that genetic factors may play some roles in children's literacy development will help us tailor our interaction based on their individual abilities and needs. However, environmental intervention can certainly change children's cognitive abilities,[59] including literacy abilities. For example, a study by Carol S. Hammer and Adele W. Miccio indicated that bilingual children from low-income backgrounds initially performed poorly on phonological awareness and letter identification tasks, but they appeared to acquire these abilities quickly in kindergarten once these abilities were emphasised in early reading instruction.[60]

Cognition

Reading is a complex process involving different mental operations in which reading-related cognitive skills play an important role. To be able to read, children have to be able to perceive sounds, store the information they hear, analyse it, recall it and recombine it in memory and problem solving. Children with good cognitive abilities tend to become fluent readers earlier with more ease.[61] However, reading also depends on language-specific cognitive abilities, such as phonological aware-ness, vocabulary and, most strongly, decoding (the ability to associate sounds and symbols with meaning).[62]

Research has shown that reading in different languages may require different activation of a different part of the brain. For example, reading Chinese invokes more activation in brain areas that are responsible for coordinating and integrating visual-spatial analyses of logographic Chinese characters compared with English.[63]

Writing is also dependent on general cognitive abilities. It may tax working memory and executive functions[64] even more than reading.[65] To write, a child must control his/her attention, set goals, plan, spell words, write sentences and revise them. The abilities to do these things are closely related to the child's cognitive abilities.

Age, gender and education

Research suggests that the age of first multilingual language exposure affects reading development in children learning to read in their multi-languages. There is definitely a reading advantage for children who are educated in multilingual schools. For example, a study compared bilingual Spanish-English children with English-speaking children in monolingual English schools. Early first bilingual language exposure had a positive effect on reading, phonological awareness and language competence in both languages: early bilinguals (age of first exposure 0–3 years) outperformed other bilingual groups (age of first exposure 3–6 years). Remarkably, schooling in two languages afforded children from monolingual English homes an advantage in phonemic awareness skills. Early bilingual exposure is best for dual language reading development, and it may have such a powerful positive impact on reading and language development that it counteracts the negative effect of low socioeconomic situation on literacy.[66]

There is also a gender difference in how children develop multiliteracy abilities. In general, girls tend to have higher reading achievement than boys. However, this effect tends to disappear when children enter high school. For example, there is no difference in SAT[67] verbal scores between girls and boys.[68]Even though the findings on gender differences in literacy are not consistent, in general, they tend to favour girls.[69]

However, gender differences in literacy may also be caused by some environmental factors. For example, research in some cultural communities, such as the Gujarati-speaking Indian Muslim community, shows that boys' achievement in reading comprehension is ahead of girls, which may reflect the particularly high status placed in their community on religious knowledge acquired by boys through a close study of texts and complex negations of meaning.[70] Similarly, in a Pakistani community in Watford, England, the view of the child as a leaner in the Qur'ānic class is undoubtedly affected by gender. The expectations of boys are different from those of girls. Parents ensure that their sons attend more regularly than their daughters and for a longer period in their lives.[71] As a result, boys tend to read better than girls.

Finally, education plays a pivotal role in whether a multilingual child is proficient in his/her multilingual literacy. When children have the opportunities to attend schools in multiple languages and when children have rich support and resources in these languages, it is likely that they will perform at the higher end of the multilingual continuum. As can be seen in the cases of Oum, Mario and Philippe, their educational opportunities certainly determined their multiliteracy competences.

Affect, emotion, motivation and identity

Children with supportive and responsive parents tend to develop better literacy skills and better attitudes towards reading. For example, secure toddlers are more likely to stay on their mother's lap and pay attention to a book while being read to,[72] and secure kindergarteners[73] are more likely to include print in their play, ask parents to read to them, and later develop good reading comprehension.[74]

When parents allow children to negotiate, children tend to be more competent communicators. When parents interact with children (joint attention) and talk to their children often, the children also tend to have better language abilities.[75] Positive emotions enhance a child's productivity and creativity. Positive emotions can also broaden thought processes and focus attention.[76] When a child feels joy or interest, the child is motivated to explore, learn, be open to new information, generate more ideas and participate in activities. Research shows that positive emotions may have this effect by altering neurotransmitters in the brain. Positive emotions are linked to small increases of dopamine in the part of the brain responsible for working memory, creative problem solving, cognitive flexibility and memory.[77] Negative emotions, such as anger and anxiety, can interfere with the information processing needed for reading and writing. If parents are sensitive and responsive when helping their children learn to read, the children are more likely to have emotionally positive encounters with print.[78] Sensitive parents tend to be better literacy coaches to their children.[79] Positive interactions during parent–child storybook reading predict greater reading fluency and a more positive attitude towards reading.[80]

Also, the emotion associated with a particular culture and language can affect how a reader may perceive words and messages differently. Eve Gregory quoted the

Russian psychologist Lev Vygotsky's comment on how the dictionary definition of the word *flag* (e.g. a piece of cloth often attached to a pole, decorated with a design and used as an emblem, signal or standard or as a means of signalling) can evoke different emotional responses from different readers (conjuring up pride and honour or humiliation or shame).[81]

Motivation is another important factor in whether a child will likely engage in heritage language literacy activities. When children see the relevance and personal meaning in engaging in heritage language reading and writing activities, they are more likely to want to learn. Conversely, children will lose motivation.

Finally, whether a person identifies him/herself with a language group or culture may determine whether the person wants to acquire or maintain the language of that group. Frequently, if being part of the group will be in an individual's favour, it is likely that the person will tend to associate with the group and feel a sense of belonging to the group.[82] Positively identifying with a heritage language has been found to be a significant predictor of success in language acquisition.[83]

Collaboration between home and school

When school and home join together and collaborate to buttress multilingual learning, children are likely to thrive and develop. For example, Jessie's teachers value her Korean heritage language asset and encourage her to share her Korean writings in class. The support from Jessie's teachers definitely made her feel positive about her heritage language and culture.[84] However, if school and teacher support is lacking, it is more challenging for children to develop multilingual literacy. Research has shown that when heritage language programmes are integrated into the school day, they tend to be successful.[85]

Unique Characteristics of Multiliteracy Learners

In a typical language-learning environment, a child is immersed in a larger cultural and linguistic community in which other adults and peers as well as the media provide a rich resource for the language and literacy-learning child. However, multilingual children, in particular those children whose major heritage language and literacy input is from their parents, often lack such constant cultural and community language experience. These children have some unique language and literacy characteristics.

Differences between heritage language learners and other types of language learners

Heritage language learners tend to be confused with other types of language learners. They are sometimes regarded as native speakers because they may be exposed to the heritage language at home as a first language, or their parents speak the language to them at home. Sometimes, they are also regarded as second language learners because they live in a mainstream language environment and are not 'fluent' in their heritage language. Occasionally, heritage language learners are even thought of as foreign language learners because they take their heritage language as a foreign language subject in school. Although researchers have long warned us about the problems of confusing these different language learners,[86] the issue is still prevalent.

Heritage language learners certainly share many commonalities with second language learners, foreign language learners[87] and native speakers. However, all these language learners also differ from each other. Even though heritage language learners may be exposed to a heritage language as the first language in their lives, their experience differs from that of native speakers. For example, it is certain that Child A, who acquires Arabic language and literacy skills in an Arabic-speaking dominant environment, differs from Child B, who learns Arabic reading and writing mainly from his/her parents in the home environment, in the speed and quality of their Arabic language and literacy acquisition. All things considered, Child A will have more advantages than Child B.

By the same token, heritage language learners may have different degrees of explicit and implicit knowledge about their heritage languages and cultures than foreign or second language learners. They often have more 'hidden' advantages in learning heritage languages than those who learn a second language or foreign language. Research suggests that heritage language learners have proficiencies and lacunae that differ from non-heritage learners such as foreign language and second language learners.[88] For instance, heritage language learners may have an advantage over second language and foreign language learners in that they may have a linguistic instinct for their heritage language. This linguistic instinct may be explained by Nick Ellis' comments in his edited book, *Implicit and Explicit Learning of Language*. If you ask a young English-speaking child how to form a plural, 'she says she does not know; ask her "here is a *wug*,[89] here is another *wug*, what have you got?" and she is able to reply, "two *wugs*"'.[90] This example shows that when a child is exposed to a linguistic model such as the heritage language model early in life, the child will form the linguistic instinct (knowledge) for that language, which may be missing for a foreign language and second language learner.

An example from my older son Léandre may further illustrate the hidden advantages of heritage language learners. Léandre once tried to convince me to buy him a video game in an e-mail (in Chinese). When he realised that his Chinese writing skills would limit him, he decided to write this message in English first and then converted it to Chinese with the Google translator. He went on to modify the Chinese translation and sent it to me. When I got this e-mail, I knew that it was the product of Léandre's Google modification. Nevertheless, I was quite happy because Léandre did know (by using his Chinese language instinct) how to modify the message and made it sound Chinese (in fact, very good Chinese). However, a friend of mine, who is a Chinese foreign language learner, sent me an e-mail in Chinese with the help of the Google translator. His lack of the Chinese linguistic instinct made his e-mail awkward and strange to a native Chinese speaker.

The matter with regard to heritage language learners is further complicated by the fact that the political, social, economic and cultural backgrounds of heritage language learners from seemingly the 'same' linguistic and cultural regions can be very different. Moreover, there are different vernacular/dialect forms that vary greatly. Using Arabic as an example, there are variations within the more than 20 Arabic-speaking countries and regions.[91]

Researchers Ludmila Issurin and Tanya Ivanova-Sullivan sum it up well with their comments on the unique characteristics of heritage language learners (in their case, Russian heritage language learners).

> Russian heritage speakers may indeed be "lost in between" in the continuum[92] of language speakers. They outperform English-speaking learners of Russian in such linguistic areas as the correct use of aspect/tense and cases, but they fall well behind the native speakers in these same areas. Moreover, they seem to be more comfortable than L2 (second language)[93] learners in using the predominantly VS (verb subject)[94] word order of Russian narrative discourse. At the same time, their mastery of that category is far from that of the native speaker. These findings are not accidental but rather are determined by the linguistic uniqueness of the population whose first language was either incompletely acquired or underwent a certain changes due to L2 influence.[95]

Challenges of blending heritage culture and heritage language

When children are interacting with more than one orthographic and grammatical system and more than one culture, they are living in simultaneous worlds,[96] and they are trying to acquire membership of different cultural, language and literacy groups in different contexts.[97] The task for these children to negotiate meanings in different languages and cultures is quite challenging.

Many heritage language-learning children are in the process of integrating practices and skills and approaches from their different literacy practices in the home and community to their mainstream culture. They mix and match both oral and texts in novel ways and they appropriate and syncretise[98] the blended forms of literacy.

In addition, many heritage language learners have to negotiate between different worlds and languages. They may speak the heritage language, yet their worldviews are often shaped or at least partly shaped by the mainstream culture. They may speak the heritage language, but lack understanding of its conventions. The Canadian researcher Rahat Naqvi gave a good example to show the negotiation of the children between their Canadian culture and their Urdu heritage culture.[99]

> Only a small part of the iceberg is visible on the surface, and the majority is submerged and visible undetected; this is similar to the comparison between the notions of peanut butter and Eid (a tradition-steeped part of Urdu-speaking culture). For Urdu-speaking children in Canada, the notion of peanut butter is

something tangible and visible, something they can easily identify with as being part of the Canadian culture. When children study Eid, it goes far below the surface and requires a much more profound understanding and development of ideas.[100]

Different pathways to literacy

The pathways for children to become literate in different languages vary among heritage language learners. Some children may develop heritage language literacy for a specific function. For example, children in an Indian heritage community in London use their different languages for different purposes. They write letters to their relatives in Gujarati, do their school homework in English and do their religious study assignments from the Madrasa in Urdu.[101]

Other children may develop heritage language literacy with the help of their mainstream language, that is, they use one language to make sense of another language. For instance, Mary checks her English dictionary to make sense of her Korean reading given to her by her Korean language schoolteachers.[102]

Still other children acquire and develop their heritage language literacy skills through formal schooling. For example, 12-year-old Jonathan goes to an American school in Beijing to study his heritage language, English.[103]

Additionally, some children acquire and develop their heritage language literacy skills at a younger age and some at an older age. Some develop their heritage language literacy skills simultaneously with their mainstream language literacy skills and some develop their mainstream and heritage language literacy skills consecutively.

As we can see, the pathways for heritage language literacy learners are not uninformed and they vary greatly according to their life's circumstances.

Needs for a Home Literacy Pedagogical Approach

Given the unique characteristics of heritage language learners,[104] it is clear that an adequate pedagogical approach is needed to support the unique needs in their multilingual literacy development, in particular, their heritage language literacy development. Currently, no pedagogical framework has been proposed specifically for teaching heritage language literacy in the home environment, even though many literacy teaching models and family literacy teaching strategies are scattered in the literature. The following literacy teaching approaches (which sometimes share similar ideas, but with different emphasis) may serve as an overarching guide.

First, the New London Group[105] proposed a pedagogical approach that involves four components:

- Situated practice.
- Overt instruction.
- Critical framing.
- Transformed practice.

These four components can be modified and applied in heritage language literacy teaching in the home environment. 'Situated practice' implies that heritage language literacy learning should occur in a specific social context, not in an isolated reading and writing activity. 'Overt instruction' means that the specific usage and cultural meaning embedded in the heritage language texts should be discussed with children explicitly. However, overt instruction does not imply direct transmission, drills or rote memorisation. The goal is conscious awareness and control over what is being learned. 'Critical framing' indicates that parents need to help children evaluate heritage language texts with a critical lens. 'Transformed practice' suggests that children should be able to show that they can implement understandings acquired through overt instruction and critical framing in practices that help them to apply and revise what they have learned, and process heritage language texts with elated understanding beyond print.

Second, Don Holdaway's theory of literacy development[106] suggests that children need to experience four basic processes in order to develop literacy competence. These processes can be modified as follows:

- Children need to observe adult literacy behaviours. For example, they need to be read to or see adults reading and writing.
- Children need to collaborate with adults who interact with them and provide encouragement, motivation and help when necessary.
- Children need to practise and experiment with reading and writing and make connections and increase skills with adult assistance.
- Children need opportunities to perform literacy skills independently.

Third, the literacy teaching principles proposed by Martha Combs[107] can also be useful to guide home teaching.

- Children develop literacy skills by being actively involved in constructing meaning from their experiences and communicating that meaning to others.
- Children develop literacy skills through modelling adults and through encouragement and opportunities to learn how to monitor and regulate their own learning.
- Children develop literacy skills in environments that are meaningful and non-threatening, where they feel valued and respected as individuals, and where they are encouraged to become independent, self-regulated learners.

Fourth, the five pillars for literacy practice proposed by Nancy DeVries Guth and Tamie Pratt-Fartro[108] can also be considered for home literacy instruction (though they were originally suggested for adolescent literacy instruction in the school environment). I modified the five areas to include the writing aspect.

- Time to read and write for enjoyment.
- Choice in reading materials and writing topics.

- Strategies for reading and writing.
- Vocabulary instruction.
- Motivation to read and write.

Moreover, when conceptualising the heritage language pedagogy in the home environment, we need to be mindful of the differences between the school literacy pedagogy and the home literacy pedagogy (even though some school literacy teaching methods are useful in the home environment). We also need to distinguish the different purposes of school literacy and home literacy. The major purpose of school literacy is for academic subject learning and the major purpose of home literacy is for social practices. In home literacy teaching, we need to go beyond the teaching and learning to read and write in only the page-bound, official (or standard) forms of a language, often the standard national (mainstream) language,[109] and broaden our understanding of literacy teaching and learning by considering the nature of heritage language literacy development outside the school environment.

Furthermore, when thinking about the pedagogy in the home environment, we need to consider the rapid change in text formats to include other modes of meaning that are dynamic representational resources, which are constantly being remade by their users as they work to achieve their purposes.[110] As Kate Pahl and Jennifer Rowsell in their edited book, *Travel Notes from the New Literacy Studies*, put it, 'Texts are increasingly multimodal. Images and words are often welded together on-screen or in children's texts'.[111] Indeed, the new communications media, such as the internet, is reshaping the way we use language (the iconographic and screen-based modes) and, thus, should be included in heritage language literacy instruction.

Finally, when considering the home heritage language pedagogy, we need to focus on flexibility in applying various teaching methods. What suits heritage language literary learners is the best method. Using an eclectic approach (taking the useful part from different methods) is the best approach. No single model can fit all.

Taken together with these literacy teaching approaches and ideas, Figure 2.1 shows how a home heritage language literacy pedagogical framework may look.

This framework contains four important key elements:

- Observation: children must have opportunities to observe how parents or other adults use literacy in the everyday context.
- Scaffolding: parents must provide support for children, such as providing overt instruction, helping them examine heritage language texts with a critical lens and taking an eclectic approach.
- Practice: children must have opportunities to practise heritage literacy skills in meaningful social contexts with different modes (e.g. printed texts or multimedia texts).
- Motivation: parents must find various ways to motivate children and help them to be lifelong heritage language readers and writers.

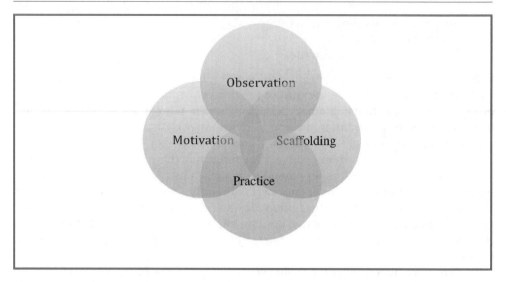

Figure 2.1 Pedagogical framework for home literacy development

In Chapters 4–6, you will see how these elements are applied in selecting heritage language literacy materials and designing heritage language literacy activities in the home teaching environment.

Summary

This chapter has touched on several important issues related to multilingual literacy learners.

A working definition of multiliteracy is proposed as reading or writing that occurs in more than one language and via more than one channel in meaningful social and cultural practices. Being multiliterate means that an individual is able to actively use more than one language in reading or writing with different levels of proficiency for a particular purpose in his/her environment.

Various factors that influence children's multiliteracy development are identified and discussed. These elements include ecological (environmental) factors, such as parents, siblings, extended family, community and society; linguistic factors, such as the convergence and divergence of a child's heritage language and mainstream language; and a child's individual factors, such as heredity, cognition, emotion, motivation and identity. In addition, a child's opportunities to practise reading and writing in the meaningful social context can affect his/her multilingual literacy attainment.

Heritage language learners' hidden advantages, unique linguistic behaviours, challenges and different pathways to literacy are addressed. A pedagogical framework consisting of four important components (observation, scaffolding, practice and motivation) is proposed to guide literacy teaching in the home environment.

Your Turn

Reflective Questions and Activities

- What could be the advantage of placing individuals at the different points on the multilingual proficiency continuum? Do you feel that this multilingual continuum helps you look at multilingual proficiency more realistically? Do you feel this continuum gives you hope in helping your children become multiliterate?
- Review the factors that influence a child's multilingual literacy development. Circle those factors that are most relevant to you (that you can control) and begin to think how you can pay attention to these areas in your multilingual and multiliteracy childrearing practice.
- By understanding the unique characteristics of heritage language literacy-learning children, do you feel more appreciative about your own heritage language-learning child and better understand her[112] challenges?
- Review the literacy approaches and ideas introduced in this chapter and underline the key elements that you believe are important in your situation. Try to apply them when you design heritage language literacy activities for your child. Alternatively, you can also use Figure 2.1 as a framework when you plan for your child's heritage language-learning activities.

Notes and References

1. The New London Group is a coalition of educational researchers from English-speaking countries. The group met in New London, New Hampshire, USA, in 1994 to discuss the important issues related to literacy and literacy education. The major ideas of this group can be found in: The New London Group (1996) A pedagogy of multiliteracies designing social futures. *Harvard Educational Review* 66 (1), 60–92.
2. I added the example of 'the Internet'.
3. Pahl, K. and Rowsell, J. (eds) (2006) *Travel Notes from the New Literacy Studies*. Clevedon: Multilingual Matters.
   The New London Group (1996) A pedagogy of multiliteracies designing social futures. *Harvard Educational Review* 66 (1), 60–92.
4. Street, B. (2000) Literacy events and literacy practices. In M. Martin-Jones and K. Jones (eds) *Multilingual Literacies: Reading and Writing Different Worlds* (pp. 17–35) Amsterdam: John Benjamins.
5. Street, B.V. and Lefstein, A. (2007) *Literacy: An Advanced Resource Book*. London: Routledge.
6. There are no standard rules for Swiss German dialect orthography. The written forms are based on different local Swiss dialects. The orthographies used in the Swiss German

literature can be roughly divided into two systems: those that try to stay as close to standard (High) German spelling as possible and those that try to represent the sounds as well as possible.

7. Wagner, D. (1993) *Literacy, Culture and Development: Becoming Literate in Morocco*. Cambridge: Cambridge University Press.
8. E-mail communication on 20 January 2010.
9. Wang, X-L. (2008) *Growing Up with Three Languages: Birth to Eleven* (pp. 17–18). Bristol: Multilingual Matters.
10. This multilingual competency continuum should not be confused with Nancy Hornberger's *Continua of Biliteracy* (see Hornberger, N.H. (2003) Continua of biliteracy. In N.H. Hornberger (ed.) *Continua of Biliteracy: An Ecological Framework for Educational Policy, Research, and Practice in Multilingual Settings* (pp. 3–34). Clevedon: Multilingual Matters), though the major ideas from Hornberger's continua framework are conveyed later in the section on the factors that influence multiliteracy development.
11. Edwards, V. (2009) *Learning to be Literate: Multilingual Perspectives*. Bristol: Multilingual Matters.
12. There are other definitions for your reference. For example, Nancy Hornberger defines biliteracy as 'any and all instances in which communication occurs in two or more languages in or around writing'. Hornberger, N.H. (2003) Continua of biliteracy. In N.H. Hornberger (ed.) *Continua of Biliteracy: An Ecological Framework for Educational Policy, Research, and Practice in Multilingual Settings* (p. xiii). Clevedon: Multilingual Matters.
13. Gregory, E. (2008) *Learning to Read in A New Language: Making Sense of Words and Worlds* (pp. 20–23). Los Angeles, CA: Sage.
14. Rosaldo, R. (1989) *Culture and Truth: The Remaking of Social Analysis* (p. 140). Boston, MA: Beacon Press.
15. Dickinson, D.K. and Tabor, P.O. (eds) (2001) *Beginning Literacy with Language*. Baltimore, MD: Paul H. Brookers.
16. Federal Interagency Forum on Child and Family Statistics (2002) *America's Children: Key National Indicators of Well-Being*. Washington, DC: U.S. Government Printing Office.
17. Adams, M.J., Treiman, R. and Pressley, M. (1998) Reading, writing, and literacy. In I. Sigel and K.A. Renninger (eds) *Handbook of Child Psychology: Child Psychology in Practice* (Vol. 4; pp. 275–355). New York: Wiley.
    Fletcher, K. and Reese, E. (2005) Picture book reading with young children: A conceptual framework. *Developmental Review* 25, 64–103.
18. DeTemple, J.M. (2001) Parents and children reading books together. In D.K. Dickinson and P.O. Tabors (eds) *Beginning Literacy with Language: Young Children Learning at Home and School* (pp. 31–51). Baltimore, MD: Paul H. Brookes.
19. Dickinson, D.K., De Temple, J.M., Hirschler, J.A. and Smith, M. (1992) Book reading with preschoolers: Construction of text at home and school. *Reading Research Quarterly 7*, 323–346.
    Snow, C. and Tabors, P. (1993) Language skills that relate to literacy development. In B. Spodek and N. Saracho (eds) *Yearbook in Early Childhood Education: Vol. 4 Language and Literacy in Early Childhood Education* (pp. 1–20). New York: Teachers Colleague Press.
    Wells, G. (1985) Preschool literacy-related activities and success in school. In D.R. Olson, N. Torrance and A. Hildyard (eds) *Literacy, Language and Learning* (pp. 229–225). Cambridge: Cambridge University Press.
20. Raikes, H., Pan, B.A., Luze, G., Tamis-LeMonda, L., Brooks-Gunn, J., Constantine, J., Tarullo, L.B., Raikes, H.A. and Rodriguez E.T. (2006) Mother-child book reading in low-income families: Correlates and outcomes during the first three years. *Child Development* 77, 924–953.

21. NICHD (2005) Pathways to reading: The role of oral language in the transition to reading. *Developmental Psychology* 41, 428–442.
Spira, E.G., Bracken, S.S. and Fischel, J.E. (2005) Predicting improvement after first-grade reading difficulties: The effects of oral language, emergent literacy, and behavior skills. *Developmental Psychology* 41, 225–234.
22. Fenson, L., Dale, P.S., Reznick, J.S. and Bates, E. (1994) Variability in early communication development. *Monographs of the Society for Research in Child Development* 59 (5), 1–189.
Hart, B. and Risle, T.R. (1995) *Meaningful Differences n the Everyday Experience of Young American Children*. Baltimore, MD: Brookes.
Hoff-Ginsberg, E. (1998) The relation of birth order and socioeconomic status to children's language experience and language development. *Applied Psycholinguistics* 19, 603–629.
Zhang, Y., Jin, X., Shen, X., Zhang, J. and Hoff, E. (2008) Correlates of early language development in Chinese children. *International Journal of Behavioral Development* 30 (2), 145–151.
23. Campbell, T.F., Dollaghan, C., Rockette, H.E., Paradise, J.L., Feldman, H.M., Shriberg, L.D., Sabao, D.L. and Kurs-Lasky, M. (2003) Risk factors for speech delay of unknown origin in 3-year-old children. *Child Development* 74, 346–357.
24. Hart, B. and Risley, R. (1995) *Meaningful Differences in the Everyday Experience of Young American Children*. Baltimore, MD: Brookes.
25. Wang, X-L. (2008) *Growing Up with Three Languages: Birth to Eleven*. Bristol: Multilingual Matters.
26. E-mail interview on 12 December 2009.
27. Anderson, J., Lenters, K. and McTavish, M. (2008) Constructing families, constructing literacy: A critical analysis of family literacy websites. *The School Community Journal* 18 (1), 61–78.
28. Kenner, C. (2005) Bilingual families as literacy eco-systems. *Early Years* 25 (3), 283–298.
However, some studies also suggest that in some families, the sibling interaction may not be conducive to support multiliteracy development if one sibling is reluctant to use the heritage language and the other prefers to use the heritage language. For more information, see Obied, V.M. (2009) How do siblings shape the language environment in bilingual families? *International Journal of Bilingual Education and Bilingualism* 12 (6), 705–720.
29. Gregory, E. (2005) Guiding lights: Siblings as literacy teacher. In J. Anderson, M. Kendrick, T. Rogers and S. Smythe (eds) *Portraits of Literacy across Families, Communities and Schools: Intersections and Tension* (pp. 21–39). Mahwah, NJ: Lawrence Erlbaum.
30. E-mail interview on 5 March 2007.
31. E-mail interview on 2 February 2007.
32. In-person interview on 20 March 2008.
33. In-person interview on 20 April 2009.
34. Example from Sneddon, R. (2007) Learning in three languages in home and community. In J. Conteh, P. Martin and L.H. Robertson (eds) *Multilingual Learning: Stories from Schools and Communities in Britain* (pp. 23–40). Stoke-on-Trent: Trentham Books.
35. Anthony, J.L. and Francis, D.J. (2005) Development of phonological awareness. *Current Directions in Psychological Sciences* 14, 255–259.
36. Rohl, M. (2000) Learning about words, sounds and letters. In C. Barrat-Pugh and M. Rohl (eds) *Literacy Learning in the Early Years* (p. 62). Buckingham: Open University Press.
37. Frith, U., Wimmer, H. and Landerl, K. (1998) Differences in phonological recoding in German- and English-speaking children. *Scientific Studies of Reading* 2, 31–54.
Wimmer, H. and Goswami, U. (1994) The influence of orthographic consistency on reading development: Word recognition in English and German Children. *Cognition* 51, 91–103.

Bentin, S., Hammer, R. and Cahan, S. (1991) The effects of aging and first-grade schooling on the development of phonological awareness. *Psychological Science* 2, 271–274.

38. Hoff, E. (2009) *Language Development* (p. 415). Belmont, CA: Wadsworth.

39. Edwards, V. (2009) *Learning to Be Literate: Multilingual Perspectives*. Bristol: Multilingual Matters.

Hoff, E. (2003) The specificity of environmental influences: Socioeconomic status affects early vocabulary development via maternal speech. *Child Development* 72, 1368–1378.

40. Hanley, J.R., Tzeng, O. and Huang, H.-S. (1999) Learning to read Chinese. In M. Harris and G. Hatano (eds) *Learning to Read and Write: A Cross-Linguistic Perspective* (pp. 173–195). New York: Cambridge University Press.

41. Barnitz, J.G. (1982) Orthographies, bilingualism and learning to read English as a second language. *Reading Teacher* 35 (5), 560–567.

Niyekawa, A.M. (1983) Biliteracy acquisition and its sociocultural effects. In M.C. Chang (ed.) *Asian- and Pacific-American Perspectives in Bilingual Education* (pp. 97–119). New York: Teachers Colleague Press.

Thonis, E. (1981) Reading instruction for language minority students. In *Schooling and Language Minority Students: A Theoretical Framework* (pp. 147–181). Los Angles: Evaluation, Dissemination and Assessment Center, California State University.

42. Edelsky, C. (1982) Writing in a bilingual program: The relation of L1 and L2 texts. *TESOL Quarterly* 16 (2), 211–228.

Fishman, J.A., Gertner, M., Lowy, E.G. and Milán, W.G. (eds) (1985) *The Rise and Fall of the Ethnic Revival: Perspectives on Language and Ethnicity* (Vol. 37). Berlin: Mouton.

Fillmore, L.W. and Valadez, C. (1986) Teaching bilingual learners. In M.C. Wittrock (ed.) *Handbook of Research on Teaching* (pp. 648–685). New York: Macmillan.

43. See Wang, X.-L. (2008) *Growing Up with Three Languages: Birth to Eleven*. Bristol: Multilingual Matters.

44. Putonghua is a standard speech used in the People's Republic of China, Taiwan (called 国语) and Singapore.

45. Pinyin is an aphetic system that is used in the People's Republic of China to help young children learn to read Chinese.

46. 注音符号 is an alphabetic system used in Taiwan to help young children learn to read Chinese.

47. Bialystok, E. (2002) Acquisition of literacy in bilingual children: A framework for research. *Language Learning* 52, 159–199.

48. Wang, M., Yang, C. and Cheng, C-X. (2009) The contributions of phonology, orthography, and morphology in Chinese-English biliteracy acquisition. *Applied Psycholinguistics* 30, 291–314.

49. Hall, D.P. and Cunningham, P.M. (2009) *Making Words: 50 Interactive Lessons that Build Phonemic Awareness, Phonics, and Spelling Skills*. Boston, MA: Allyn & Bacon.

50. Adams, M.J. (1990) *Beginning to Read: Thinking and Learning about Print*. Cambridge: MIT Press.

Cunningham, P. (2005) *Phonics They Use*. Boston: Allyn and Bacon.

51. Wang, M., Yang, C. and Cheng, C-X. (2009) The contributions of phonology, orthography, and morphology in Chinese-English biliteracy acquisition. *Applied Psycholinguistics* 30, 291–314.

52. Shanahan, T. (2006) Relations among oral language, reading, and writing development. In C.A. MacArthur, S. Graham and J. Fitzgerald (eds) *Handbook of Writing Research* (pp. 171–183). New York: Guilford.

53. Street, B. (1988) A critical look at Walter Ong and the Great Divide. *Literacy Research Center* 4 (1), 1–5.

54. Heath, S.B. (1983) *Ways with Words: Language, Life and Work in Communities and Classrooms*. New York: Cambridge University Press.
55. Wang, X.-L., Bernas, R. and Eberhard, P. (2002) Variations in maternal support to children's early literacy development in Chinese and Native American families: Implications for early childhood educators. *International Journal of Early Childhood* 34 (1), 9–23.
56. Trzesniewski, K., Moffitt, T., Caspi, A., Taylor, A. and Maughan, B. (2006) Revisiting the association between reading achievement and antisocial behavior: New evidence of an environmental explanation from a twin study. *Child Development* 77, 72–88.
    Harlaar, N., Dale, P.S. and Plomin, R. (2007) From learning to read to reading to learn: Substantial and stable genetic influence. *Child Development* 78, 116–131.
57. Trzesniewski, K., Moffitt, T., Caspi, A., Taylor, A. and Maughan, B. (2006) Revisiting the association between reading achievement and antisocial behavior: New evidence of an environmental explanation from a twin study. *Child Development* 77, 72–88.
58. Oliver, B.R., Dale, P.S. and Plomin, R. (2005) Predicting literacy at age 7 from preliteracy at age 4: A longitudinal genetic analysis. *Psychological Science* 16, 861–865.
59. Kraus, N. and Banai, K. (2007) Auditory-processing malleability: Focus on language and music. *Current Directions in Psychological Science* 16, 105–110.
60. Hammer, C.S. and Miccio, A.W. (2006) early language and reading development of bilingual preschoolers from low-income families. *Topics in Language Disorders* 26 (4), 322–337.
61. Jenkins, J.R., Fuchs, L.S., van den Broek, P., Espin, C. and Deno, S.L. (2003) Sources of individual differences in reading comprehension and reading fluency. *Journal of Educational Psychology* 95, 719–729.
    Whitehurst, G.J. and Lonigan, C.J. (1998) Child development and emergent literacy. *Child Development* 69, 848–872.
62. Swanson, H.L., Trainin, G., Necoechea, D.M. and Hammill, D.D. (2003) Rapid naming, phonological awareness, and reading: A meta-analysis of the correlation evidence. *Review of Educational Research* 73, 407–440.
63. Liu, Y. and Perfetti, C.A. (2003) The time course of brain activity in reading English and Chinese: An ERP study of Chinese bilinguals. *Human Brain Mapping* 18, 167–175.
    Tan, L.H., Liu, H.-L., Perfetti, C.A., Spinks, J.A., Fox, P.T. and Gao, J.-H. (2001) The neural system underlying Chinese logographic reading. *NeuroImage* 13, 836–846.
    Tan, L.H., Spinks, J.A., Feng, C.M., Siok, W.T., Perfetti, C.A., Xiong, J., Fox, P. and Gao, J.H. (2003) Neural systems of second language reading are shaped by native language. *Human Brain Mapping* 18, 158–166.
64. Executive function means processes such as selective attention, rehearsal, elaboration and organization that influence encoding, storage and retrieval of information in memory.
65. Ransdell, S., Levy, C.M. and Kellogg, R.T. (2002) The structure of writing processes as revealed by secondary task demands. *L1-Educational Studies in Language and Literature* 2, 141–163.
66. Kovelman, I., Baker, S.A. and Petitto, L.A. (2008) Age of first bilingual language exposure as a new window into bilingual reading development. *Bilingualism: Language and Cognition* 11 (2), 203–223.
67. SAT stands for Scholastic Aptitude Test. It is a test used for college admission in the USA.
68. Benbow, C., Lubinski, D., Shea, D. and Eftekhari-Sanjani, H. (2000) Sex differences in mathematical reasoning ability at age 13: Their status 20 years later. *Psychological Science* 11, 474–480.
69. Halpern, D.F. (2000) *Sex Differences in Cognitive Abilities* (p. 94). Mahwah, NJ: Erlbaum.

70. Sneddon, R. (2007) Learning in three languages in home and community. In J. Conteh, P. Martin and L.H. Robertson (eds) *Multilingual Learning: Stories from Schools and Communities in Britain* (pp. 23–40). Stoke-on-Trent: Trentham Books.

71. Robertson, L.H. (2007) The story of bilingual children learning to read. In J. Conteh, P. Martin and Robertson, L.H. (eds) *Multilingual Learning: Stories from Schools and Communities in Britain* (pp. 41–85). Stoke-on-Trent: Trentham Books.

72. van Ijzendoorn, M.H., Dikstra, J. and Bus, A. (1995) Attachment, intelligence, and language: A meta-analysis. *Social Development* 4 (2), 115–128.
Bus, A.G., Belsky, J., van Ijzendoorn, M.H. and Crnic, K. (1997) Attachment and book reading patterns: A study of mothers, fathers, and their toddlers. *Early Childhood Research Quarterly* 12, 81–98.

73. Kindergarten age in the US public systems is between 5 and 6. It is the first year of compulsory education in most public schools. The rough equivalent in Australia, New Zealand and some parts of the UK is Year One.

74. Bus, A.G. and van Ijzendoorn, M.H. (1988) Attachment and early reading: A longitudinal study. *The Journal of Genetic Psychology* 149, 199–210.
Pianta, R.C. and Harbers, K. (1996) Observing mother and child behavior in a problem-solving situation at school entry: Relations with academic achievement. *Journal of School Psychology* 67, 307–322.

75. Tomasello, M. (2007) Cooperation and communication in the 2nd year of life. *Child Development Perspectives* 1, 8–12.

76. Fredrickson, B.L. (2001) The role of positive emotions in positive psychology: The broaden-and-build theory of positive emotions. *American Psychologist* 56, 218–226.
Izard, C.E. (2007) Basic emotions, natural kinds, emotion schemas, and a new paradigm. *Perspectives on Psychological Science* 2, 260–280.

77. Ashby, F.G., Isen, A.M. and Turken, A.U. (1999) A neuropsychological theory of positive affect and its influence on cognition. *Psychological Review* 106, 529–550.

78. Bus, A.G. and van Ijzendoorn, M.H. (1988) Attachment and early reading: A longitudinal study. *The Journal of Genetic Psychology* 149, 199–210.

79. Clingenpeel, B.T. and Pianta, R.C. (2007) Mothers' sensitivity and book-reading interactions with first graders. *Early Education and Development* 18, 1–22.

80. Bergin, C. (2001) The parent-child relationship during beginning reading. *Journal of Literacy Research* 33, 681–706.
Bergin, D. and Bergin, C. (2011) *Child and Adolescent Development in Your Classroom.* Florence, KY: Cengage Learning. Please note that the information on pp. 25, 29, 30 and 31 was obtained either directly or indirectly from this reference.

81. Gregory, E. (2008) *Learning to Read in A New Language: Making Sense of Words and Worlds* (pp. 28–29). Los Angeles, CA: Sage.

82. Tse, L. (1998) Affecting affect: The impact of heritage language programs on student attitudes. In S.D. Krashen, L. Tse and J. McQuilan (eds) *Heritage Language Development* (pp. 51–72). Culver City, CA: Language Education Associates.

83. Wang, X-L. (2008) *Growing Up with Three Languages: Birth to Eleven.* Bristol: Multilingual Matters.

84. See Note 26.

85. Tse, L. (1998) Affecting affect: The impact of heritage language programs on student attitudes. In S.D. Krashen, L. Tse and J. McQuilan (eds) *Heritage Language Development* (pp. 51–72). Culver City, CA: Language Education Associates.

86. Valdés, G. (2001) Heritage language students: Profiles and possibilities. In J.K. Peyton, D.A. Ranard and S. McGinnis (eds) *Heritage Languages in America: Preserving a National Resource* (pp. 37–77). Washington, DC: Center for Applied Linguistics and Delta Systems.

87. Kagan, O. (2005) In support of a proficiency-based definition of heritage language learners: The case of Russian. *The International Journal of Bilingual Education and Bilingualism* 8 (2 & 3), 213–221.

88. Kagan, O. (2005) In support of a proficiency-based definition of heritage language learners: The case of Russian. *The International Journal of Bilingual Education and Bilingualism* 8 (2 &3), 213–221.
Schwartz, A.M. (2001) Preparing teachers to work with heritage language learners. In J.K. Peyton, D.A. Ranard and S. McGinnis (eds) *Heritage Languages in America: Preserving a National Resource* (pp. 229–252). McHenry, IL: Centre for Applied Linguistics and Delta Systems Co.
Kagan, O. and Dillon, K. (2001) A new perspective on teaching Russian: Focus on the heritage leaner. *The Slavic and East European Journal* 45 (3), 507–518.

89. 'Wug' is a word coined by language researcher Jean Berko Gleason to investigate English-speaking children's acquisition of plural forms and other inflectional morphemes.

90. Ellis, N. (1997) Implicit and explicit language learning—An overview. In N.C. Ellis (ed.) *Implicit and Explicit Learning of Languages* (pp. 1–31). London: Academic Press.

91. Anderson, J. (2008) Toward an integrated second-language pedagogy for foreign and community/heritage language in multilingual Britain. *Language Learning Journal* 36 (1), 79–89.

92. Dorian, N.C. (1981) *Language Death: The Life Cycle of a Scottish Gaelic Dialect*. Philadelphia, PA: University of Pennsylvania Press.
Hornberger, N.H. (1994) Continua of biliteracy. In B.M. Ferdman, R.M. Weber and A.G. Ramirez (eds) *Literacy across Language and Cultures* (pp. 103–139). New York: New York State University Press.

93. Explained by the author of this book.

94. Explained by the author of this book.

95. Isurin, L. and Ivanova-Sullivan, T. (2008) Lost in between: The case of Russian heritage speakers. *Heritage Language Journal* 6 (1), 72–104.

96. Kenner, C. (2004) *Becoming Biliterate: Young Children Learning Different Writing Systems* (p. 55). Stoke-on-Trent: Trentham Books.

97. Gregory, E. (2008) *Learning to Read in A New Language: Making Sense of Words and Worlds* (p. 25). Los Angeles, CA: Sage.

98. Robertson, L.H. (2007) The story of bilingual children learning to read. In J. Conteh, P. Martin and L.H. Robertson (eds) *Multilingual Learning: Stories from Schools and Communities in Britain* (pp. 41–61). Stoke-on-Trent: Trentham Books.

99. Weaver, G.R. (1993) Understanding and coping with cross-cultural adjustment stress. In R.M. Paige (ed.) *Education for the Intercultural Experience* (pp. 122–139). Yarmouth, ME: Intercultural Press.

100. Naqvi, R. (2008) From peanut butter to Eid…blending perspectives: Teaching Urdu to children in Canada. *Diaspora, Indigenous, and Minority Education* 2, 154–164.

101. Sneddon, R. (2007) Learning in three languages in home and community. In J. Conteh, P. Martin and L.H. Robertson (eds) *Multilingual Learning: Stories from Schools and Communities in Britain* (pp. 23–40). Stoke-on-Trent: Trentham Books.

102. See Note 30.

103. E-mail communication on 23 May 2009.

104. Chevalier, J.F. (2004) Heritage language literacy: Theory and practice. *Heritage Language Journal* 2 (1), 1–9.
Kondo-Brown, K. (2003) Heritage language instruction for post-secondary students from immigrant backgrounds. *Heritage Language Journal* 1 (10), 1–25.

105. The New London Group (1996) A pedagogy of multiliteracies designing social futures. *Harvard Educational Review* 66 (1), 60–92.
   Garcia, G.E. and Willis, A.I. (2001) Frameworks for understanding multicultural literacies. In P.R. Schmidt and P.B. Mosenthal (eds) *Reconceptualizing Literacy in the New Age of Multiculturalism and Pluralism* (pp. 3–31). Greenwich, CT: Information Age Publishing.
106. Holdaway, D. (1986) The structure of natural learning as a basis for literacy instruction. In M. Sampson (ed.) *The Pursuit of Literacy: Early Reading and Writing.* Dubuque, IA: Kendall/Hunt.
   Holdaway, D. (1979) *The Foundation of Literacy.* Sydney: Ashton Scholastic.
107. Combs, M. (2006) *Readers and Writers in Primary Grades: A Balanced and Integrated Approach* (pp. 8–22). Upper Saddle River, NJ: Merrill Prentice Hall.
108. DeVries Guth, N. and Pratt-Fartro, T. (2010) *Literacy Coaching to Build Adolescent Learning: 5 Pillars of Practice.* Thousand Oaks, CA: Corwin.
109. Cazden, C., Cope, B., Fairclough, N., Gee, J., Kalantzis, M., Kress, G., Luke, A., Luke, C., Michaels, S. and Nakata, M. (1996) A pedagogy of multilingual literacies: Designing social futures. *Harvard Educational Review* 66 (1), 60–92.
110. The New London Group (1996) A pedagogy of multiliteracies designing social futures. *Harvard Educational Review* 66 (1), 60–92.
111. Pahl, K. and Rowsell, J. (2006) Introduction. In K. Pahl and J. Rowsell (eds) *Travel Notes from the New Literacy Studies: Instances of Practice* (p. 9). Clevedon: Multilingual Matters.
112. I sometimes use 'her' or 'she' and 'him' or 'he' alternately in the book.

Chapter 3
The Importance of Active Planning

This chapter examines the necessity and importance of active planning during the process of helping your children develop heritage language literacy skills in the home environment. You are encouraged to evaluate your individual situation carefully before rushing into home literacy teaching. You are urged to develop a home literacy teaching plan to guide your practice and use suitable home literacy assessment methods to monitor your children's literacy progress. You are invited to use the ongoing self-reflection as an impetus to improve your home literacy teaching quality. At the end of the chapter, a set of activities and reflective questions are presented to provide opportunities for you to relate your own situation to the content discussed in this chapter.

A Lesson Learned from Ms Andersson

I begin this chapter by telling a story about a parent, Ms Andersson, to emphasise the significance of planning and how it can affect children's multilingual and multiliterate development outcomes.

Ms Andersson moved to the USA from Stockholm in 1979 after she married an American. Two years later, she gave birth to a son and then a daughter three years later. She worked as a CEO for a textile company. Despite her demanding work schedule, Ms Andersson decided to bring up her children bilingual and biliterate in English and Swedish.

Ms Andersson tried to speak Swedish to her children early in their lives and read Swedish children's books to them whenever she could. However, when Ms Andersson realised that her children seemed to prefer English to Swedish, she began to switch to English. One day, she met a Swedish friend who shared her successful story of raising three bilingual and biliterate children. Inspired by her friend, Ms Andersson decided to re-engage her children in Swedish and she resumed speaking Swedish to them. However, her action did not bring about much change in her children. When her children were in elementary school, she finally abandoned trying to speak Swedish to them because she felt that she was not able to get her children to cooperate.

Nonetheless, her hope to bring up her children bilingual and biliterate did not diminish completely. She thought that even if she could not make her children speak Swedish, she could at least help them read and write in Swedish. She found some Swedish language textbooks and tried to work through the books with her children. However, because of her busy work schedule, she could only work with them on a sporadic basis. She constantly struggled to keep her children concentrated on their Swedish language learning tasks. It was an excruciating experience for Ms Andersson. She continued to drag along like this for about two years, employing different methods that she had heard about from her friends. Her children did not seem to make any progress in their Swedish literacy skills. Ms Andersson was frustrated and finally gave up her dream of bringing up her children bilingual and biliterate.

When reflecting on her experience, Ms Andersson made the following comments:

> I didn't really know what I was doing. I tried many things without a plan and direction... and I didn't know where I was heading. I didn't know how to get my children interested...If I had known what I know now, it would have made a difference with my children.[1]

We can learn several things from Ms Andersson's experience. First, Ms Andersson did not evaluate her own situation carefully before starting her practice. She did not examine her reality and find out how she could adapt her busy work schedule to her children's Swedish learning at home. Second, she did not think her teaching strategies through before using them (e.g. when she heard about the strategies used by her friends, she copied them without thinking about her own situation). Finally and most importantly, other than wanting to bring up her children bilingual and biliterate, Ms Andersson did not have a plan on how to help her children achieve the goal.

Planning is especially important in the home literacy teaching and learning environment. Unlike in the school system, there is no set curriculum to guide what parents do at home. Thus, thinking through what you do can help you be better prepared for the possible challenges ahead, avoid unnecessary mistakes and become more confident.[2] The following analogy illustrates how important it is to plan ahead.

Suppose two young couples Jacque and Susanne and Pierre and Jacqueline from Geneva decide to take a trip to Amsterdam. This is their first long distance road trip since they recently received their driver's licenses. They plan to reach Amsterdam in two days in separate cars. The two couples will take different approaches with regard to the preparation of the trip: Jacque and Susanne will use their instinct to get to Amsterdam without much planning and Pierre and Jacqueline will make out a careful plan before the trip.

Pierre and Jacqueline first do a thorough search on Google maps to find out the possible roads that lead to Amsterdam and the time needed to reach there. They also search for available hotels. Once they have the information, Pierre and Jacqueline begin to evaluate their suitability for the trip. They ask themselves whether they are able to drive a long distance because they are new drivers and whether they can afford the trip since they are on a budget. After pondering on these factors, Pierre and Jacqueline decide that they want to bring their friend Danielle along on the trip because he is an experienced driver and traveller, and he can offer help and advice when needed. In addition, Pierre and Jacqueline decide to use the autobahn in Germany instead of using the French autoroute to save money (to avoid paying tolls).

They also decide to drive an extra 30 km in order to stay in a budget hotel. They will leave early in the morning to avoid road construction delays.

It is obvious that Pierre and Jacqueline are better prepared for the trip than Jacque and Susanne. Pierre and Jacqueline will most likely accomplish their journey with less surprises and frustrations than Jacque and Susanne. Pierre and Jacqueline's planning is active because they do all they can to get themselves ready for their trip. Thus, the active planning process serves the purpose of preparation, anticipation and confidence.

Since the language and literacy learning experience provided by parents will certainly influence children's heritage language and literacy development outcome,[3] you will want to make sure that what you do in their heritage language learning will yield the best results, even though you may still encounter challenges and surprises (just like Pierre and Jacqueline will probably still encounter surprises on their trip; they, however, are better prepared than Jacque and Susanne to deal with the surprises). In the remaining part of this chapter, I will discuss the important aspects involved in the active planning process.

Evaluating Your Situation

Your availability

If you are a parent who spends a lot of time working outside the home, if you travel often, if you are a single parent[4] or if you have any other factors that prevent you from spending time with your children, can you still raise a multilingual and multiliterate child? The answer is probably. Spending less time with your children is indeed a serious challenge with regard to their heritage language and literacy learning. However, spending less time with your children does not necessarily mean that you cannot help them with their heritage language and literacy development.

If you are an often-absent parent, realistically estimating how much time you are able to devote to your children's heritage language and literacy learning on a daily or weekly basis can help you budget your time effectively. When you are conscious about your time constraints, you tend to be more inclined to focus on the tasks and use every available minute.

Another way to deal with the time limitation issue is to prioritise the important things that you must do in your life. If you set your children's heritage language literacy learning as one of your life's priorities, you will probably be able to find time creatively. For instance, often-absent and busy parents can make heritage literacy teaching and learning happen by using technology: talking and reading to your children via webcam and using the internet, e-mails and pre-recorded videos/audios.[5]

If, after seriously examining your availability, you conclude that you are unable to spend enough time teaching your children, you may want to find other options, such as hiring a tutor, sending your children to a community heritage language school, enrolling them in a school heritage language after-school programme or an international school.

Your ability

Knowing your ability in teaching heritage language literacy is also crucial. As discussed in Chapter 1, the teaching quality determines children's learning outcomes. Before you commit to any strategy, you may want to think about the following things.

First, you may want to evaluate your own heritage language literacy competency. If you think that you are not confident with your own competence in your heritage language literacy, it is likely that the outcome of your children's learning will be affected by your heritage literacy limitation. In this case, you may want to look for other support in your environment to help your children develop heritage language literacy skills, such as the types of heritage language schools and programmes mentioned above, or you can find tutors or other parents who are more proficient in your heritage language literacy to help you. However, even though your heritage literacy level may be limited, your role as a supporting parent is still very important. For example, you can help monitor your children while they are doing the tasks given by the tutor or the language schoolteacher. You can find heritage language reading materials for your children. You can motivate them to continue with their heritage language literacy learning.

Second, you may want to evaluate your comfort level with teaching your child at home. Some parents feel at ease in working with their children in the home environment and others feel less at ease in the same situation. However, none of us are born to be good teachers, yet we can each try to improve. We can perfect our teaching abilities by constantly thinking about what we do, learning from our experiences and informing ourselves through reading.

Your support

Evaluating what kinds of support you will get in your environment (your family, community and school) and knowing the available resources you will have access to will help you effectively allocate your time and effort. You may want to examine your support by thinking about the following questions:

- Are you the only major heritage language input provider?
- Can your spouse or other family members help?
- Can you find other heritage language speakers, such as babysitters, childcare providers or tutors?
- Do you have friends who share the same heritage language background? If so, can you team up with them?
- Does your community have a heritage language school or class?
- Where do you find resources for your children's literacy development? Do you have access to them and can you afford them? If not, what are your options?

Think through each of these questions very carefully and plan your strategies accordingly. If you think your support is meagre, you might want to come up with a plan that will make your home literacy teaching possible.

Your childrearing beliefs

In Chapter 2, we discussed how parents' childrearing beliefs about the purpose of literacy can influence how they interact with their children in heritage language literacy learning activities. Many studies conducted in different cultural communities have shown that children's language and literacy development outcomes are closely associated with the parents' cultural childrearing beliefs.[6] If your child lives in an environment that holds different teaching and learning beliefs than the ones in your heritage culture, it may be important for you to negotiate the differences for the benefit of your child.

For example, if your culture emphasises parent-centred teaching (the parents decide the direction of teaching and learning) and your child's mainstream culture values child-centred teaching and learning (focus on the learning needs of the children), your child might resist your methods of teaching. Whether you want to follow your cultural beliefs in teaching or not is absolutely your choice as long as your child's interests are seriously considered.

Your child

Understanding your children's learning characteristics and needs can help you teach them effectively. Some strategies that you have read or heard about may work well with other children but not yours. Your children should be the yardstick to measure what is suitable for them. You might want to take into consideration your children's temperament, interests, age and ability when you decide what kinds of teaching strategies to use.

Your expectation

While we all want our children to achieve the highest proficiency in their heritage language literacy, the reality is that every family situation is different and every child is different. Given the challenges and complexity of becoming multilingual readers and writers, as discussed in Chapter 2, the expectation that we have for our children needs to be realistic and achievable to prevent frustration and disappointment.

In addition, if your children have more than one heritage language, for example, one from the father and one from the mother, you will have to think very carefully based on all the factors in your situation whether you want to help your children to develop literacy skills in all their heritage languages or only one heritage language. You may also want to determine at what age you will begin the literacy learning process.[7]

After ruminating on your situation, if you feel that you are able to take up the challenge to help your children develop their heritage language literacy skills at home, you can begin to think about the next step in the active planning process, that is, to develop a home teaching and learning plan to guide your practice.

Developing an Active Home Teaching and Learning Plan

The planning process in home language and literacy teaching is rarely discussed in the literature. This is probably due to the popular belief that home teaching is spontaneous and casual. Although the nature of the home teaching environment is not the same as the school environment, it is worth noting that unlike oral language acquisition, reading and writing is a learned ability,[8] which requires more systematic and targeted efforts. Ms Andersson's lament, 'I didn't really know what I was doing. I tried many things without a plan and direction... and I didn't know where I was heading. I didn't know how to get my children interested', is a powerful reminder for us to take home teaching and learning planning seriously. In fact, research confirms that careful planning can lead to children's successful multilingual and multiliteracy attainment.[9]

The following is an active planning process that I propose for you to consider:

- Setting home literacy teaching and learning goals (the overall literacy development goals that you want your children to achieve, the areas of competence that you want your children to develop and how you can help your children to obtain the areas of competence that you have identified).
- Deciding on which home literacy assessment methods to use (the measures that you will use to help you know whether your children are doing well in the areas that you have identified).
- Designing a home literacy activity plan or action plan (the concrete activities that you plan to carry out with your children).
- Reflecting on the process and results (how your children responded to the activities you designed, whether your strategies worked and what action you need to take for the next cycle of learning).

Although these components are described in a linear order, they should be treated as an ongoing operation, that is, the beginning and end are not clearly separated and they are merged continuously (see Figure 3.1). I will elaborate on this process below.

Home literacy teaching and learning goals

Effective planning requires establishing clear goals, and clear goals serve as a roadmap to guide you where you intend to go. When thinking about the goals of your children's heritage language literacy learning, you may want to set long-term and short-term goals based on your specific situation. The short-term goals may be

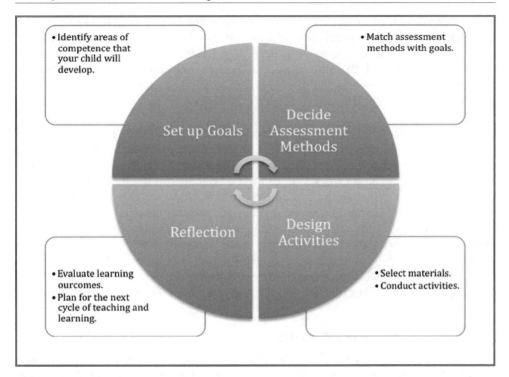

Set up Goals
• Identify areas of competence that your child will develop.

Decide Assessment Methods
• Match assessment methods with goals.

Reflection
• Evaluate learning ourcomes.
• Plan for the next cycle of teaching and learning.

Design Activities
• Select materials.
• Conduct activities.

Figure 3.1 Home literacy planning process

what your children can achieve daily or weekly and the long-term goals may be what your children can accomplish monthly, quarterly or yearly.

There are several areas that you may want to consider when you set goals for your children. First, you need to match your long-term and short-term goals with the factors discussed earlier, such as your availability, your ability, your support, your beliefs and your child's developmental level. This reality check may help you see whether the goals you set are possible to achieve. A mother once shared with me her heritage language teaching plan for her 13-year-old son. She planned to teach her son 20 new words daily in addition to a five-page grammar exercise, plus one heritage language book per week. This mother's plan was ambitious in her family situation. Her son already had a full schedule for his schoolwork, sports and musical activities. Both parents had to work fulltime. It is not hard to imagine how this mother's plan would end.[10]

Second, the short-term and long-term goals you set for your children should be concrete and measurable. For example, the goal 'be able to use the new words in writing' is concrete and measurable, whereas the goal 'be able to appreciate the author's writing style' is not concrete and is hard to measure. This does not mean that children's ability to 'appreciate' is not important to measure. Rather, it means that your children's 'appreciation' should be measured in a concrete term, for example, by identifying the areas where they have demonstrated 'appreciation' (e.g. the child noticed that the author used different adjectives to describe the protagonist's deep feeling or the child noticed that the author often used exaggerated terms to draw the reader's attention to the inner world of the protagonist).

Third, it is always productive to plan short-term and long-term goals together with your children, even young children. When doing so, your children will feel empowered and motivated. For example, my older son Léandre complained that, because of his heavy homework load in high school, he did not have time to do the Chinese language exercises that I planned for him. However, as soon as I began to involve him in the planning process, asking his opinion on what he could do, he began to cooperate with me. Occasionally, he even came up with some brilliant ideas on how to carry out OUR plan in a more effective way.

Finally, the short-term and long-term goals should not be inflexible; they can be revised or changed based on your children's learning experience. If you notice that your goals are not realistic, you should not hesitate to modify or even abandon them.

Home literacy assessment methods

The nature of teaching and learning heritage language literacy skills in the home environment makes assessing children's progress even more critical because this is the way that you know how well you and your children are doing. Traditionally, the assessment takes place only at the end of a teaching activity. The backward curriculum design model (or understanding by design)[11] moves the assessment step before a teaching activity actually happens. The advantage of thinking about the assessment before designing teaching activities is that it can help us focus on the goals when conducting activities and avoid assessing aspects that are not relevant to the goals.

Moreover, the assessment methods for a child's language and literacy development are often norm-referenced standardised language tests (compared with other children). There are several problems associated with using norm-referenced standardised literacy achievement tests to evaluate children in the home learning environment. First, there is no norm for children who are learning language and literacy in different home environments. Second, norm-referenced standardised tests do not reflect children's ability to use language and literacy in real-life situations. Thus, it is inadequate to use norm-referenced standardised literacy tests to assess children who are learning heritage language literacy in the home environment. The Australian educator Collette Taylor believes that children need to be given many opportunities to demonstrate their literacy competence and progress. She recommends that the key to helping children develop and learn is to capture the widely diverse ways that they may demonstrate capacities and then use these to document progress and assist them with their new understandings. Verbal, written, technological, artistic and dramatic expressions all contribute to the demonstration of literacy competence.[12]

Given the nature of children who develop heritage language literacy in the home environment, I recommend six easy-to-do assessment methods that may be useful to evaluate your children's heritage language literacy progress. In Chapters 5 and 6, I will introduce additional assessment methods to meet the needs of children during middle childhood and adolescent periods.

Observation log

You can keep an observation log while you are working with your children on their heritage language literacy activities. The value of keeping an observation log is to help you mark the important progress that your children have made and attend to the areas that need improvement. Overall, the observation log serves the functions of recording what happens in your children's heritage language literacy learning. There is really no standard way of keeping an observation log; it can be detailed or brief. You will get a feel for it once you begin to use it. The following is an example of an observation log. You can use it as a template and add or delete the items to suit your needs.

Date of observation	
Learning activity or task	
Child's motivation	
Child's learning behaviour	
Child's learning outcome	
Further action plan (what you want to do next)	
Other comments	

Checklists

You can also use a checklist to help you track whether your children are making progress in the areas that you have taught them. A checklist is a quick way to find out at the end of a task whether your children are able or unable to attain the skills. Below is an example of a checklist; you can modify it based on your needs.

Skills or areas taught	Mastered	Not Mastered	Other comments
Skill 1	x		
Skill 2		x	
Skill 3	x		
Skill 4		x	

Sibling review

As children become more proficient in their heritage language, you can begin to ask them to offer sibling critiques or reviews. For example, you can ask one sibling to read a paragraph and ask the other to check whether the words are pronounced correctly. You can also ask one sibling to check the other's spelling or grammar. Often, the older sibling or the one with more heritage language proficiency can function better in sibling critique. However, the younger or less proficient sibling can also play an important role in sibling review. They can serve as a learning partner or a monitor to move things along.

Self-assessment

You can also help your children develop abilities to examine their own work and progress. Encourage your children to revisit or revise their work. For example, you can develop a chart for them to facilitate their self-assessment. Suppose you want your child to assess her reading comprehension of a heritage language text, the following chart may help your child track her progress.

Date	
Text title	
What I understood	
What I did not understand	
What I need help with	
My overall reading experience in this text	
Other comments	

This chart is perhaps more useful for older children, however, you can also begin such self-assessment processes with younger children by modelling the steps in this chart orally. The advantage of self-assessment is that children can feel empowered by contributing to their own evaluations and see their own progress or areas that need improvement.

Portfolio assessment

A portfolio, similar to a work folder, contains various samples of a child's work. The portfolio assessment is a holistic way of measuring children's literacy progress[13] and a rich documentation of children's efforts, progress and achievements based on observation and analysis of their meaningful literacy experiences in real-life situations. In other words, children are evaluated based on the way they use language and literacy skills to solve real-life problems at their developmental levels. For example, a 3-year-old child who can identify the symbols (words) of her favourite cereal from a Turkish catalogue is regarded as having an emergent literacy skill even though she does not know how to write the words.

The portfolio assessment is not norm-referenced (not compared with other children), but it is criterion-referenced (the criteria you have determined as progress).[14] The power of the portfolio assessment is that it allows both parents and children to see progress overtime. For example, when using a portfolio to assess a child's writing progress in a heritage language, you can see the child's journey of becoming a writer: from simple illustrations and random letters to writing complete sentences and paragraphs.

Your children's involvement is central in the portfolio assessment process.[15] You can empower them by letting them choose the items to be included in their portfolios. The biggest advantage that I see in using the portfolio assessment method in the home teaching and learning environment is the motivation factor: when children realise how far they have progressed, they feel encouraged to go on. In Chapter 4, I will demonstrate how the portfolio assessment method can be used.

Audio and video recordings

Audio and video recordings are also a useful way for you to track the progress of your children' heritage language literacy progress. Suppose you want to know whether your child has improved his reading fluency, you can record his reading at a certain point and then record him again, say, two months later. The recordings are a useful way for you and your child to see what he has achieved over a period of time and what needs to be improved.

Home literacy activity plan

A home literacy activity plan is an outline of the activities that you want to carry out in order to fulfil the goals and objectives that you have set for your children. In essence, it is an action plan. The merit of having an activity plan or action plan is that you can think through what you plan to do before rushing into action. Writing down your teaching ideas can help keep you on track. When you begin the process, you can write down what you plan to do in detail. As you become more comfortable, an outline of what you plan to do should be sufficient (see Example 3.1 for an activity plan sample).

When planning an activity on a particular teaching topic, it is always helpful to involve children, even young children. The benefit of planning together with children is that they can see the purpose, provide input and they also tend to be more motivated and cooperative.

Parental self-reflection

You may find it odd to put the reflection in the planning process. Your question could be, 'I have not even started, how can I reflect?' Earlier in this chapter, I mentioned that the four elements in planning should be regarded as an ongoing process. Even though at this point, you are just planning, I put reflection here as a place holder to show that this step is as important as the other steps and that it is the beginning of the next teaching and learning cycle (see Figure 3.1).

Refection is an integral part of planning. After you try out the activities you have planned, you will want to know how you are doing and how your children respond to your strategies. This process is quite important in determining your next teaching cycle. Thinking about what works and what does not work may help you adjust your plan. In my own multilingual childrearing practice, I find that keeping a reflective journal on what I do helps me a great deal in my interactions with my children. This process seems to be tedious. However, you will notice that over time you are able to see how far you have come and that your past frustrations may be your present opportunities. In Chapter 7, you will meet some parents who found reflective notes/journals helpful in their home teaching.

Example 3.1

Example of a Home Activity Plan
Main Objective of the Activities (Short-Term Goals)

- Understand the meaning of the Chinese measurement word 串 (string, bunch and cluster) such as in 一串珠子 (a string of beads), 一串葡萄 (a cluster of grapes), 一串钥匙 (a bunch of keys).
- Know how to use it correctly in daily conversations.
- Recognise it in reading materials.
- Know how to use it correctly in writing.

Relation to the Long-Term Goals
Know how to use 150 frequently used measurement words.

Time Allocation
One week

Age
8 years old

Literacy Assessment Plan

- Give directions by using the measurement word and see whether the child understands it.
- Provide opportunities and see whether he can use the measurement word correctly.

Materials, Resources and Technology

- Beads, grapes and keys.
- Paper and pencil.
- The internet and Chinese software.

Procedures

- Introduce the measurement word 串 by stringing beads together. Ask the child 把珠子串成串 (to string the beads together) and see whether he understands 串. If he does not understand it, go through the cycle again until he understands the meaning of 串.
- During breakfast, ask the child to bring you 一串葡萄 (a cluster of grapes) and see whether he is able to follow you. If not, demonstrate.
- When you go to your car, ask your child to bring you your 一串钥匙 (a bunch of keys).
- Show your child how to write 串 (pay attention to the order of the strokes).
- Ask your child to practise how to write the word by doing some relevant tasks such as finishing your shopping list by filling in all the places that need 串. As in 买五 (   ) 葡萄 (buy five — of grapes) in the grocery store and 六 (   ) 珠子 (buy six — of beads) in the craft store.
- Play the Chinese measurement word software online.
- Leave a note on the refrigerator door (or send your child an e-mail) and ask him 你吃点心时要几串葡萄 (how many clusters of grapes do you want for your snack?).

Note: The activities do not have to follow the same order.

Supplemental Activities
Teach your child the song '一串红葡萄' (A String of Red Grapes) to get more exposure to the use of 串.

Note: You can creatively extend the activities to different everyday settings.

Assessment and Evaluation
Document your child's process in learning the measurement of 串. For example:

- document some examples of when your child used the measurement word correctly or incorrectly in daily conversations;
- document some examples of when your child was able to recognise or not able to recognise the word in reading;
- document some examples of when your child wrote the word correctly or incorrectly;
- look at all the representative examples you have collected with your child together, identify the progress he has made and the issues that still exist.

Reflection

- Are you successful in the activities that you planned?
- Any issues that you have encountered?
- Have you found anything that surprises you? How did you respond to it?
- Is your child interested in the tasks?
- What has your child learned in the activities that you carried out?
- Do you need to make any adjustment for your next teaching task?

After reading the planning process and steps, some of you may feel discouraged. You may think it is too cumbersome to do all these things. If you feel this way, it is all right. You do not have to go through all the steps I suggested. However, to avoid Ms Andersson's mistakes, some level of planning before you implement any strategy in your practice is necessary. You may want to at least think about the larger goals in your children's heritage language literacy development and how you go about achieving these goals.

Summary

This chapter has discussed the importance and necessity of active planning in the process of helping children become multiliterate. It shows that examining your availability, ability, support, childrearing beliefs and expectations can help you determine whether you are prepared to take on the challenge of bringing up your children multiliterate in the home environment. A four-step ongoing planning process is introduced, which includes setting up home literacy goals, determining assessment methods, designing activity plans and reflecting on the teaching and learning experience. This planning process helps keep you focused on the goals that you set for your children's heritage language literacy development and achieve a better outcome. When you are actively planning, you are likely to be better prepared to respond to the possible challenges ahead and minimise your frustrations.

Your Turn

Now that you have had an opportunity to read about the important steps involved in making an active plan. The following are some activities and questions for you to connect what you read in this chapter to your reality.

Activities and Reflective Questions

- Based on the information you read in this chapter and based on your current family situation, design a home heritage language literacy plan for your child at her specific age level.
- Think about your reality, e.g. the areas identified earlier in the chapter (your availability, your ability, your support, your childrearing beliefs and your expectations). Do you think you are ready to achieve the goals you set in your home literacy plan that you designed?
- Are your goals in your home literacy plan realistic for you and your child? Do you need to make any adjustments in your home literacy plan to make your child's heritage language literacy learning possible?
- Observe your child for a period of time (a day or a week). Write down the areas that you have not noticed before (you can also videotape him). How does this experience help you understand your child? If you have learned anything from this activity, would you like to continue the process in the future?
- Think about a topic you plan to teach your child. Try to develop an activity plan using the model provided in Example 3.1. Try the activities with your child. Do you think your plan helps you reach your child better? If so, how? Write down your thoughts and reflection on this particular experience. Look at your reflection one month later. What have you found in rereading your earlier reflection?

Notes and References

1. This story was shared in the parent workshop on 24 November 2008. Consent was given by Ms Andersson to include her story in this book.
2. Wang, X-L. (2008) *Growing Up with Three Languages: Birth to Eleven*. Bristol: Multilingual Matters.
3. Nordtveit, H. (2005) Family literacy. Paper commissioned by the Education for All Global Monitoring Report.
4. If you are a single parent and your former spouse is not living with your children, you still can raise multilingual children. Read this article, which may give you some insights. Obied, V.M. (2010) Can one-parent families or divorced families produce two-language children? An investigation into how Portuguese-English bilingual children acquire biliteracy within diverse family structures. *Pedagogy, Culture & Society* 18 (2), 227–243.
5. Wang, X-L. (2009) Interview with Xiao-lei Wang: Author of *Growing up with Three Languages. Multilingual Living Magazine* 4 (1), 22–24.

6. Heath, S.B. (1983) *Ways with Words: Language, Life, and Work in Communities and Classrooms*. Cambridge: Cambridge University Press.
    Ochs, E. and Schieffelin, B.B. (1984) Language acquisition and socialization: Three developmental stories and their implications. In R.A. Shweder and R.A. LeVine (eds) *Culture Theory: Essays on Mind, Self, and Emotion* (pp. 276–320). Cambridge: Cambridge University Press.
7. For detailed information about how to make decisions in these aspects, please see Wang, X-L. (2008) *Growing Up with Three Languages: Birth to Eleven*. Bristol: Multilingual Matters.
8. Garton, A. and Pratt, C. (1998) *Learning to Be Literate: The Development of Spoken and Written Language*. Oxford: Blackwell.
9. Cuero, K. and Romo, H. (2007) Raising a multicultural multilingual child. Paper presented at The Annual Meeting of the American Sociological Association, New York, 10 August.
    Wang, X-L. (2008) *Growing Up with Three Languages: Birth to Eleven*. Bristol: Multilingual Matters.
10. Example from the parent workshop conducted on 8 February 2009.
11. Wiggins, G. and McTighe, J. (2005) *Understanding by Designing* (2nd edn). Alexandria, VA: ACSD.
12. Tayler, C. (2000) Monitoring young children's literacy learning. In C. Barrat-Pugh and M. Rohl (eds) *Literacy Learning in the Early Years* (p. 211). Buckingham: Open University Press.
13. Cohen, J.H. and Wiener, R.B. (2003) *Literacy Portfolios: Improving Assessment, Teaching, and Learning* (2nd edn). Upper Saddle River, NJ: Merill Prentice Hall.
    Grinffin, P. Smith, P.G. and Burrill, L.E. (1995) *The American Literacy Profiles Scales: A Framework for Authentic Assessment*. Portsmouth, NH: Heinemann.
14. Grinffin, P., Smith, P.G. and Burrill, L.E. (1995) *The American Literacy Profiles Scales: A Framework for Authentic Assessment*. Portsmouth, NH: Heinemann.
15. Fleet, A. and Lockwood, V. (2002) Authentic literacy assessment. In L. Makin and C. J. Diaz (eds) *Literacies in Early Childhood: Changing Views, Challenging Practices* (pp. 135–153). Sydney: Maclennan & Petty.

Chapter 4

Infancy and Early Childhood (Birth–5 Years)[1]

This chapter discusses how to help infants and young children develop emergent heritage language literacy skills, including beginning multimedia literacy skills, in the home environment. It begins with a brief overview of the learning characteristics of infants and young children to justify the strategies recommended in the chapter. It then examines various ways to select suitable literacy materials and conduct engaging activities. The chapter concludes with a discussion on how to monitor and assess children's emergent heritage language literacy progress using the portfolio assessment method. At the end of each main section, you are provided with an opportunity to reflect or act on the suggested strategies in light of your own situation.

Typical Learning Characteristics

The typical learning characteristics during infancy and early childhood are marked by curiosity, exploration and discovery.[2] It is quite accurate for people to compare a sponge to the natural learning drives of infants and young children because they always seem ready to explore and learn as long as the environment presents them with the opportunity.

The cognitive development of infants and young children goes through at least two major stages. Initially, infants tend to focus on the objects and people in their immediate environment. Anything beyond their immediate environment does not seem to concern them. In the latter part of the second year, children begin to develop symbolic thought (early signs already shown in late infancy[3]), that is, they can think and talk about things beyond their immediate experience. However, they tend to focus on one aspect of a situation at a time and not to consider multiple perspectives. For example, a 4-year-old child is likely to insist that a tall container contains more water than a short one even though the same amount of water is poured into the two containers. In addition, children during this period tend not to understand the function of rules. You have probably noticed that children are not able to follow rules when playing a game and they often change the rules of a game to suit their needs.

Given the learning characteristics of infants and young children, the best way to encourage their learning (language and literacy learning included) is to provide them with a rich environment and ample support. Therefore, you may want to consider the following approaches as a general guideline when interacting with your children:

- Providing a stimulating environment[4] that encourages children to explore and imagine.
- Taking cues from children when interacting with them.
- Explaining things with concrete examples.
- Being responsive to children's requests and signals.
- Providing scaffolding (support) to help children expand their interests.
- Initiating teaching activities that are meaningful to children.
- Focusing on positive feedback and avoiding negative comments.
- Providing choices for children.

When parents interact with infants and children in these supportive ways, children will make headway in all aspects of their development. The learning experience they gain during these early years is critical for their future cognitive, language, literacy and social-personality development.

Multiliteracy Development Focus

It was once thought that literacy activities should not begin until children were formally schooled. It is now widely endorsed by educators and researchers that the literacy process begins at birth and continues throughout children's lives.[5] In the case of a child who is exposed to more than one language, the early start of the multilingual literacy development process may be beneficial.

Based on infants and young children's learning characteristics that I have just discussed, the home literacy focus during this period needs to be on helping children build emergent literacy skills[6] and beginning multimedia literacy skills.[7] Although most children at this stage will not have developed conventional reading and writing competencies in any language, they can begin to construct meaning from the multilingual prints that they encounter in their surroundings[8] and begin to accumulate knowledge about them. For example, even though 3-year-old Ommar does not know how to read Arabic and English, he has developed his knowledge to distinguish the two different scripts; thus, when his father asked him to fetch the Arabic newspaper, Ommar successfully accomplished the task without confusing the English newspaper with the Arabic one.[9] Similarly, most children at this stage will not have developed the ability to use multimedia literacy independently, such as surfing the internet or using e-mails. They can, however, develop the concept of multimedia literacy by observing their parents and older siblings. For example, 4-year-old Ayati often observed her mother downloading pictures from the internet. One day, she requested her mother to print a picture from the computer (the internet) of a dish served in the Indian Diwali[10] celebration, for her 'Show and Tell' in her English nursery school.[11]

However, the emergence of literacy and multimedia skills during infancy and early childhood may be characterised by spurts, plateaus and even regression, because development is often not smoothly uniform and cumulative, but asynchronous (not at the same time) and non-linear.[12] Nevertheless, the print and multimedia concept as well as the metalinguistic abilities (e.g. the ability to notice the differences between scripts) developed during this early period will most definitely pave the way for children's future multiliteracy advancement.

Thus, when planning the home literacy activities for this period in the home environment, the focus should be on helping young children develop emergent multilingual literacy and multimedia literacy skills, for example how symbols (such as letters) and sounds are related in different languages, how word order differs in different languages, how text layouts differ in different languages and how the printed text form differs from the multimedia text form.

Selecting Literacy Materials

Once you have reviewed the home literacy teaching framework discussed in Chapter 2 and noted the important elements involved in it and once you have gone through the planning stage as suggested in Chapter 3, you can now begin the process of choosing suitable literacy materials to carry out your plan. The right kind of literacy materials can facilitate children's emergent literacy development in general. They are even more important for children who are developing heritage language literacy in a non-heritage environment where heritage literacy materials may be remote from their lives. The following are some ideas for you to consider when choosing heritage language literacy materials for your children during infancy and the early childhood period.

Environmental print

The literacy materials used to help children start their heritage language literacy is not necessarily always from good quality children's literature. They can be from unexpected sources such as number plates, clothing labels, cereal boxes, road signs, shop windows or birthday cards. This kind of print is called environmental print because it is present in children's daily surroundings. Environmental print is usually contextualised, and children are able to use the clues from the print to derive meaning and learn the purpose associated with it.[13] For example, each time 3-year-old Lori sees the GAP store sign, she would call out GAP! She associated the letters G-A-P with the clothing store because she had been in the store with her mom on many occasions. Her experience with the store helped Lori understand that the symbol 'GAP' represents the name of the store.[14] Research shows that environmental print helps infants and young children decipher the meaning of the printed word in their everyday lives.[15]

Heritage environmental print is often lacking in heritage language learning children's environment. However, with some creativity, it is possible for parents to use it to help infants and young children start the heritage language literacy process. For example, Mrs Shokhirev from Connecticut wants to give her 10-month-old son an early start with his heritage language Russian. When she gives her son breakfast in the morning, she often points at the Russian words that she purposefully glues onto the infant cereal boxes and playfully sounds out the letters.[16] Similarly, Mrs Minami from New Jersey asks her 5-year-old daughter to help her shelve groceries with Japanese on the packages after each trip back from the Japanese supermarket.[17] Likewise, Mrs Xu from New York labelled many of her household objects in Chinese for her 4-year-old son.[18] What these mothers do in common is that they creatively use environmental print to draw their young children's attention to heritage language print in a meaningful context.

In fact, researchers have found that many immigrant parents in Canada, the UK and the USA are successful in using heritage language environmental print, such as newspapers, television programme guides,[19] magazines and catalogues[20] to help their young children begin the heritage language literacy learning process.

Dual/multiliteracy materials

Despite past criticism that using dual language or multi-language texts would encourage children to read the easier language,[21] recent studies found that children who are reading dual or multiliteracy materials can transfer the literacy skills and concepts developed in one language to another (often a stronger one to a weaker one) and promote overall literacy skill development.[22]

There are several benefits in using dual or multiliteracy materials. First, they provide predictability from one language to another. Literacy experts have long advocated that using repeated reading materials helps facilitate comprehension and introduce children to the way print works.[23] For example, Mr Demir read a Turkish version of *Snow White* to his 3-year-old son Kabil; two weeks later, Kabil's English babysitter read him the same book in English. Even though this was the first time Kabil was read the English version, he could talk about the story in English.[24] Second, dual or multiliteracy materials provide children with an opportunity to compare and contrast the texts and develop metalinguistic ability (ability to notice the different features in different languages). For example, when Mrs Zhang read the English and Chinese dual version of Dr. Seuss's book *Horton Hears A Who!*[25] (霍顿听到了呼呼的声音) to her 2-year-old daughter, her child noticed the different use of onomatopoeia in English and Chinese.[26]

If you cannot find dual or multi-language texts for your children, you can try to find materials in your child's mainstream language and make your own dual or multi-language books by adding your heritage language texts next to the mainstream language texts. With the advancement of computer technology and software, it is possible for you to create your own version of dual or multi-language books or multimedia books.

Multimedia literacy

As discussed in Chapter 1, multimedia (or hybrid) texts have increasingly become a dominant text form in our lives.[27] The recent publication of the *vooks* (video books that mash together text, video and web features)[28] is yet another example of how the text format has been fundamentally changed with the application of multimedia components. Therefore, it is important to include multimedia literacy skills as part of multilingual literacy development.

Infants and young children obviously have some physical and cognitive constraints in using multimedia literacy. For example, they have not fully developed their fine motor skills, therefore they are unable to play with much interactive literacy software via the computer or the internet. Similarly, they are not capable of searching for information on the internet. However, introducing them early to multimedia modality can help them acquire the basic concepts necessary for their heritage language literacy development later.

There are many ways you can help infants and young children begin to explore the multimedia world. Touch-sensitive devices are now available for infants and young children to engage in multimedia interactive books and games. You may want to take advantage of these multimedia devices. There are several merits in using multimedia literacy materials at an early age. First, these materials introduce infants and young children to multimedia modality and help them learn how to interact with multimedia texts. Second, multimedia materials are interactive and fun. Third, these materials often have the possibility to switch from one language to another. Finally, these materials provide multiple inputs (such as sounds and colours). Many studies have pointed out the advantages of multimedia materials in facilitating young children's emergent literacy. For example, children who are introduced to different types of literacy software were found to improve in their spelling and story writing.[29]

However, you may need to examine the multimedia software and interactive storybooks and materials first before introducing them to infants or young children. When choosing software and interactive storybooks for your infants and young children, you can ask yourself the following questions:

- What does this software or interactive book intend to teach?
- Is it age-appropriate?
- Does it provide visual stimulation? For example, is it colourful and attractive?
- Is it interactive?
- Can your infant and young child benefit from using it?
- Do you enjoy playing with the game? (Your infants and young children will notice whether you enjoy the game or not. Your reaction to the game will affect them.)

Some researchers suggest that software that asks children to engage in activities such as 'print-and-complete' or 'click-and-action' exercises, which require adult involvement in order for children to understand the tasks, may inhibit young children becoming independent users of multimedia.[30]

Children's literature

The literature written for or told to children is often an important resource for children's early literacy development. Almost every culture has stories written, told or sung for children (e.g. oral forms in Native American cultures[31] and dancing and musical forms in Aboriginal cultures[32]). Using children's literature for children's early heritage language literacy development has several important benefits. First, children's literature written or told in heritage languages provides a way to introduce them into their heritage cultures.[33] Since these children do not live in the heritage cultures/countries, heritage children's literature can help children leap between their current environment and the environment in their heritage cultures. Second, the language, pictures and content presented in children's literature are usually targeted at children's age level, and are a good way to introduce children to the world of literacy. Third, children's literature provides a framework for experience. Literacy experts suggest that children can use the stories to relate to their own experience and talk about them. Many experiences with books help children understand their own emotional reactions and provide a manageable context or a metaphor for their real experiences. Young children often do not have the language to explain their emotional reactions or fears. The language and shared knowledge in children's literature can allow opportunities for this expression. Literature provides opportunities to experience excitement and fear in a safe environment. It can push children's language development to the limit in their attempts to express their feelings.[34] Thus, you may want to take advantage of children's literature to help your children enter the door of heritage language literacy.

The following suggestions may help you choose children's literature in your heritage language.

Using developmentally sensitive literacy materials

Developmentally sensitive literature can help elicit better responses from children. For heritage language learning children, the initial process may determine whether they will stay on course with their heritage language literacy development.

Infants tend to enjoy books that have strong rhythm and onomatopoeia. For example, infants often enjoy lullabies. Books that have simple texts accompanied by bright, primary colours or contrasting black and white images are ideal for infants.[35] In addition, books with the themes of family, friends, parents, animals, toys and teddies are usually attractive to infants.[36]

Young children, while continuing to enjoy the same kinds of books as infants, can now appreciate simple and repetitive texts with a clear beginning, middle and end. As time goes on, young children begin to enjoy books such as the popular English book *The Very Hungry Caterpillar* by Eric Carle.[37] In this book, children learn how a caterpillar becomes a butterfly. The information is conveyed through simple narrative and vibrant, collaged illustrations.[38]

Appendix B provides a list of English children's literature for infants and young children. Although these books are written in English and recommended by English-speaking literacy experts, they may be used as a reference to help you determine the type of books that you may consider in your heritage language. Sometimes, you may not be able to find suitable books for infants and children in your heritage language. In such cases, you can purchase mainstream language books for infants and young children and make your own heritage language books by replacing the mainstream language texts with your heritage language texts.

As mentioned in Chapter 2, your beliefs in language and literacy socialisation determine how you choose reading materials for your children. Because of your cultural beliefs, you may feel strongly about what kinds of children's literature your children should read in your heritage language. You obviously have the right to choose whatever books you deem suitable for your children. However, you may also want to be mindful of your children's developmental needs during this period. The best way to test the suitability of your choice is to observe your children's reaction to the books and materials you select for them. If they embrace the books you chose, you have the green light to continue.

Utilising books with illustrations

Young children often rely on contextual cues to recognise and identify print.[39] This also applies to children who are developing their heritage language literacy skills. Research has shown that visual texts, such as books containing pictures, can provide further layers of meaning that allow children's continued enjoyment of the interactions between the words and pictures. These books can help young children to remember and interpret. They can also help them to express their cognitive, cultural and affective (emotional) understanding before they can read the print and link it to their own experience to make meaning.[40]

A good book with funny and attractive illustrations is a rich resource and can often provide an impetus to assist young children understand the content of a book. Moreover, they can also provide a good opportunity for parents to model different kinds of narratives. When choosing heritage language books for young children, consider choosing books that have pictures, which will help your children understand and construct meanings from the books and their experiences.

Choosing books that can help phonological awareness

You may want to choose books that can help young children develop overall phonological awareness, such as books that will help children understand the symbol–sound relationship and the patterns in words. Books such as *The Cat in the Hat*[41] and *Green Eggs and Ham* by Dr. Seuss[42] or traditional nursery rhymes are the best books to help young children develop phonological awareness. You can use some of the books listed in Appendix B as a guide to choosing books for your young children in your heritage language.

Focusing on the relevance to children's lives

When books are relevant to their lives, children are more likely to enjoy them. The top priority in choosing heritage language books for children is to find books that appeal to them[43] and that they can relate to. You may want to look for heritage language materials that are of interest to your children living in a specific region. For example, reading material related to winter, skiing, camping, jam, maple syrup and peanut butter may be more relevant to Urdu heritage language learning children who live in some parts of Canada than materials from their heritage regions.[44] I don't mean to say that reading materials from the heritage regions should be avoided. Rather, the point is that at this early stage, it is likely that children care more about what is in their immediate environment and what appeals to them than something that is remote. In Chapter 6, I will address how to incorporate cultural knowledge and heritage cultures into children's reading.

Avoiding banal texts

Reading materials selected for young children should be simple. However, simplicity of language does not imply banality of ideas or messages. A case in point is the writing style of the American writer Earnest Hemmingway. Although the language used in his works, such as *The Old Man and the Sea,*[45] is simple, the ideas conveyed between the lines are profound. Some literacy experts suggest that texts selected for young children should go beyond over-simplified language for the purpose of helping beginning readers and should challenge the readers and help them respond or contribute meanings.[46] Texts for young children should be simple, but should not be simply written. This means that texts should be written at children's age level, but should at the same time provoke their reactions and questions, and invite them to imagine and participate in meaning-making. Darlene Witte-Townsend and Emily DiGiulio recommend a good criterion to measure an author's ability to convey profound meaning through simple texts:

> The measure of authors' genius, however, is that their books are far from simplistic. The stories are very child-friendly, warm, charming and attractive and, most importantly, they are intellectually interesting. They present a challenge to the mind and return our attention continually to the contemplation of issues of the soul.[47]

Good examples of simple text that contains deep meaning and can elicit young children's responses are books such as *The Very Hungry Caterpillar,*[48] *The Very Busy Spider*[49] and *The Grouchy Ladybug* by Eric Carle,[50] *Something from Nothing* by Phoebe Gilman[51] and *Joseph Had a Little Overcoat*[52] by Simms Taback. You can use these books as a guide when selecting heritage language reading materials for your infants and young children or when creating your own books.

Using different genres

Different genres of books can provide different vocabulary for children and guide them to broader subject areas. Chances are that the more genres children are exposed to, the greater the variety of vocabulary and expressions they develop. For heritage language learners, this may be significant because they often do not have opportunities to hear different subjects being discussed in their immediate environment. Thus, different genres of literature in their heritage languages may help bridge the gap.

You may want to select different genres of heritage language children's books using the books listed in Appendix B as a reference.

Using good quality 'scary' books

Children, including young children, tend to be attracted to scary books. It is often the parents, rather than their children, who are scared when encountering these books.[53] What makes a book scary for a child is quite different from what an adult interprets as scary.[54] Many educational experts now try to allay the adults' fear of scary books by providing the following advice: 'Scary books themselves do not cause fear.[55] Don't let a good scare frighten you'. In fact, almost every culture has scary tales and stories for children.[56] Some researchers believe that scary tales, books and movies are popular because the world is an unpredictable place for children as well as for adults.[57] Young children typically tend to have imaginary fears and some children may even have fears and worries because of their life experiences. Thus, quality scary books and tales can help children deal with their fears and anxieties.[58] Studies have shown that using good quality chillers can promote children's early literacy skills.[59] Nevertheless, it is absolutely your call as a parent whether you feel comfortable or not to introduce these kinds of books to your young children.

Letting children choose their own reading materials

All said, the most attractive and engaging early literacy materials for young children are those chosen by children themselves. However, young children usually have very little power over their book selection.[60] Adults (e.g. publishers, booksellers, parents and teachers) are usually the people who decide what is suitable for children.

To provide children with a choice of what they want to read during early childhood can motivate them to stay the course in heritage language literacy learning. It is a simple fact that people are more motivated to do what they have chosen. Our young children are no exception.

Your Turn

Now you have been introduced to some ideas on how to select heritage language literacy materials for infants and young children. It is your turn to reflect a moment on the suggestions that I have just made. The following activity and questions are designed to help you relate these recommendations to your own situation.

Activities and Reflective Questions

- Look around your house or apartment. Can you identify any heritage language environmental print? If so, think about ways that you might be able to utilise them to help your child develop initial heritage language literacy in your own reality. If you do not have any heritage language print around, is it possible for you to acquire some, for example, by getting food labels in a heritage grocery store or on the internet?
- Search online or talk to your friends or relatives who live in your heritage country/region/culture. Identify some popular heritage language media materials. Get hold of some and read them yourself. Do you find them interesting? Do you think any of them can be used as a carrot to attract your child to begin heritage language literacy development?
- Analyse a children's book in your heritage language. Determine whether the language and content in this book suit your child (your perspective). Then show the same book to your child. Find out your child's reaction (your child's perspective). Is your reaction to the book similar to or different from your child's? What have you learned from this experience?
- If you have difficulties locating good heritage language reading materials for your child, look at the books listed in Appendix B. Replace (cover) the English texts with your heritage language texts. Read the books to your child and observe his reaction.
- When choosing a multimedia interactive book or software for your child, what is the most important criterion you use to determine whether it is suitable for your child? Try one of your selections with your child. What is your child's reaction?
- Show a popular culture material (such as a cartoon) in your heritage language to your child. Observe your child's reaction. What does your child's reaction tell you about using popular culture materials for heritage language literacy learning?
- After reading this section and reflecting on these questions and activities, come up with some of your own creative ideas on selecting heritage language literacy materials. Write them down and try them out with your child. Think about why they worked and did not work.

Conducting Literacy Activities

As discussed in Chapter 1, finding time to carry out heritage language literacy activities is often not easy for busy parents. The emergent literacy activities introduced below are designed with this situation in mind as they can be carried out in the everyday context. Before you try any of the following activities, please revisit the home literacy teaching framework (in Chapter 2) and review the four-step home literacy planning process and the home activity plan template introduced in Chapter 3 (Example 3.1) and try to situate the activities introduced below in your plan. In other words, think about how these activities fit your long-term or short-term goals.

Providing opportunities to observe adult literacy activities

Research has shown that very young children are able to take note of the symbols being used for writing and reading and the overall purpose of literacy events in their daily encounters in the world.[61] For example, a 4-year-old boy from a Punjabi-Hindu family living in Southall, West London, is already able to distinguish among the Gurmukhi (Punjabi), Devanagari (Hindi) and the Roman (English) scripts by observing his grandparents and parents using these scripts in their daily activities, such as writing shopping lists, letters and reading magazines.[62] Similarly, a 4-year-old girl from a Gujarati-speaking family living in South London can spontaneously produce her own version of emergent Gujarati symbols modelled after her mother's writing without instruction.[63] Even at a young age, children can observe the purpose of literacy. Six-year-old Dior can summarise the different purposes of literacy in her household for various occasions:[64]

- For gaining information – newspaper, Time magazine, television.
- For pleasure – books, magazines, stories, newspapers, television, e-mail.
- For social interaction – birthday cards.
- For gaining further qualifications – computer assignments.
- For work – reports.
- For school–home reader.

You may want to deliberately create opportunities for children to observe how literacy including language is used in the everyday context. When children are exposed to an environment where the heritage language is used, they will notice and gradually understand the purposes.

Sometimes, you can purposely draw children's attention to your own literacy activities such as reading newspapers. For example, when Hanna reads her heritage language German newspaper every Sunday morning, she always makes sure to read it out loud to her 3-year-old son, pointing at the interesting photos and reading the captions underneath the photos.[65] This is a good way to engage the child to associate the print (captions) with the meaning (photos).

Including everyday talk in your heritage language literacy teaching

The foundations of literacy are far wider than reading and writing. Everyday talk can serve as a form of literacy practice during early childhood.[66] Thus, you can provide opportunities for your young children to use heritage language across a wide range of activities and experiences. For example, when Sonya takes a walk with her 4-year-old son in a park near her apartment in London, she plays a game she invented in her heritage language Dutch *'Who Can Find the First Car'*. In this game, the person who finds the first car has to name the colour (e.g. red, white, black and yellow), the size (e.g. huge, big, medium, small and tiny) and the initial letter of the maker (e.g. T in Toyota, N in Nissan, and M in Mercedes Benz).[67]

Research has shown that some cultures have different narrative structures from English.[68] When talking to young children, you can begin to model the typical narrative style in your heritage culture by constructing oral texts with a variety of themes. This practice may help your young children become conscious about the differences between mainstream and heritage narrative styles. In the long run, this may enrich their thinking and future writing.

One word of caution: while modelling and guidance in the use of the heritage language in everyday conversation is important, you may not want to replace your children's inventions with your 'correct' convention. Appreciating your children's creative use of language may help you understand their perspective[69] and find more suitable ways to reach them.

Incorporating play into heritage literacy learning

Play is an essential way that young children learn during the early childhood period.[70] Play provides holistic, natural and fun ways for young children to explore and to experiment in a safe and enjoyable setting.[71]

There are many ways that you can help young children develop their emergent literacy concepts and skills through play. This is not to say that you interfere with their spontaneous play. Rather, this means that you take advantage of their play and scaffold them to develop emergent heritage language literacy skills through what they like to do. Example 4.1 demonstrates how this can be done.

Example 4.1[72]
Orientating Children to Print through Play

Child: People keep coming into the restaurant with all their animals. If they do it again I want you to come and put them in jail and tell them off, and not let them do it again.

Adult: Have you got any animals in the restaurant at the moment?

Child: No. Only babies. Darren's got a baby and it's not a dog any more ... only babies.

Adult:	What are you going to do if someone else tries to bring a dog in?
Child:	I'm gonna get you. To tell you to tell them it's not allowed. It's breaking the law so we can phone the police.
Adult:	Have you got a sign which says 'No dogs allowed'?
Child:	You mean like … I know … You mean like when you tell people not to smoke and that. We've got 'No smoking' sign.
Adult:	Do you think it would help if you had a 'No animals' sign?
Child:	Yeah! Then they'd know cause it would say so.
Adult:	Why don't you make one them? If you think it would help.
…	

In this example, the adult takes advantage of this child's spontaneous play and cleverly helps him understand what words can do, that is, (in this case) influencing people's behaviour (don't bring animals into the restaurant).

Encouraging visual and multimodal activities

In the early childhood period, you can encourage young children to explore a plethora of visual (such as drawing and painting) and multimodal activities (such as building blocks and playing video games). Through engaging in such visual representational activities, children can learn how to manipulate an array of signs, icons, moving and still images, which can help them understand how meanings are made and represented through different visual images,[73] and eventually, lead them to understand (for example) how print works.

You can paint together with young children and deliberately draw their attention to the fact that image and colour can represent meanings (such as emotions). For instance, the colour *blue* may express the sentiment of melancholy. Suppose a little boy lost his favourite toy, you use the blue colour to express his mood. Through exploration like this, young children will begin to understand that colours can be used to attract, persuade or inform other people[74] and images can represent meaning, just as later they will realise that words can achieve the same effect.

You can also help your children take advantage of devices such as digital cameras and video cameras to develop their early literacy skills. A friend of mind told me that she took a walk with her 4-year-old daughter in her neighbourhood. The girl took lots of pictures with her digital camera. She spent two weeks downloading the pictures to the computer, labelling them and writing stories on the pictures with the help of her mother. The little girl was enthralled by this activity, and her emergent literacy skills were developing as a result.

The advantage of encouraging visual and multimodal activities in early child-hood is that these activities are enjoyable. Many young children are already spontaneously engaged in them.

Using children's music

Children's music often contains lyrics that are simple and fun. Taking advantage of children's music can engage children in early literacy learning. For example, my two children could sing and recite many of the lyrics by the Swiss-French singer Henri Dès during their early childhood years. The vocabulary in these songs enriched their French vocabulary greatly.

Using children's work to support literacy development

Children's early literacy work tends to be scribbles, drawings, paintings and non-conventional spontaneous writing. This kind of children's work often demonstrates their knowledge and understanding of the world including literacy. Some researchers believe that if such self-expression by children is not encouraged, children cannot easily demonstrate what they know, what they can do, and what they hold dear or what they are fear.[75]

Thus, in the heritage language learning process, you may want to take advantage of your children's spontaneous productions and use them as an opportunity to talk about the meanings that they want to represent and gradually help them move their non-conventional expression to conventional expression. For example, when Sonja's (I mentioned her earlier in this chapter) 4-year-old son drew many lines on a piece of paper one day, she asked what he wanted 'to say' in his drawing. The boy replied that he was building roads. Sonja took this opportunity to help her son label the roads in Dutch.

Engaging children in literacy activities that are relevant to their lives

Early heritage language literacy activities should be relevant to children's lives and mean something to them.[76] Children are likely to see the meaning of print when they are relevant to their lives. The best way to help children make connections to the literacy event is to involve them in everyday activities. For example, Mrs Lek brought a shopping list she wrote in Thai to the Thai grocery store and asked her 5-year-old daughter to check if the items that she placed in the shopping cart corresponded to the list.[77] You can involve your children in literacy learning in any daily routines, such as making a shopping list, planning a birthday party and writing invitation cards.

Doing activities, such as sport, with your children is also an excellent opportunity for them to develop their heritage language and literacy. In these activities, children learn new expressions, grammatical structures and rules of language through your modelling.[78]

Reading to your children

Even though reading has been depicted in the research literature as contributing to children's literacy development, studies show that not all storybook reading in family settings influences children's school success in their later life.[79] Therefore, just reading books to children may not be enough. You may want to pay attention to how you read.

Paying attention to your reading styles

How to read to your infants and young children can influence their experience with early literacy. They can find reading either interesting or boring. There are different ways that you can make this early literacy experience enjoyable. You can role-play the story in the book; you can draw and paint the story together with your young child; and you can sing and dance the story with your child. You can also let your child 'read' (tell) the story to you and ask your child to interpret the story in her own words. When you read to your child, sharing the meaning of the book is also a vital part in making reading attractive: talking about the ideas so that you can help your child derive rich understandings of the meanings involved.[80]

Practising print-focused reading

Since reading is a learned ability and since heritage language learning children tend to have fewer exposures in their environment to heritage literacy, explicit and print-focused parent–child interaction is particularly important. Researcher Laura Justice and associates have recommended that adults use verbal and non-verbal techniques to heighten children's attention to and interest in print within the storybook. The simple techniques include *asking questions about print* (e.g. 'Do you see the letter S on this page?'), *commenting on print* (e.g. 'That word says SPLASH!') and *tracing one's finger along the text while reading*. Their research has found that when preschool children are exposed to this explicit print referencing style of reading, they tend to achieve significant gains in print concept knowledge, alphabetic knowledge and name writing abilities as compared to the children who are not exposed to this reading style.[81]

Therefore, you may want to provide guidance for your children to focus on heritage language print. For example, use model reading (parents read to children) and guided reading (parents read together with children). This kind of guidance will eventually lead to children's independent reading (children read on their own).

Fostering reading for pleasure

Even though different cultures may have different beliefs about whether reading should be treated as work or pleasure (see Chapter 2), it is important to make initial reading an enjoyable experience. In her study, Lucy Tse found that adults who have high levels of heritage literacy tend to read for pleasure.[82] Reading for pleasure will ensure children's heritage language learning motivation. As mentioned earlier, using materials that are relevant and meaningful to children as well as providing children with choice can help young children appreciate reading and find it enjoyable.

Literacy experts have suggested that the following factors may increase the pleasure associated with reading:

- Find a comfortable place to read. For infants and young children, the most comfortable and secure place is on their parent's lap.
- Relate the books to children's immediate experiences and talk to them about the book and their experience.
- Reading time is used for reading only; try to avoid other distractions.
- Try to avoid monotone and use an animated voice when reading to infants and young children.

When children associate the reading experience with pleasure, they are likely to be continuously engaged in such activities.

Reciprocating mainstream emergent literacy and heritage literacy

Research has long suggested that building literacy skills in one language can facilitate the development of literacy skills in another language. One way that some parents have tried is to use mainstream language children's literature as a base to introduce heritage language. For example, the English-speaking neighbour of 2-year-old Eddie lent him the popular English book, *The Very Hungry Caterpillar*. Eddie liked it very much. So, his mother decided to read the book to him in English and then they discussed the book in their heritage language Arabic.[83] This process can be reversed as well.

Emergent writing

During the early childhood period, building knowledge about writing is key. The relevant basic knowledge includes the development of the concept of a writing system (scripts and concepts), the function of communication through print and parental scaffolding (assistance).

Handwriting

Different languages have different writing systems, thereby requiring different kinds of practice. When the writing system in a child's mainstream language is similar to that in the heritage language, the knowledge and skills (mechanics) in one writing system can transfer easily to the other. However, when writing systems are different, children may need more time to practise. For example, my two children did not have any problems transferring their knowledge and skills in French to English and vice versa. They did have to practise a lot harder on writing Chinese script than their English and French scripts. The key during early childhood is to provide opportunities for children to practice and understand how the writing system works (e.g. the spaces between words, writing from left to right in French and from right to left in Arabic).

Although some parents and cultures emphasise the correctness and neatness of handwriting,[84] literacy experts suggest that during early childhood, experimentation with writing scripts is more important than correct script formation and neatness. In fact, researchers have shown that when children (and adults) consciously control their handwriting, it is detrimental to their handwriting automaticity, which is more important in overall handwriting competence.[85]

Learning to compose

The traditional view holds that children should not begin the writing process until they start school. In reality, most children who live in print-rich environments do not wait until they go to school to write. They are already investigating the written world around them, finding out what graphic symbols stand for and how they can be used to communicate with others.[86] Typically, children begin attempting to write between the ages of 3 and 7,[87] though their writing is very different from conventional writing. Taking advantage of children's early spontaneous writing attempts can help them move forward in their writing development.[88]

During the early childhood period, helping children construct meaning in what they want to express is far more important than the writing mechanics (such as correct punctuation and spelling). Helping children discover the principles of writing, the concept of print and the function and purpose of written communication should be the focus.

Moreover, there is a great deal of overlap in the skills that children must master when learning to read and write, and much of what a child learns while engaging in one of these activities will be of relevance and benefit to the other.[89] Therefore, the strategies discussed previously on reading can also be applied in helping children begin to write.

Co-writing with children

The concept of scaffolding[90] is based on the work of the Russian psychologist Lev Vygotsky, who proposed that with an adult's assistance, children could accomplish tasks that they ordinarily could not perform independently. During the scaffolding process, adults help children move from their current cognitive level to a more advanced level (potential level) by providing adequate support. Co-writing (you write together with your child) is a good application of Vygotsky's scaffolding concept. It allows children to write at a level slightly beyond what they are able to do on their own by working with a more proficient and mature writer.

As the early childhood educator Caroline Barratt-Pugh so rightly points out, by introducing frameworks through discussing the purpose, content and structure of the writing, children are able to organise their ideas, learn new vocabulary and try out new language structures within a 'safe' context.[91] Hence, modelling writing is an excellent way of demonstrating the writing process, the styles and the genres.

Writing together with your children also helps them contrast different writing styles in different cultural and linguistic systems and understand cultural norms in writing. You may begin to show them explicitly the different cultural expressions of the same idea. Early exposure to different cultural writing styles can help broaden young children's cognitive horizons.

Your Turn

Before we move on to the next section, let's look at how to connect your reality to the activities that I have just discussed.

Activities and Reflective Questions

(1) Make a list of the typical activities that you have done together with your child in the past month.

- Can you identify the purpose of these activities?
- Have any of these activities helped your child develop her heritage language and literacy development in any way? If so, identify the specific areas (e.g. awareness of heritage language print or sound and symbol/letter relationships).
- What are the similarities and differences between your activities and the activities that I have suggested in this chapter? What have you learned in the process?
- Do any of the strategies recommended in this chapter confirm or make you rethink what you are doing?

(2) When you read to your child in your heritage language, how do you usually do it? Compare your method with the strategies introduced in this book. What have you learned in this comparison?

(3) Explore children's software in your heritage language. Identify the areas you think your child might be interested in and benefit from. Try some samples with your child. Does he find it interesting? If not, what could be the issues?

(4) When your child makes a spontaneous drawing, ask her to explain the meaning of the drawing to you. What have you learned about your child? How would you link her drawing to heritage language literacy learning?

(5) Examine one of your child's spontaneous productions (drawings or spontaneous writing) and ask yourself the following questions:

- Have you noticed any emergent literacy abilities in your child's work?
- Has your child demonstrated any understanding about literacy?
- What could you do to provide your child with more literacy experience using your child's spontaneous work?

---

(6) Reflect on how you have done when you finish trying all or some of the strategies I recommended in this chapter. Were you successful? Was your child interested in the activities? What do you need to improve? If possible, write your thoughts down and revisit them when you finish the next teaching cycle.

Monitoring and Assessing Progress

Six assessment methods were introduced in Chapter 3. In this chapter, I will demonstrate how to use the portfolio assessment method to document young children's heritage language literacy development progress because this assessment method is more complex than the others. The portfolio assessment can be divided into several steps:

Step 1: Collecting representative samples of your child's spontaneous work (such as drawing and writing samples) at the beginning of a learning process. The evidence you have documented serves as a baseline for your later comparison. Please note that not all artefacts produced by your child should be included in the assessment portfolio. Only those artefacts that can show your child's typical performance should be included.

Step 2: Documenting your child's representative samples again in the middle of the learning process. The samples collected during this stage serve the functions of checking whether your child has made any progress due to your intentional interaction (strategies, activities or materials) and whether you need to adjust your strategies or use different materials. You may also want to include your observational and reflective notes here.

Step 3: At the end of a learning cycle, collecting your child's representative artefacts produced. Compare the samples collected at the beginning, middle and the end. These samples, documented at different stages, can give you a good idea of what your child has achieved and what he/she needs to improve, as well as whether your strategies have worked. If possible, write a brief reflection (or comments) on your child's learning process and your teaching (interactive) process.

It is important that the evidence collected in the portfolio should illustrate young children's particular skills, abilities or interests. Samples and artefacts collected in the portfolio should include a range of topics and genres to provide a comprehensive picture of a child as a 'writer' or a 'reader'. Even though young children's speech, writing and drawing samples may be brief and cryptic,[92] you may want to 'unpack' (study carefully) their unconventional products. Sometimes, through close examination of your children's speech and writing samples, you may be surprised to find that they actually understand more than they seem able to express. Videotaping children's naturalistic everyday samples is also an option (a video portfolio). At this stage, children are not self-conscious about it and usually enjoying watching themselves. The video can also be used to initiate conversations.

When evaluating your child's portfolio, the following questions may help guide you:

- What is your child able to do in solving real-life literacy problems?
- How does this information demonstrate a change in your child's emergent literacy skills and in what context?
- What skills does your child need to develop next?
- How can the results inform you of the next step and do your strategies need to be modified?

Finally, children should be involved in the entire portfolio assessment process. When children participate in selecting samples for their portfolio and comparing their own work at different stages, they will realise their own achievements, and will be more motivated to go on.

Your Turn

Activities and Reflective Questions

- How do you usually assess and evaluate your child's literacy accomplishments? Is your method similar to or different from the portfolio assessment method described in this chapter? What are your thoughts on this comparison?
- Review the steps of the portfolio assessment shown above and try to use it to document your child's progress in a learning activity. Do you find it helpful to document your child's progress in this way? Show the portfolio to your child. What is her reaction?

Summary

This chapter describes the learning characteristics of infancy and early childhood and identifies developing emergent multiliteracy skills as the focus during this period. It suggests strategies on how to select heritage language materials that can promote emergent literacy development (such as environmental print, children's literature, multimedia and dual or multilingual literacy materials) and points out the kinds of literacy materials that can hinder children's emergent literacy development (such as banal and simplistic texts). It proposes various engaging activities that can facilitate children's early multilingual literacy development, such as observing adult literacy activities, using everyday talk, engaging in play, music, visual and multimodal activities and children's literature. It recommends useful ways of how to read and write with your children and how to help them build emergent skills for future multilingual literacy development. Finally, you are shown how to use the portfolio assessment method to document and evaluate your children's progress in emergent multilingual literacy development.

The strategies and activities suggested in this chapter are not meant to be prescriptive. They are only presented as references for you to consider. There are endless activities that you can come up with in your own family context.

Notes and References

1. The age range included in this chapter is determined by the period before most children formally attend schools in 31 countries. For more information, see http://eacea.ec.eur opa.eu/education/eurydice/eurybase_en.php#description.
2. Copley, J.V. (2000) *The Young Child and Mathematics*. Washington, DC: National Association for the Education of Young Children.
3. Piaget, J. (1962) *Play, Dreams, and Imitation in Childhood*. New York: W.W. Norton.
4. One word of caution, stimulation does not mean pushing. Bombarding young children with over-stimulating environments and developmentally inappropriate expectations can be disconcerting to young children and can impede their optimal psychosocial and cognitive development, causing stress.
   See Gunnar, M.R. (1996) *Quality of Care and Buffering of Stress Physiology: Its Potential in Protecting the Developing Human Brain*. Minneapolis, MN: University of Minnesota Institute of Child Development.
   Black, J.K. and Puckett, M.B. (1996) *The Young Child: Development from Prebirth Through Age Eight*. Englewood Cliffs, NJ: Prentice Hall.
5. Wangmann, J. (2002) Forward. In L. Makin and C.J. Diaz (eds) *Literacies in Early Childhood: Changing Views, Challenging Practices* (p. xi). Sydney: MacLennan & Petty.
6. Teale, W.H. and Sulzby, E. (1986) Emergent literacy: Writing and reading. In M. Farr (ed.) *Advances in Writing Research*. Norwood, NJ: Ablex.
7. Jalongo, M.R. (2003) *Early Childhood Language Arts*. Boston, MA: Pearson Education Group.
8. Reyes, I. and Azuara, P. (2008) Emergent biliteracy in young Mexican immigrant children. *Reading Research Quarterly* 43 (4), 374–398.
9. This example was provided by Ommar's mother in the parent workshop on 28 November 2008.
10. Diwali is an Indian festival (the Festival of Lights).
11. This example was provided by Ayati's mother in the parent workshop on 28 November 2008.
12. Reyes, I. and Azuara, P. (2008) Emergent biliteracy in young Mexican immigrant children. *Reading Research Quarterly* 43 (4), 347–398.
13. Barratt-Pugh, C. (2000) Literacies in more than one language. In C. Barratt-Pugh and M. Rohl (eds) *Literacy Learning in the Early Years* (pp. 172–196). Buckingham: Open University Press.
14. Example provided by Lori's mother (personal communication).
15. Neumann, M., Hood, M. and Neumann, D.L. (2009) The scaffolding of emergent literacy skills in the home environment: A case study. *Early Childhood Education Journal* 36, 313–319.
16. This example was contributed by the Shokhirev family in the parent workshop on 29 April 2009.
17. This example was contributed by the Minami family in the parent workshop in 29 April 2009.
18. Personal communication.
19. Xu, H. (1999) Young Chinese ESL children's home literacy experiences. *Reading Horizon* 40 (1), 47–64.

Li, G-F. (2002) *East Is East, West Is West?: Home Literacy, Culture, and Schooling*. New York: Peter Lang.

20. Hurst, K. (1998) Pre-school literacy experiences of children in Punjabi, Urdu and Gujarati speaking families in England. *British Educational Research Journal* 24 (4), 415–429.
21. Multilingual Resources for Teachers Project (1995) *Building Bridges: Multilingual Resources for Children*. Clevedon: Multilingual Matters.
22. Sneddon, R. (2008) Young bilingual children learning to read with dual language books. *English Teaching: Practice and Critique* 7 (2), 71–84.
23. Clay, M. (1991) *Becoming Literate: The Construction of Inner Control*. Portsmouth, NH: Heinemann.
    Sipe, L. (2000) The construction of literacy understanding by first and second graders in oral response to picture storybook read-alouds. *Reading Research Quarterly* 35 (2), 252–275.
24. This example was contributed by Kabil's father in the parent workshop on 27 September 2008.
25. Dr. Seuss (1954 and 1982) *Horton Hears A Who!* New York: Random House.
26. Personal communication.
27. Pahl, K. and Rowsell, J. (eds) (2006) *Travel Notes from the New Literacy Studies: Instances of Practice*. Clevedon: Multilingual Matters.
    Wild, M. (2000) Information communicating technologies and literacy learning. In C. Barratt-Pugh and M. Rohl (eds) *Literacy Learning in the Early Years* (pp. 129–151). Buckingham: Open University Press.
28. Rich, M. (2009) Curling up with hybrid books, videos included. *New York Times*, 1 October.
29. Liang, P. and Johnson, J. (1999) Using technology to enhance early literacy through play. *Computers in Schools* 15 (1), 55–64.
30. Lankshear, C. and Knobel, M. (2003) *New Literacies: Changing Knowledge and Classroom Learning*. Milton Keynes: Open University Press.
    Marsh, J. (2006) Global, local/public, private: Young children's engagement in digital literacy practices in the home. In K. Pahl and J. Rowsell (eds) *Travel Notes from the New Literacy Studies: Instances of Practice* (pp. 19–38). Clevedon: Multilingual Matters.
31. Wang, X-L., Bernas, R. and Eberhard, P. (2002) Variations in maternal support to children's early literacy development in Chinese and Native American families: Implications for early childhood educators. *International Journal of Early Childhood* 34 (1), 9–23.
32. Cusworth, R. and Simons, R. (1997) *Beyond the Scripts: Drama in the Classroom*. Newton: Primary English Teaching Association.
33. Sheridan, C. (2000) Children's literature and literacy learning. In C. Barratt-Pugh and M. Rohl (eds) *Literacy Learning in the Early Years* (pp. 105–128). Buckingham: Open University Press.
34. Sheridan, C. (2000) Children's literature and literacy learning. In C. Barratt-Pugh and M. Rohl (eds) *Literacy Learning in the Early Years* (pp. 105–128). Buckingham: Open University Press.
35. Neuman, S.B. and Wright, J.S. (2007) *Reading with Your Young Child*. New York: Scholastic Inc.
36. Braxton, B. (2007) Read-abounds: Choosing right book. *Teacher Librarian* 34 (3), 52–53.
37. Carle, E. (1969) *The Very Hungry Caterpillar*. New York: Philomel Books.
38. Neuman, S.B. and Wright, J.S. (2007) *Reading with Your Young Child*. New York: Scholastic Inc.
39. Romero, G. (1983) Print awareness of the preschool bilingual Spanish-English speaking child. Doctoral dissertation, University of Arizona.

40. Walsh, M. (2003) 'Reading' pictures: What do they reveal? Young children's reading of visual texts. *Reading* 37 (3), 123–130.
41. Dr. Seuss (1957) *The Cat in the Hat.* New York: Random House.
42. Dr. Seuss (1960) *Green Eggs and Ham.* New York: Random House.
43. Sheridan, C. (2000) Children's literature and literacy learning. In C. Barratt-Pugh and M. Rohl (eds) *Literacy Learning in the Early Years* (pp. 105–128). Buckingham: Open University Press.
44. The ideas were borrowed from Naqvi, R. (2008) From peanut butter to Eid... blending perspectives: Teaching Urdu to children in Canada. *Diaspora, Indigenous, and Minority Education* 2, 154–164.
45. Hemingway, E. (1952 and 1994) *The Old Man and the Sea.* New York: Collier Books.
46. Fleet, A. and Lockwood, V. (2002) Authentic literacy assessment. In L. Makin and C. J. Diaz (eds) *Literacies in Early Childhood: Changing Views, Challenging Practices* (pp. 135–153). Sydney: MacLennan & Petty.
    Paul, L. (2000) The naked truth about being literate. *Language Arts* 77 (4), 335–342.
47. Witte-Townsend, D.L. and DiGiulio, E. (2004) Something from nothing: Exploring dimensions of children's knowing through the repeated reading of favourite books. *International Journal of Children's Spirituality* 9 (2), 127–142.
    Estes, C.P. (1992) *Women Who Run with the Wolves: Myths and Stories of the Wild Woman Archetype.* New York: Ballantine Books.
48. Carle, E. (1969) *The Very Hungry Caterpillar.* New York: Philomel Books.
49. Carle, E. (1984) *The Very Busy Spider.* New York: Philomel Books.
50. Carle, E. (1996) *The Grouchy Lady Bug.* New York: HarperCollins.
51. Gilman, P. (1992) *Something from Nothing.* New York: Scholastic Inc.
52. Taback, S. (1999) *Joseph had a Little Overcoat.* New York: Viking-Penguin.
53. Stone, K. (1981) Marchen to fairy tales: An unmagical transformation. *Western Folklore* 40, 232–244.
54. Kellerman, J. (1981) *Helping the Fearful Child.* New York: Norton.
55. Lewis, C.S. (1996) *Of Other Word: Essays and Stories.* New York: Harcourt Brace.
56. Richards, P.O., Thatcher, D.H., Shreeves, M., Timmons, P. and Barker, S. (1999) Don't let a good care frighten you: Choosing and using quality chillers to promote reading. *The Reading Teacher* 52 (8), 830–840.
57. Tomlinson, C. and Lynch-Brown, C. (1996) *Essentials of Children's Literature.* Boston, MA: Allyn & Bacon.
58. Crosser, S. (1994) When young children are afraid. *Day Care and Early Education* 22 (1), 7–11.
    Bettelheim, B. (1976) *The Uses of Enchantment.* New York: Knopf.
    Lewis, C.S. (1996) *Of Other Word: Essays and Stories.* New York: Harcourt Brace.
59. Richards, P.O., Thatcher, D.H., Shreeves, M., Timmons, P. and Barker, S. (1999) Don't let a good care frighten you: Choosing and using quality chillers to promote reading. *The Reading Teacher* 52 (8), 830–840.
60. Sheridan, C. (2000) Children's literature and literacy learning. In C. Barratt-Pugh and M. Rohl (eds) *Literacy Learning in the Early Years* (pp. 105–128). Buckingham: Open University Press.
61. Kenner, C. and Gregory, E. (2003) Becoming biliterate. In N. Hall, J. Larson and J. March (eds) *Handbook of Early Childhood Literacy* (pp. 178–188). New York: Sage.
62. Saxena, M. (1994) Literacies amongst the Punjabis in Southall (Britain). In J. Maybin (ed.) *Language and Literacy in Social Practice* (pp. 96–116). Clevedon: Multilingual Matters.
63. Kenner, C. (2000) Biliteracy in a monolingual school system? English and Gujarati in South London. *Language, Culture and Curriculum* 13 (1), 13–30.

64. Barratt-Pugh, C. (2000) The socio-cultural context of literacy learning. In C. Barrat-Pugh and M. Rohl (eds) *Literacy Learning in the Early Years* (pp. 1–26). Buckingham: Open University Press.

65. E-mail communication on 20 March 2009.

66. Wang, X-L. (2008*) Growing Up with Three Languages*. Bristol: Multilingual Matters.

67. Example from an e-mail exchange with Sonia.

68. Makin, L. Campbell, J. and Diaz, C. (1995) *One Childhood Many Languages. Guidelines for Early Childhood Education in Australia*. Pymble: Harper Educational.

69. Danby, S. (2002) Language and social practices: Everyday talk constructing school-literate practices. In L. Makin and C.J. Diaz (eds) *Literacies in Early Childhood: Changing Views, Challenging Practices* (pp. 55–70). Sydney: MacLennan & Petty.

70. Leong, D. and Bodrova, E. (2003) Building language and literacy through play. *Early Childhood Today*. October Issue. On WWW at http://www2.scholastic.com/browse/article.jsp?id = 3747175.

71. Ramey, S.L. and Ramey, C.T. (1999) *Going to School: How to Help Your Child Succeed*. New York: Goddard Press.

72. This example is modified from Hall, N. and Robinson, A. (2000) Play and literacy learning. In C. Barratt-Pugh and M. Rohl (eds) *Literacy Learning in the Early Years* (p. 95). Buckingham: Open University Press.

73. Martello, J. (2002) Many roads through many modes: Becoming literate in early childhood. In L. Makin and C.J. Diaz (eds) *Literacies in Early Childhood: Changing Views, Challenging Practices* (pp. 35–52). Sydney: MacLennan & Petty.

74. Martello, J. (2002) Many roads through many modes: Becoming literate in early childhood. In L. Makin and C.J. Diaz (eds) *Literacies in Early Childhood: Changing Views, Challenging Practices* (pp. 35–52). Sydney: MacLennan & Petty.

75. Markin, L. and Groom, S. (2002) Literacy transitions. In L. Makin and C.J. Diaz (eds) *Literacies in Early Childhood: Changing Views, Challenging Practices* (pp. 71–91). Sydney: MacLennan & Petty.

76. Harris, P. (2002) Children as readers. In L. Makin and C.J. Diaz (eds) *Literacies in Early Childhood: Changing Views, Challenging Practices* (pp. 117–134). Sydney: MacLennan & Petty.

77. E-mail communication on 11 March 2009.

78. Giambo, D.A. and Szecsi, T. (2005) Parents can guide children through the world of two languages. *Childhood Education* 81 (3), 164–165.

79. Orellana, M.F., Reynolds, J., Dorner, L. and Meza, M. (2003) In other words: Translating or "para-phrasing" as a family literacy practice in immigrant households. *Reading Research Quarterly* 38 (1), 13–34.
    Purcell-Gates, V. (2000). Family literacy. In M.L. Kamil, P.B. Mosenthal, P.D. Pearson and R. Barr (eds) *Handbook of Reading Research: Volume III* (pp. 853–870). Mahwah, NJ: Lawrence Erlbaum Associates.
    Scarborough, H. and Dobrich, W. (1994) On the efficacy of reading to preschoolers. *Developmental Review* 14, 245–302.

80. Sheridan, C. (2000) Children's literature and literacy learning. In C. Barratt-Pugh and M. Rohl (eds) *Literacy Learning in the Early Years* (pp. 105–128). Buckingham: Open University Press.

81. Justice, L.M., Kaderavek, J.N., Fan, X., Sofka, A. and Hunt, A. (2009) Accelerating preschoolers' early literacy development through class-based teacher-child story reading and explicit print referencing. *Language, Speech, and Hearing Services in Schools* 40, 67–85.
    Wang, X-L., Delaney, K. and Eberhard, P. (2009) Effects of teachers' strategies on children's early literacy development: A comparative study of Chinese and American

early literacy programs. Paper presented at the 16th European Conference on Reading, Braga, Portugal, 20 July.
82. Tse, L. (2001) Heritage language literacy: A study of US biliterates. *Language, Culture and Curriculum* 14 (3), 256–268.
83. Example provided by Eddie's mother at the November 2008 parent workshop.
84. An, R. (1999) Learning in two languages and cultures: The experience of Mainland Chinese families in Britain. Doctoral dissertation, University of Reading.
85. Tucha, O. Tucha, L. and Lange, K. W. (2008) Graphonomics, automaticity and hand-writing assessment. *Literacy* 42 (3), 145–155.
86. Kenner, C. (2004) *Becoming Biliterate*. Stoke-on-Trent: Trentham Books.
87. Garton, A and Pratt, C. (1998) *Learning to be Literate: The Development of Spoken and Written Language*. Oxford: Blackwell.
88. Martello, J. (2002) Many roads through many modes: Becoming literate in early childhood. In L. Makin and C.J. Diaz (eds) *Literacies in Early Childhood: Changing Views, Challenging Practices* (pp. 35–52). Sydney: MacLennan & Petty.
89. Garton, A. and Pratt, C. (1998) *Learning to be Literate: The Development of Spoken and Written Language*. Oxford: Blackwell.
90. Bruner, J.S. (1975) The ontogenesis of speech acts. *Journal of Child Language* 2, 1–40.
91. Barratt-Pugh, C. (2000) Literacies in more than one language. In C. Barratt-Pugh and M. Rohl (eds) *Literacy Learning in the Early Years* (pp. 172–196). Buckingham: Open University Press.
92. Harris, P. (2002) Children as readers. In L. Makin and C.J. Diaz (eds) *Literacies in Early Childhood: Changing Views, Challenging Practices* (pp. 117–134). Sydney: MacLennan & Petty.

Chapter 5

Middle Childhood (6–11 Years)[1]

This chapter briefly addresses the learning characteristics of middle childhood and identifies the focus of heritage language literacy development during this period. Various suggestions are made to assist you in selecting home language literacy materials and conducting learning activities that complement your children's school literacy experience. The assessment priority is identified for this period and methods are introduced to help you monitor your children's progress. At the end of each section, opportunities are provided to practise the recommended strategies and reflect on how to incorporate these strategies to fit your personal circumstances.

Typical Learning Characteristics

During the middle childhood period, children gradually develop logical and systematic thinking by incorporating multiple pieces of information. They begin to perceive underlying reality despite superficial appearance. This is also the time when children begin to understand, appreciate and use rules. Most importantly, children begin to develop the ability to think effectively about their own knowledge and processes of thought (that is, metacognition – the ability to think about thinking).[2] Swiss psychologist Jean Piaget viewed this period as a major cognitive turning point: children make the striking transition from the preoperational stage where their thoughts are not yet logical, to the concrete operational stage where their thoughts become logical, flexible and organised. Recent research, however, indicates that the transition from early childhood to middle childhood does not involve as dramatic a transformation in cognitive abilities as Piaget once thought. Instead, the major cognitive development of middle childhood appears to involve refinement and a more widespread use of skills that existed in primitive forms during early childhood.[3]

Nevertheless, children do show major improvements in their attention and memory during middle childhood. They develop increasingly effective strategies for directing and maintaining attention and they also develop memory strategies to retain information.

However, despite all the cognitive advancements, children at this stage still have some limitations. For example, they tend not to think abstractly and hypothetically. Their reasoning tends to be confined to their own concrete experiences. They sometimes have trouble using a skill they possess as part of a larger problem-solving system. Thus, when solving problems, on the one hand, they tend to be too narrow in scope and tied to a particular experience or context (e.g. 'an apple is something you eat for lunch'), and on the other hand, too broad in scope and incapable of differentiating between words and other related concepts (e.g. 'a cat is a pet').[4]

Thus, in order to help your children develop home language literacy more effectively during middle childhood, I will offer the following recommendations for you to consider when working with them.

- Provide opportunities for your children to engage in authentic home language literacy activities (that is, activities close to their real-life experiences, e.g. write about a recent sport event, write an e-mail to a friend, write a letter to grandparents or read the instruction manual of a video game).
- Supply contextual clues and hints to help your children understand home language reading materials.
- Introduce heritage language grammatical rules (this is a good time for you to introduce home language grammatical rules as children begin to understand the importance of rules in general).
- Help your children perform challenging home language literacy tasks through scaffolding (assistance) and apprenticeships[5] (help your children practise literacy skills in the real world just like a master carpenter helps his apprentice learn carpeting skills by asking him/her to observe and practice).
- Allow your children to appropriate[6] the home language knowledge introduced by you (allow your children the freedom to apply heritage language literacy knowledge in their own understanding and manner).

If you are cognisant of your children's learning characteristics when planning and conducting home language literacy learning activities, your children will tend to learn better and you will tend to feel less frustrated and happier to interact with them.

Home Language Literacy Development Focus

Most children begin formal education at the beginning of middle childhood (around age 6). If a child's home language and school (or mainstream) language are the same, the child's emergent literacy skills developed in early childhood tend to be automatically replaced by conventional literacy skills[7] in school.

For those children whose home language is different from that of their school (or mainstream) language, the home language literacy development path is often different. Although their emergent heritage language literacy skills developed at home in early childhood will no doubt benefit their school literacy development, their emergent literacy skills will not automatically become conventional home language literacy skills unless special efforts are made.

As these children become more involved in mainstream school learning as well as extracurricular activities, they have less time for home language literacy activities. Without extra effort, it is unlikely that these children's home language literacy will develop any further and may even terminate. Therefore, the focus for home language literacy development during middle childhood is to facilitate the transition from the emergent home language literacy skills to conventional home language literacy skills, to use the literacy skills developed at home and in school to support each other, to negotiate home language literacy activities with extracurricular activities and to cultivate motivation for continuous home language literacy development.

Selecting Literacy Materials

While you are reading the following suggestions, think about how to link them to the home literacy teaching framework discussed in Chapter 2 and the four-step home literacy teaching process discussed in Chapter 3.

Choosing right level reading materials

Choosing the right level of home language reading materials is essential in helping children gain confidence to continue their home language literacy development during middle childhood. When a text is too easy, a child may feel bored and lose interest in it. When a text is too difficult, a child may feel discouraged and unable to continue. When measuring the suitability of a text for your children, three areas need to be considered: linguistic level, content suitability and exploitability.[8]

The linguistic level of a text refers to whether a child is familiar with the vocabulary, grammatical structure and idioms of a text. Reading experts have suggested many ways to measure the linguistic difficulty level of reading materials (particularly for beginning readers). Some suggest that if a child reads 90–94% of the words correctly in a text and is able to answer at least 75% of the questions, the text is at the right level for the child with adult help. If a child can read 95% or more of the words correctly, the text is appropriate for the child to read independently. However, if a child's word recognition is less than 90% or comprehension is 50% or less, the text is too difficult for the child (the frustration level).[9] Others suggest that when choosing books for children, one good test is to take a page from the text you are considering, photocopy it and cover up (or whiten) about 20 words scattered throughout the page. You can then give your child a cloze test with the photocopied page (a cloze test is a test in which words are removed from a text and replaced with blank spaces). The child's task is to fill in the spaces with the missing words or suitable words. If your child can complete over 80% of the sentences with the correct words or reasonable alternatives, the text is at the right level for your child. Otherwise, the text is too difficult.[10]

Content suitability of a text refers to whether a text appeals to a child, whether the content is at the child's developmental level and whether a child has the cultural background information to understand the text. For example, even though 12-year-old Jingjing (Liz), who lives in Vancouver, has no problem understanding the vocabulary of the simplified version of the Chinese classic novel 红楼梦[11] (*The Dream of the Red Chamber*), she has tremendous problems in understanding the complicated power relationship among the characters in the novel. As she told her mother, 'I know most of the Chinese characters in the book. But, I am so confused about what they say and do to each other.'[12] Therefore, when judging whether a heritage language text content is suitable for your children, you may want to consider whether they have the social or cultural knowledge or experience to comprehend the text. This point is particularly important to stress because children who are not living in heritage cultures often face the same challenge as Jingjing. In general, the most reliable measure for you to decide the text content suitability is to ask your children or observe their reaction.

Exploitability of a text means whether a child can use a text as a springboard to learn and develop high-order thinking abilities. Christine Nuttall suggests that when selecting a text for a child, teachers (in this case, parents) should consider what a text could do for the child. The following questions, proposed by Nuttall, may be able to guide you to look for the exploitability of a heritage language text:[13]

- Will the text do one or more of these things?
  o   Tell the children things they don't already know.
  o   Introduce them to new and relevant ideas and make them think about things they have not thought about before.
  o   Help them to understand the way other people feel or think (e.g. people with different backgrounds, problems or attitudes from their own).
  o   Make them want to read for themselves (to continue a story and find out more about a subject).
- Does the text challenge the children's intelligence without making unreasonable demands on their knowledge of the language?
- If there are new words, are they worth learning at this stage and not too numerous? (If these new words are not worth learning, consider replacing them with words that the children already know). Are some of them understandable by means of inference from the context? (If not, can you build in some additional clues to make this possible)?
- Does the text lend itself to further study? Does it enable you to ask good questions or devise other forms of exploitation? For example:
  o   Make a map, diagram or graphic based on the information in the text.
  o   Reprocess the information from the text.
  o   Debate, discuss or role-play (e.g. between you and your child or between siblings).

Sometimes, if it is too difficult for you to find the right level of home language texts for your children, you may consider simplifying original heritage language texts. I have tried to do this for my children. For example, some classic Chinese texts contain too many non-common and non-contemporary words and concepts; without my rewriting (simplifying) them, my children would not have been able to understand them.

However, simplification of a text for the purpose of helping comprehension needs to be done with caution. When you simplify a text, you may eliminate the barriers of understanding, but you may also make the text too explicit, which will cause your children to be unable to deduce. Thus, it has been suggested that you should not insert explicit connectives, such as *because* or *although*, so that your child deduces the relationships between sentences without them. When you simplify a text, retain as much as possible of the quality and structure of the original and remove only difficult vocabulary and complex sentences.[14]

Including a variety of reading materials

To help your children enlarge the scope of their home language reading materials, it is important to provide opportunities for them to read a variety of genres and topics. Mrs Cho (whom you met in Chapter 2) is exemplary in this respect. She makes sure that her daughter Jessie reads a variety of Korean language materials. For example, when her daughter was 11 years old, Mrs Cho gave her a different text every weekday (with different genres and topics): Monday, a text on animals (non-fiction, fiction and poetry on animals); Tuesday, a paragraph on different transportation tools: trains, airplanes or cars (non-fiction); Wednesday, a paragraph on plants (poetry and non-fiction); Thursday, a paragraph from a Korean fable (fiction and prose); and Friday, a text on cooking (non-fiction). Mrs Cho has been doing this ever since her daughter entered elementary school. She consistently tries to incorporate different topics and genres in her daughter's Korean language reading. According to Mrs Cho, her daughter enjoys the different types of reading materials, and the information she retains from reading Korean materials has also benefited her academic performance in school. One of her daughter's teachers told Mrs Cho that Jessie was far more versatile than her peers.[15]

Perhaps it is hard for many of us to do what Mrs Cho does and very few children are as cooperative and motivated as Jessie. Nevertheless, Mrs Cho's practice is commendable in that she introduces her child to different genres (fiction, non-fiction, prose and poetry) and topics (animal, transportation tools, plants, cooking and fables) when choosing Korean reading materials. In doing so, Jessie has had the opportunity to learn different vocabulary, expressions and information. In addition, Jessie is not bored with the same type of reading materials. Most importantly, Jessie's home language reading has contributed to her learning in school. Mrs Cho's teaching approach is particularly helpful for children who are developing heritage language literacy in a non-heritage language environment.

Balancing intensive and extensive reading materials

There are two types of reading: intensive and extensive. Both are important for heritage language learners in developing their literacy skills. Middle childhood is a good time to begin to distinguish between these two types of reading approaches when selecting reading material for your children.

Intensive reading is slow and careful reading. In many ways, intensive reading is more of a method of language study than a form of reading. Intensive reading is useful for language study because its slow speed allows children to stop and look up new words in the dictionary and allows them to pause and carefully study long or difficult sentences to get a better understanding.

However, intensive reading alone will not make children good readers. In fact, too much intensive reading may actually cause them to develop bad reading habits. For example, because intensive reading requires readers to pay attention to every detail, it often encourages the habit of paying more attention to the vocabulary and grammar of a text than to its overall meaning. It also encourages the habit of reading very slowly, and children who become accustomed to reading in this way often never learn to read any faster. Finally, intensive reading tends to be relatively boring, so children who fall into the habit of reading everything in this manner may ultimately grow to dislike reading.[16]

The main purpose of most reading is to understand the meaning of a text, usually as quickly as possible. This kind of reading is called extensive reading – an approach that requires a child to rapidly read large amounts of text. Extensive reading is more like 'real' reading than intensive reading. To become good readers, children need to read a lot (entire books or magazines) instead of just short articles or passages from textbooks. Just like a musician must practise sight reading a lot in order to understand the meaning of the music notes and demonstrate such understanding while playing a musical instrument; a good reader needs to read a lot to recognise the grammatical structure of a text and understand the meaning at the same time.

Moreover, extensive reading skills are essential to function in the real world (e.g. to obtain a general understanding of a subject or for pleasure). In reading, speed, enjoyment and comprehension are closely linked with one another.[17] To achieve these three areas, a proficient reader will not read word by word. Instead, she will read a meaningful unit at a time. If a reader reads too slowly, she will forget what she has read.

There are several benefits associated with reading extensively in a heritage language. It helps children to:

- build confidence;
- increase motivation to read;
- facilitate prediction skills;
- develop reading automaticity;
- enlarge vocabulary;
- increase knowledge.

Although it is sometimes useful for children to read intensively so that they can study a text's grammar and vocabulary to get a better understanding of their heritage language, it is more important for them to spend time reading extensively, focusing mainly on the meaning of the text, not stopping to look up every new word. Experts have suggested that more access to books leads to more reading, and more reading results in higher levels of grammatical accuracy, a larger vocabulary and greater reading comprehension.[18] Thus, when you select heritage language reading materials for your children, you may want to consider the balance between intensive reading and extensive reading materials.

Matching school and home reading materials

There is often an incompatibility between school language reading materials and home language materials. When multilingual children begin to receive formal literacy education in their mainstream language in school, they tend to accelerate in their mainstream literacy skills and regress or make little progress in their home language literacy development. Thus, it is beneficial to encourage simultaneous literacy development in your home language and school language.

One way to match school reading with home reading is to employ the dual/ multilingual reading materials addressed in Chapter 4. During middle childhood, dual/multilingual literacy materials may play an even more important role in children's heritage language literacy development. You may want to consider introducing similar reading materials in your heritage language to match the school reading materials. Obtain the list of your children's reading materials in an academic year and try to find similar topics in your heritage language or dual-/ multi-language versions. If you cannot find an exact version in your heritage language, materials with the same topic or genre can help as well.

There are several benefits in matching home language literacy skills with school literacy skills. First, your children can acquire similar vocabulary in different languages. Second, the concept acquired through one language (either home language or mainstream language) can help your children understand the same concepts in the other language. According to Mrs Cho, her daughter found it easier to understand her subject areas in English because the concepts she read in the Korean materials helped her (an incidental bonus[19]). Third, the relevance to children's school knowledge may motivate them to read home language texts.

If your child's heritage language literacy level is not as advanced as his school literacy level, you can choose home language reading materials that are simpler, but contain information that will help him learn school subject content areas. By connecting school literacy with home literacy, you may avoid teaching home language literacy as a separate and isolated activity.

Taking advantage of situational readings

In Chapter 4, I addressed the benefits of using environmental print as a resource for your children's emergent home language literacy development. During middle childhood, you may want to consider extending the same practice by using situational reading materials (materials used in real-life occasions) to help your children acquire heritage language literacy skills. For example, heritage restaurant menus, community newsletters, religious texts, holiday messages, letters or e-mails from relatives, recipes, wedding or birth announcements, birthday invitations and game instruction manuals are good sources of situational reading materials.

Situational reading materials are connected to real-life events. They can show your children how literacy is used in a specific real-world situation. For example, 8-year-old Diya has learned to read and recite many beautiful verses and poems by reading wedding invitation cards her family had received in Hindi.[20]

Exploring multimedia reading materials

Multimedia modality has increasingly become part of children's daily routines. For example, according to a recent report from the Kaiser Family Foundation, an average American child between the ages of 8 and 18 spends seven and a half hours a day using a smart phone, a computer or another electronic device and watching television.[21] As mentioned in Chapter 1, reading in this multimedia format provides a kind of visual input different from reading in traditional books. Unlike reading traditional books, multimedia reading is interactive and multidimensional: a combination of text, pictures, video and sound.

Taking advantage of multimedia reading can facilitate your children's heritage language literacy development. Mr Belinsky reported that he found it very useful for his 10-year-old daughter Sasha to learn her heritage language Russian through the multimedia modality. Every Saturday, Mr Belinsky would spend a couple of hours with Sasha looking for information on different Russian websites for doll collections (her hobby) and guide her to some targeted readings about dolls that he had selected beforehand. Similarly, one of my older son Léandre's hobbies was Märklin trains. He used to spend hours surfing the internet and reading about different models of trains in French (one of his heritage languages). His father would show him the different links about Märklin. Surfing the internet has no doubt motivated multilingual children like Sasha and Léandre to read their heritage languages.

However, you may want to monitor your children's use of multimedia devices such as the internet surfing activities. You can discuss internet safety with your children. Based on your situation, you can also establish certain rules with your children.

Valuing popular culture

Popular culture sources such as children's television programmes, cartoons, video games, comic books, magazines and game cards have been prevalent in our children's lives, and they serve the purpose of entertainment and information. Though many parents have concerns about the educational values and moral corruption of these materials, educators and researchers now believe that when used appropriately, these materials can provide incentives for children to engage in literacy learning.[22] Some researchers and educators go further to suggest that ignoring materials from popular culture is to devalue the children's perspective,[23] because children are enthusiastic about these popular cultural materials. Recent research has shown that popular media texts can be seen as a valuable resource for learning to read and write.[24] For example, Jeff Kinney's *Diary of a Wimpy Kid* series[25] has had an astronomical success among American elementary and early middle school children. I once asked my younger son Dominique why he found the book interesting (he finished one of the books in two hours). He replied, 'because I can relate to the kid in the book'.

The advantage of using popular culture to help initiate the heritage language developing process is that these materials can provide a familiar context (territory) for children, that is, popular culture is part of their reality. It is an attractive way to lead children into the world of literacy. Moreover, the contents of these materials often go beyond the here and now in their environment and provide possibilities for children to look at past and future events. Furthermore, for children who are developing more than one language, using popular culture materials may be especially meaningful in a number of important ways. First, there is often no immediate incentive for heritage language learning children to read heritage language materials. Since popular culture materials are often humorous, they can help attract children to read their heritage language. Second, children can compare popular materials in their mainstream culture with those in their heritage culture and thus, develop the critical ability to evaluate reading materials from a very early age.[26]

However, popular cultural materials may contain information that is not suitable for children. Therefore, you may want to screen these materials before introducing them to your children.

Using children's literature

Good children's literature is often written by writers who understand children and have a good command of their language. Therefore, children's literature tends to be more suitable in both language and content. During middle childhood, you may want to use good children's literature to attract your children to read their heritage language and help them become more conscious of their heritage language conventions.

Using children's literature to attract children to read

We all tend to read books that interest us, and our children are no exception. Having access to interesting, comprehensible heritage language children's literature will help children develop home language literacy.

However, what counts as interesting and captivating children's literature depends on the reader. It is possible that what you (as an adult) find interesting is entirely different from what your children find interesting. For example, as discussed in the previous chapter, parents often fear scary children's books and hesitate to introduce them to their children. On the contrary, children are often drawn to these books.

Giving children the freedom to choose literature for their own reading can help you avoid imposing your view of what counts as an interesting book and, consequently, encourage them to read in their heritage language. There are many ways you can discretely help your children choose books. For example, you can introduce your children to books with funny illustrations or books with catchy titles. You can read them an interesting episode from a book. By doing so, you draw your children's attention to these books and maybe entice them to read the books.[27] Most of all, you can make your children see that reading is enjoyable. There is evidence to suggest that self-selected reading can increase a child's interest, therefore, it may be effective for heritage language learners.[28]

Using children's literature to learn heritage language convention

If popular culture reading materials can lure your children to heritage language reading, what good children's literature can do is to help move their heritage language literacy to a more conventional level. As stated earlier, good heritage language children's literature is often written by writers who are masters of their language and who can provide good language models for children on how to use words and sentences. Good children's books (or trade books[29]) also tend to contain simple and commonly used words. In addition, the storylines in these books are usually easy to understand.

Every language has its own seminal children's books. If you are willing to look around, you are likely to find some. Marissa used to complain that she could not find good Tagalog children's books for her elementary school-age children. After doing some research, she was pleasantly surprised that such books did exist.[30]

Creating heritage language books

Encouraging your children to create their own versions of home language reading materials or books is an interesting way to engage your children in home language literacy learning. Children can create their own reading materials and books by cutting out pictures from advertisements, magazines and newspapers or printing them from the internet. You can work together with your children to label pictures and photos or you can help your children write about the materials they collect. This is an innovative way to engage your children in heritage language literacy learning.

Self-made reading materials can increase children's motivation to read the materials. Karl from Germany, who now lives in Shanghai, has helped his 7-year-old son create his own German books by cutting out pictures from the German magazines he receives monthly. According to Karl, his son is very interested in making his version of German *Bücher* (books). The boy has begun to learn to read and write German through these self-made books.[31]

In case you just cannot find good children's literature in your heritage language, you can try to write your own books for your children. To some parents, this may sound quite challenging. However, Karen, who lives in London, found that she enjoys writing books for her three kids in Swahili. Over the years, she, her husband and her children have made many Swahili books with attractive illustrations, family photos and interesting texts. Her children enjoy reading these homemade books immensely.[32] They are a vivid record of her children's heritage language learning journey.

With the advancement in computer software, it is now easier for you to create books in your heritage language. When writing your books in your heritage language, you may want to follow these guidelines:

- Use vocabulary and grammatical structures that are frequent in your conventional heritage language use.
- Use easily readable fonts (in your word processor) or handwriting.
- Compose interesting texts.
- Include interesting clip art or illustrations.
- Follow the conventions of your heritage language writing.

You can also try to translate some good mainstream children's literature into your heritage language. There are at least two advantages of doing so. First, your children may be familiar with the story. It is likely that they have heard of it in their mainstream language. Second, these books are probably written for a specific age group. Therefore, the content is suitable for your children. However, when translating books from mainstream language to heritage language, you may want to be mindful of not injecting one culture's convention into the other because the major point in learning a heritage language is also learning the heritage culture.

Your Turn

Having read the suggestions I have made for choosing heritage language literacy materials during middle childhood, this is a good time for you to stop and relate what you have read so far to your own situation. The following activities and reflective questions may help you begin.

Activities and Reflective Questions

- Research your heritage language reading materials through the internet, your local bookstore and library catalogues. Compile a list of your heritage language reading materials that you want your child to read.
  - ○ Sort the list into genres and topics. Does your selection contain different genres and topics? If not, you may want to redo the list and try to include diverse reading materials.
  - ○ Check whether these materials are the right level for your child by using the information provided earlier in this chapter (linguistic level, content and exploitability).
  - ○ Decide which materials you want to use for intensive reading and which for extensive reading.

    ○ Divide these materials into monthly, weekly and daily readings. Is the amount that you want your child to read doable?

    ○ Do you see the benefits of going through the above activities in selecting home language reading materials?

- Obtain a list of mainstream language reading materials from your child's school (preferably, the materials used in your child's current grade). Sort them into different genres and topics. Then try to research similar books with similar genres and topics in your heritage language. Read one of these heritage language books to your child or let your child read it. Observe your child's reaction. Is he interested in the material? Does the familiarity of the subject help him comprehend the heritage language text?

- If you cannot find suitable heritage language reading materials for your child, try to simplify (rewrite) some. Based on the suggestions you read in this chapter, what do you need to do so that you will not compromise your child's ability to infer from the text?

- Visit a heritage language bookstore (if available in your area) or look online together with your child. Ask her to choose the books that she would like to read. Observe what she picks. Do your child's book choices give you some insights on selecting reading materials for her?

- Talk to your child about the idea of creating his own book. Observe his reaction. If he is interested in this idea, how would go about helping him realise it?

- Talk to your child about the idea of creating an interactive, multimedia online book. If she is interested in the idea, can you find a way to make this book creating process an opportunity to attract her to read your heritage language? Alternatively, you can explore how to create an interactive, online book yourself and show your child.

Conducting Literacy Activities

There is absolutely no reason to think that children's reading activities have to precede writing. In fact, children often start writing before they can read.[33] Similarly, there is no real reason why reading activities need to be separated from writing activities. Reading and writing are both part of a child's total literacy development. However, for ease of discussion, I will begin with how to conduct activities with reading and then show how to conduct activities with writing in the home environment.

Reading

Unlike oral language acquisition, reading is an acquired skill, and reading development needs more adult deliberate guidance. The basic skills involved in reading include script (orthography) knowledge, symbol-sound correspondence, syllables, parsing (segmenting phonemes and syllables), phonemic awareness,[34] morphological awareness, semantic awareness (meaning) and vocabulary knowledge. Helping your children acquire these basic skills in your heritage language will ensure their success in their heritage language reading development.

Developing decoding skills

Decoding is the ability to apply the knowledge of symbol-sound (such as letter-sound) relationships to make sense of words in print. It is an essential skill for reading development in any language. Over the years, researchers have found that phonological awareness, morphological awareness, orthographic awareness and semantic awareness need to be developed before a child can read, that is, decode the print. Phonological awareness generally refers to the ability to perceive and manipulate sound units in a spoken language (such as syllables and rhymes). Morphological awareness means children's understanding of the morphemic structures of words and their ability to perceive and manipulate that structure (e.g. the meaning of -ed in *worked* and -s in *works*). Orthographic awareness refers to children's understanding of the conventions used in the writing system of their language.[35] Semantic awareness refers to children's understanding of the meaning of words.

In general, these reading-related decoding and cognitive skills can be developed in school when children are learning mainstream language literacy. Some of the skills that children develop in school can be easily transferred to their home language literacy and vice versa. For example, research has shown that phonological skills can be transferred from a sound-based language (such as English) to a meaning-based language (such as Chinese) and vice versa.[36] It has also been shown that certain cognitive skills necessary for reading development are not attached to a specific language. Once they are learned, they are available for learning other languages,[37] although the school (dominant) language literacy skills tend to have a stronger effect of transfer on heritage language literacy skills than the other way around.[38]

Multilingual research expert Viv Edwards, however, questions the cross-linguistic transfers and cautions us to pay attention to language specificity. For example, in English, [d] as in *Dan* and [ð] as in *than* are two separate phonemes. By contrast, in Spanish, they are one phoneme such as /dado/ (given), the initial /d/ is always pronounced as [d] at the beginning of a word and as [ð] in the middle or at the end. Also, in English, /k/ is aspirated (or followed by a puff of air) at the beginning of a word, but not in the middle or the end. In Panjabi, both variants can occur at any position in the word, [pʰul], for instance, means 'fruit' while [pul] means 'moment'. In this example, there is one phoneme in English and two phonemes in Panjabi.[39]

Some children develop decoding strategies over time with little direct instruction. Others may need some one-on-one teaching to help them learn the decoding strategies. Nevertheless, research indicates that most children do benefit from deliberate training in reading-related decoding and cognitive skills (e.g. phonological, morphological, orthographic and semantic awareness).[40]

Thus, when you help your children develop heritage reading abilities, you can be more conscious of teaching them decoding skills. Some strategies are suggested below.

When helping your children develop decoding skills in their heritage language, you can help them relate sounds to symbols (such as letters) by reminding them of what they already know. Using English as an example, if your child already knows *'tr'* at the beginning of the word *train*, you can remind him/her of this when he/she reads the new word *truck*. You can also help him/her to look at how words are formed. Using another example in English, *raincoat* is formed with two words *rain* and *coat*.[41] Additionally, you can draw your child's attention to the word parts (the orthographic chunks). Still using English as an example, when looking at the word *habitat*, you can help your child become aware of (decode) these multisyllabic parts *'ha'*, *'bi'*, *'tat'*.

When you help your children develop decoding skills, be sure to make this activity as enjoyable as possible and avoid turning it into a boring exercise. Playing games with your children is an interesting and engaging way to help them pay attention to the parts of words they are reading. For instance, you can try to play word hunt games (by looking for words that have vowels) or play word-sorting games (by sorting words that contain two vowels and one consonant).

Building vocabulary knowledge

Vocabulary is a basic building block of literacy and is closely linked to children's reading comprehension. Therefore, during middle childhood, helping your children build heritage language vocabulary should be one of your top priorities in their literacy development. Some literacy experts argue that word learning cannot just rely on children's spontaneous engagement with words on their own. Rather, effective word learning must be deliberately taught.[42] Research has shown that systematic, explicit and direct teaching of vocabulary can indeed enhance a child's reading proficiency.[43] The following are some strategies for you to consider.

Using contextual clues

You can start to help your children learn the meanings of new words by using the contextual clues in the reading material. For example, if your child comes across new vocabulary, you can help him/her by looking for the clues in the reading material, such as illustrations and background information. You can use guiding questions to help your child understand the meaning. For instance, when reading a Chinese text on 谁干什么? (Who Is Doing What?), my older son Léandre did not know the Chinese words 锄地 (plough fields). I asked him to find the meaning of the words by looking for clues in the illustration in which a farmer is ploughing. Because Léandre had been speaking Chinese since birth, he could use the words in speech, but was unable to recognise them in print. By providing clues such as the illustration of a farmer ploughing, it was easy for him to get the meaning of 锄地 (plough fields).

Learning more words through connections

You can help your children enlarge their heritage language vocabulary by learning words connected by their specific features. Additionally, you can help your children learn more words by building on what they already know and expand on their word knowledge. Suppose a child already knows the word *act*, a new word *interact* can be introduced.[44] Similarly, after Léandre learned the characters 锄地 (plough), I could teach him many additional characters and radicals (部首/essential elements of Chinese characters): 钅 (a radical for words that have a metal component such as 针/needle and 锅/pot), 且 (but), 力 (strength), 土 (earth) and 也 (also).

Moreover, you can teach your children more words that logically belong together in the context. For example, *eavesdrop* and *gregarious* do not have an apparent connection. However, you can make them belong together by creating a context. Suppose if someone reports you to a teacher for talking to a friend, this person is *eavesdropping* and you are being *gregarious*.[45]

Furthermore, you can help your children learn more words by employing the idea of a word web[46] (a visual representation resembling a web of concepts and subordinating ideas with connecting lines to show relationships[47]) or accumulative vocabulary teaching.[48] Suppose you teach the word *shoe* in your heritage language, you can draw different kinds of connections with this word and help your children not only learn more vocabulary related to this word, but also increase their knowledge of the concept. This approach is illustrated in Figure 5.1. You can extend the idea suggested in Figure 5.1 and make your children's vocabulary learning more interesting.

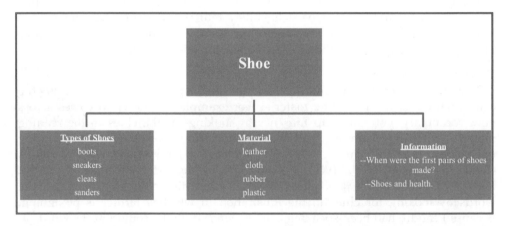

Figure 5.1 Word web

Increasing vocabulary through synonyms and antonyms

Synonyms are words that have almost the same meaning as other words. Antonyms are words with opposite meanings.[49] Take the following as an example: some synonyms of the adjective *kind* are *nice, hospitable* and *tender*. Some antonyms of the word are *cruel* and *heartless*. Using synonyms and antonyms can help your children enlarge their heritage language vocabulary. At the same time, it is also a meaningful way to make connections between words. However, you might want to be cautious when using synonyms and antonyms by explaining the differences (sometimes very subtle differences) to your children.

Deciding which words to teach

Not all words need to be taught to children. According to literacy expert Isabel Beck and colleagues, a mature literate individual's vocabulary comprises three tiers. The first tier consists of the most basic words, such as *clock, baby, happy* and *walk*. Words in this tier rarely require purposeful instructions because they are embedded in our everyday environment. The second tier contains words that are of high frequency for mature language users and are found across a variety of domains. Examples of these include *coincidence, absurd, industrious* and *fortunate*. Because of the large role these words play in a language user's repertoire, mastering them can have a powerful impact on an individual's literacy development. Therefore, instructions directed towards tier two words can be most useful. The third tier is made up of words that are infrequently used or limited to a specific domain, such as *isotope* and *lathe*. Beck and colleagues suggest three criteria for selecting tier two words.[50]

- Importance and utility: words that are characteristic of mature language users and appear frequently across a variety of domains.
- Instructional potential: words that can be worked with in a variety of ways so that children can build rich representations of them and their connections to other words and concepts.
- Conceptual understanding: words that can help children understand the general concept and assist children in describing the concept with precision and specificity.

Beck and colleagues also commented that the lines between tiers are not clear-cut. Everyone may have different selections. However, thinking in terms of tiers is just a starting point, a way of framing the task of choosing candidate words for instruction.

Using dictionaries

When children reach middle childhood, you can begin to teach them how to use reference works, such as dictionaries and online resources, to help them understand heritage language texts. However, Beck and colleagues argue that it is not suitable to use a dictionary at the beginning of literacy development. They point out several problems.[51]

First, a dictionary often has weak definitions of words. For example, *conspicuous* is defined in a junior dictionary as 'easily seen'. This definition weakly differentiates *conspicuous* from the general domain of 'visible'. Unless it is dark or someone has poor vision, nearly everything is easily seen. Something conspicuous is not just easy to see but rather pops out at you because of its size or colour or inappropriateness to a situation.

Second, a dictionary definition is often stated in such vague language that it provides little information. For example, *typical* is defined as 'being a type'. A child might ask 'a type of what?'

Third, a dictionary definition may suggest a meaning that is not intended and it may lead a child to use familiar words in unfamiliar ways. For example, the word *devious* is defined as 'straying from the right course; not straightforward'. The idea of straying from a course is likely to be interpreted in a concrete, physical way. A child in middle childhood (still in the concrete operational stage as described by Piaget) may conclude that *devious* has to do with crooked walking or getting lost.

Finally, some dictionary definitions give multiple pieces of information, but offer no guideline on how they should be integrated. Using the word *exotic* as an example, the definition is 'foreign; strange; not native'. A child might wonder what relationship to draw among these parts. Is something exotic if it is strange but not foreign? Or only if it is both foreign and strange?

Given these problematic features, children may not be able to learn effectively from dictionary definitions. One way to remedy this is to help your children get the initial heritage language word meaning in context and provide them with opportunities to use the words or observe the use of the words.

There are, however, good dictionaries that can help children study, discover and follow up on interesting words. Checking more than one dictionary can help children see the openness and flexibility of language. It has been suggested that using learner's dictionaries is more beneficial to children. These dictionaries are tailored to language learners and provide discursive explanations unlike traditional dictionaries. You may want to research different sources of your heritage language dictionaries (including online dictionaries and thesauri) before you encourage your children to use them.

Employing text talk approach

You can help your children develop their vocabulary knowledge through text talk[52] – a method that is often used for young children. However, I find it very useful for older children as well, particularly in the home environment. Text talk is an effective vocabulary teaching method in which parents ask children questions regarding the ideas in a text, talk about them and make connections among them as the reading moves along, thereby enhancing vocabulary development. There are different ways that you can help your children engage in text talk. For example, you can ask open-ended questions that encourage your children to move beyond simple responses and use the words that they read when having conversations with you. You can also use follow-up questions that aim at assisting your children's thinking by encouraging them to elaborate and develop ideas that they read in a book. You can ask your children to explain challenging words. You can help your children understand vocabulary by smartly tapping into their past experiences and knowledge.

The advantage of this approach is that you can engage your children in actively using words through speaking, which enriches and deepens their understanding of word meanings. Additionally, you can incorporate these types of activities into your busy schedule (e.g. talking/teaching while you are cooking or cleaning).

Teaching literacy skills explicitly

Literacy skills require explicit teaching. Research has shown that effective literacy skills instruction helps children become more proficient readers. Given the environmental constraints for heritage language learners, purposeful instruction on heritage language literacy proves to be even more important. You may want to provide your children with guidance in at least two areas.

First, help your children develop reading comprehension in heritage language reading materials. Literacy expert Lesley Morrow, in her book *Literacy Development in the Early Years: Helping Children Read and Write*,[53] used a very vivid quotation from the English poet, Samuel Taylor Coleridge, to explain reading comprehension:

> There are four kinds of readers. The first is like an hourglass, and their reading being as the sand, it runs out, and leaves not a vestige behind. The second is like the sponge, which imbibes everything and returns in nearly the same state, only a little dirtier. The third is like a jelly bag, allowing all that is pure to pass away, and retaining only the refuse. And the fourth is like the workers in the diamond mine of Golconda, who cast aside all that is worthless and retain only pure gems.

When reading with your children, you may want to help them cast aside unnecessary or less important information and retain the pure gems (important information). To do so, you may want to explicitly teach your children the following.[54]

- Encourage your children to look for information that may help them with clarification.
- Re-read the information that is relevant to what they want to remember.
- Help your children anticipate the content of the text based on prior knowledge about the topic.
- Help your children reflect on ideas in the text by creating summaries about what they have read.
- Help your children refer to the text for important information to clarify issues.

In addition, you can also teach your children how to use graphic maps to check their reading comprehension (see the assessment section later in this chapter).

Second, middle childhood is the time when children can understand and appreciate rules in general (as discussed previously in the section on the learning characteristics of middle childhood). Therefore, this is a good time for you to draw their attention to grammatical rules and specific language features (such as conjugations in French, classifiers in Chinese or cases in German). Grammatical rules and language-specific features can help your children become proficient language users. The best way to teach grammatical rules and specific language features is to show your children how these rules and specific features are used in their reading materials and provide them with opportunities to practise. Often, grammatical rule drills in heritage language learning are not effective.

Practising reciprocal interaction

Reciprocal teaching[55] (I modify the term here to *reciprocal interaction* to suit the home teaching and learning environment) is a successful reading instructional approach widely used in US classrooms. This approach includes four strategies:

- Predicting: anticipating what points an author is apt to make in later sentences or paragraphs.
- Questioning: asking questions to check comprehension of ideas.
- Clarifying: taking steps to better understand confusing points.
- Summarising: identifying the main ideas of a text.

The reciprocal interaction approach (some people also use the term *guided* or *mediated* reading) requires that parents and children read a piece of text together, occasionally stopping to discuss and process the text. Initially, parents lead the discussion, asking questions about the text to promote summarizing, questions, clarifying and predicting. Parents then gradually turn the 'teaching' role over to the children and let them ask questions. Eventually, the children can read and discuss a text almost independently. Example 5.1 provides some sample questions for you to consider when using the reciprocal interaction approach with your children.

Example 5.1

Sample Questions for Reciprocal Interaction

Predicting	Questioning	Clarifying	Summarizing
Why do you suppose the author chose the title for the book? By looking at the title, can you predict what this text/story is about?	How does the author's use of adjectives reveal her character's emotion? How does this chapter relate or connect to your life?	Are there any words or phrases that confused you? Are there any cultural or religious references that you don't understand	What is important and/or not important in this section of the text? What do you suppose was the author's intent in this chapter?

After reading this first chapter or paragraph of the book/text, what specifics do you expect to learn from the information you read?	Are you intrigued by what you read? Why?	or you would like clarification on? How might you have responded in the particular situation in which the main character found himself?	How would you characterise the overall tone of the opening section?
What is likely to happen next? Can you predict how the main character will react to the situation?			

The merit of the reciprocal interaction is that it provides opportunities for parents (more skilful readers) and children (novice readers) to work together,[56] and parents to provide modelling and guidance for their children.

Engaging in shared reading

Like reciprocal interaction, shared reading involves parents and children reading books together. This approach can be used when your children are not yet able to read heritage language materials independently. In shared reading, parents usually read books aloud and model fluent reading. They read the materials again and again for a few days. The focus for the first reading is on enjoyment. During the next couple of readings, parents draw attention to language features and comprehension.[57]

Children are actively involved in shared reading. They are encouraged to make predictions and pay attention to language features (similar to the ideas suggested in the previous section on reciprocal interaction).

Learning to read and reading to learn

It was once thought that in the early elementary school years (usually grades 1–3), the major literacy learning goal was to learn how to read and write. From the fourth grade onwards, children began to use reading and writing skills to learn subject contents (such as math, history, geography and science). We now know that learning to read and reading to learn occur concurrently from the very beginning.[58] This also applies to heritage language learning.

When helping your children to learn a heritage language, focus on using the heritage language to learn subject content and vice versa. Recall Mrs Cho's practice, she applied this principle well in providing different topics and genres for her daughter. She made reading the heritage language an opportunity to learn different subject areas. At the same time, her daughter learned her heritage language through reading.

Writing

A competent writer needs to master several important skills: she must be fluent in handwriting or keyboard use, know accurate spelling, have adequate vocabulary and have acquired cognitive strategies, such as how to organise ideas before starting. All these skills need some level of explicit instruction.

Teaching handwriting explicitly

It is well established that handwriting fluency places constraints on the quality of writing[59] and affects a child's early writing development.[60] Just as young readers must learn to decode fluently so that they can focus on comprehension, young writers must develop fluent and legible handwriting (as well as master other transcription skills such as spelling) so that they can focus on generating and organising ideas in writing.

During middle childhood, children's fine motor skills improve greatly compared with early childhood; therefore, this is the time when you can begin formal handwriting instruction. The focus is to help children develop fluency and legibility.

Young writers typically have to cope with the multiple demands of handwriting and composing by minimising the composing process (e.g. planning and organising). As handwriting skills become more automatic and less cognitively demanding, children's attention and resources for carrying out other writing processes, including those involving more reflection and careful composing, become available. Some researchers believe that handwriting fluency needs to occur relatively early in a child's life, because the later that handwriting fluency develops, the more difficult it is for the child to move to composing.[61]

There are two major writing systems in world languages: the meaning-based system (such as Hanzi[62]) and the sound-based system (such as Italian). Within these writing systems, there are different representations of scripts (such as Arabic, Hanzi and Roman).[63] Children whose home language and mainstream language share similar script features have it easier because they receive instruction and practise in school. The handwriting skills developed in the mainstream language can be transferred, e.g. from English to French.

However, for those children whose home language script is different from the mainstream language, explicit teaching of the home language script is important. There is considerable scientific evidence demonstrating that direct handwriting teaching enhances legibility and fluency.[64] Handwriting expert Steve Graham suggests that the basic goal of handwriting instruction is to help children develop legible writing that can be produced quickly with little conscious attention.

A critical ingredient in achieving this goal is teaching children an efficient pattern for forming individual symbols (e.g. letters).[65]

You may ask how much time is needed for handwriting teaching. It has been suggested that during kindergarten[66] and grades 1–3,[67] about 50–100 minutes a week need to be devoted to the mastery of handwriting.[68] In my own teaching experience with my two children's Chinese handwriting practice, 10 minutes a day during early middle childhood (grades 1–2) was doable and effective.

Effective handwriting teaching does not only mean copying and rewriting; it involves other components. For example, observing parents writing, tracing scripts based on models or marked directions, dictations and real-life or relevant writing. The goal of handwriting instruction is to make it a fun experience and, at the same time, help children develop speed and legibility.[69]

With the increasing use of keyboard writing in our children's lives, you may ask whether it is necessary to practise handwriting at all. Research on this question is not conclusive. A recent study conducted on 300 primary school children does suggest that handwriting speed is consistently faster than keyboarding speed across all ages. Children's compositional quality is superior in handwritten scripts as opposed to the keyboarded scripts. Keyboarded scripts tend to be up to two years behind handwritten scripts in development. In addition, writing with keyboards does not necessarily lead to improvements in script quality.[70] Of course, more research is needed for us to understand how handwriting and keyboard writing can contribute to children's writing (composition) development. Nevertheless, it is beneficial to help your children develop their handwriting fluency.

Teaching the writing process

Helping children understand the process of writing is important in their heritage language writing development. Although children may be taught about the writing process in school, providing additional help in this area at home in your heritage language can strengthen their school literacy development and promote their overall cognitive development. There are five general steps in the writing process you may want to focus on.

- Prewriting: you can show your children how to choose a topic, explore it and organise and plan what to put in the writing (e.g. you can orient them by providing the information on 'who, where, when, and what happens'). You can incorporate this step into your daily routines (e.g. while you are cooking, eating or in the car).
- Drafting: you can model by showing your children how to put the ideas in print.
- Revising: you can show your children how to make changes to improve their draft, e.g. check word choice and mechanics (spelling, grammar and punctuation).

- Proofread: you can show your children how to edit their writing and fix mistakes.
- Final version: you can show your children how to finalise and complete the final copy of the writing.

Introducing the basic writing process in the heritage language will likely help your children to write better.

Creating more opportunities to write

Although handwriting fluency and an understanding of the writing process are essential in writing development, these are not what writing is all about. It is important that you help your children write (put their ideas in print) without being stifled by excess emphasis on handwriting or spelling or grammatical rules. To become proficient writers in any language, children must have ample opportunities to write.

There are many natural opportunities for your children to write in their daily routines that are fun and attractive. For instance, Isha gives her 10-year-old son many practical opportunities to write in Panjabi by asking him to drop her notes reminding her to get him his favourite snacks on her way home, by asking him to send birthday party invitations and by asking him to exchange e-mails with his cousin in Pakistan.

Using language-experience approach

The language-experience approach (LEA) is a method in which children's own words are written down by parents and used as materials or background for literacy instruction (e.g. reading, writing, spelling, listening and speaking). The advantage of this approach is that it is personalised, meaningful and motivating.[71] In this section, I will focus on how to use this approach to help your children with their heritage language writing (you can certainly use the same approach to help your children develop abilities in other areas such as reading).

The basic procedure of this method involves:

- Discussing with your child what to write about.
- Brainstorming with your child about the topic, title and content of what he wants to write.
- Dictating the story that your child narrates.
- Using your child's own words.
- Reading and showing the version of your dictation to your child (e.g. spacing between words and conventional spelling). This procedure is particularly important when your home language script is different from the mainstream script.

Example 5.2 shows how Mrs Edwards, who lives in Beijing, used the LEA to help her 10-year-old son write in English (his heritage language).

Example 5.2[72]

Mother: What do you want to write about?

Child: I'm not sure.

Mother: How about your trip to your grandma's last summer?

Child: Kentucky?

No. I don't feel like. I want to write about my trip to the Grand Canyon.

Mother: Great. How do you want to do that?

Child: (no response.)

Mother: How do you want to write the beginning of the story?

Child: (no response.)

Mother: How about you tell me the story and I write it down for you?

Child: Ok, then. We got up early and drove to our destination. It was dark. 500 miles later, we stopped for a break. We stayed in a shabby hotel, there was no food service there. We had to go out for dinner...)

Mother: Good. Let's look at your story. You can help me make sure that I didn't miss anything you said. You said, 'We got up early in the morning and drove to our destination'. You used the word *destination*, good word choice. You said, 'We drove 500 hundred miles that day. It was dark when we found a hotel'. Or a motel. A motel is a hotel for people with a vehicle. Let me see what else you said, oh, you said, 'We stayed in a shabby hotel or motel'. You used another good word *shabby*; I agree the motel we stayed was shabby. You said, 'We had to go out for dinner *because* there was no food service in our motel...'

Do you have anything to add?

. . .

In this example, the mother helped her son decide the topic, brainstorm what should be included in the story and then recorded his narration. Notice that the mother wrote down her child's story mostly based on his vocabulary and sentence structure (even though they were not the best). The mother used the child's own version as a base for writing instruction. There were several advantages to this mother's approach. First, the mother showed the child that she valued his version (motivation). Second, the child was interested in looking at his own story (relevance) than perhaps other topics that his mother would ask him to do. Third, the mother drew the child's attention to the use of vocabulary by praising the child for his good choice of words. At the same time, she discreetly tried to teach the child to use a more precise word *motel* instead of *hotel*. Finally, the mother tried to teach the use of the conjunctive link *because* by discretely inserting it in the child's narration, 'We had to go out for dinner *because* there was no food service in our motel'.

One word of caution in using LEA: some people noticed that children might not be eager to do their own writing because they prefer the adult's 'perfect' writing to their own childish writing.[73] To avoid this situation, you may want to gradually relinquish the writing task to your children. When they become more skilful in the heritage language, you can scaffold them to move more towards conventional writing. For example, once a child decides a topic to write about, you can negotiate what should be put in writing, you can suggest ways to express ideas better, you can guide your child throughout the sequence of ideas and writing mechanics (such as where to put a punctuation mark). You can help your child revise and edit. All these guided efforts are called shared writing: you write together with your child and provide modelling and guidance.

Learning to write and writing to learn

Promoting heritage writing can help your children learn and develop in many areas. For example,[74] writing can help children learn to read. Thus, when children write or observe you writing, you can purposefully help them pay attention to how symbols (e.g. letters or strokes) form words, how words form sentences, and how words make meanings. You can help your children think about sequence, cause and effect, and other reading comprehension skills.

Writing can help your children learn how to plan and make decisions. You can discuss explicitly how to plan writing and help your children think about not only what they want to write about, but also how they write about it, who will read it and which words will communicate more effectively.

Writing may also help your children learn to become sensitive to the views of others. For example, when writing to someone else, a child may need to think about her audience's views. You have to be able to see another's point of view to communicate effectively.

Finally, you can help your children express their emotions through writing. Children can learn to use writing as a medium to express their emotions, vent frustrations and anger in a more constructive way.

Valuing invented spelling

Children who are exposed to a print-rich environment, often spontaneously attempt to represent words in print through invented spellings (you probably notice this when your children are in their early childhood). Initially, the invented spellings bear little resemblance to conventional spellings. Over time, their invented spellings become more phonologically accurate and orthographically complex.[75] In other words, their invented spellings look more and more like conventional ones. A child's spelling of the word *'monster'* as *'MSTR'*[76] and writing the sentence *'Are you deaf?'* as *'RUDF'*[77] tells us about the sophistication of that child's understanding of the way words work.

However, children's invented spellings are often regarded as spelling errors. Research findings show us otherwise. Invented spellings spontaneously produced by children are often principle driven rather than random mistakes,[78] as shown in *'MSTR'* and *'RUDF'*. Children's early attempts to experiment with putting words into print can promote and facilitate literacy development. The invented spellings created by children may allow them to explore and analyse the written codes and begin to make important associations between phonology (sound) and orthographic or symbol (word in print) representation. Moreover, research confirms that children who are better at invented spelling are better readers at the start of school.[79]

Furthermore, research shows that children can improve their phonemic awareness after invented spelling training.[80] Thus, during the initial stage in middle childhood, you may want to create opportunities for your children to produce words on their own and then provide feedback. You may get an idea of how this training can be done by looking at a recent study conducted by Gene Ouellette and Monique Sénécha.[81]

A group of children were trained to increase the sophistication of their naturally occurring invented English spellings. The training words were presented, one at a time, in both picture form and orally by a teacher. Each word was spoken out loud by the teacher at a normal speech rate. It was then repeated in a stretched manner with exaggerated articulation but with no pausing between the phonemes. The teacher said the word a third time (at a normal speech rate) and the children were asked to repeat the word out loud. The word was said a fourth time and the children were each instructed to print the word in the notebook provided. The children were instructed to print the word how they thought it would look. They were repeatedly encouraged to do their best and told that their spelling did not have to be the same as an adult's spelling.

After each word was printed, the teacher went around the table offering individually tailored feedback in which each invented spelling was contrasted with a teacher-generated invented spelling (just a minimal increase in sophistication; see the *eel* example below). This feedback was provided in the context of praising the child's invented spelling and then of showing another way to write the word; the corrected form typically contained one additional phoneme. For example, a child who spelled *eel* as *ekxn* would be shown a teacher-generated spelling with one additional level of sophistication – in this example the correct final phoneme. The teacher would thus copy the child's spelling, replacing the last letter with a conventional representation of the final phoneme (*ekxl*). Following the fourth session, feedback also included drawing the children's attention to any extra letters within their invented spellings. This was done to coincide with the phonological awareness group's switch to phoneme counting, as well as to offer additional help to the weaker spellers by focusing their attention on the correspondence between sounds within a word and the letters in their spellings. In the example mentioned previously, the corrected feedback given to the child's *ekxn* was to add the final *l* and remove the unnecessary letters, yielding *el*.

Note that the procedure of providing feedback in the form of a model with one additional element of complexity resulted in providing the conventional spelling only when the child's production was one element away from being (conventionally) correct. For example, *eel* was only provided as the corrected spelling if the child produced *el* on his or her own; here, the one additional level of sophistication is to go from the accurate phonetic spelling to the conventional form. Following the individualised feedback, children turned to a clean page in their notebooks, and the procedure was repeated using the same word.

The result of the teacher's practice shows that invented spelling coupled with feedback encourages an analytical approach and facilitates the integration of phonological and orthographic knowledge, thereby facilitating the acquisition of reading. This kind of training in children's invented spelling has been successful with Portuguese-speaking children as well.[82]

It is likely that children who are learning more than one language may invent spellings that are different from children who are learning one language. Currently, research information is sparse in this area. However, the best thing you can do is appreciate your children's invented spellings and value their attempts to make meaning. You can use your children's invented spelling as an opportunity to guide them to learn conventional spelling in your heritage language.

Beyond Reading and Writing

Using the retelling procedure

Some years ago, I came across a book titled *Read and Retell* co-written by a school teacher, Hazel Brown, and a researcher, Brian Cambourne, in Australia.[83] I was intrigued by the method introduced in the book and tried it successfully with my children in their heritage language literacy learning activities. I would like to share it here with you.

The retelling procedure is an effective way to engage children in literacy learning by asking them to 'spillover'[84] what they read or what they hear when read to. The approach is easy to implement and can be used with children throughout the middle childhood period.

There are four forms of retelling. You can use any of them when you engage your children in heritage language learning activities.

- Oral-to-oral retelling: a child listens to a parent reading aloud a text and then retells it orally.
- Oral-to-written retelling: a child listens to a parent reading aloud a text and then retells it in writing.
- Written-to-oral retelling: a child reads a text and retells it orally.
- Written-to-written retelling: a child reads a text and retells it in writing.

You can begin by either reading to your children or asking them to read a text and then tell you either orally or in writing what they have heard or read. You can tell them to relax and not to worry about spelling and neatness. The goal is to tell or write whatever they are able to. Initially, your children's retelling (orally or in writing) may be very brief. Overtime, their writing will become more sophisticated. You can also model the procedure by retelling the text yourself (orally or in written form). After your children's retelling, you may ask them to re-read or re-listen to the original texts and compare their version with the original texts (note that the purpose is not to make children feel bad about their version, but to expose them to a more sophisticated version). To avoid boredom, you can vary your request for their retelling by saying things like, 'Your cousin has not read the story, you may want to write to him and tell him what you read or heard'; 'this book/text is really interesting, you may want to tell your friend what it is about'.

According to Brown and Cambourne's research and experience (my own experience as well), children who are immersed in the retelling procedure can gradually spillover the vocabulary, phrases, sentences and other 'accoutrements' of text structure. I agree with Brown and Cambourne that such a process in approaching literacy learning is natural in the sense that it is similar to how a child acquires oral language in a natural learning environment.

The retelling procedure helps children develop their literacy abilities in listening, reading, speaking, thinking and writing simultaneously.

Talking literacy

In Chapter 1, I addressed the time constraint issue that parents face when struggling between the everyday activities of life, work and their children's heritage language teaching and learning. One practice that may help you deal with the situation is to use the *talking literacy* method. *Talk literacy* means that you talk about reading and writing with your children during everyday activities (e.g. while you are driving them somewhere or in the middle of cooking). You can, for example, teach them vocabulary or grammatical usages. You can brainstorm ideas on a composition by discussing what ideas should be included in the writing, how to develop the ideas and how to make the conclusion. You can model what you would write and ask your children to tell you first what they plan to do in writing. You can also ask your children about the material they have just read and help them digest it. You can also use talk literacy as an assessment method to check your children's comprehension of their reading materials by asking them a series of questions that relate to the reading materials.

Through talk literacy practice, you can help your children construct knowledge of their heritage language by creating additional times for deliberate discussion.

Applying heritage language literacy in real-life problem solving

You can create opportunities for your children to use their heritage language literacy to solve real-life problems. For example, Mrs Xie, who lives in the Flushing area of New York city, shared a very interesting practice. She often brings her

11-year-old daughter to local banks, where bank clerks use Chinese and bank forms are also printed in Chinese. She would ask her daughter to help her fill in the information in Chinese. When they bought their first apartment, Mrs Xie made sure that her daughter read the information in Chinese together with her.[85]

What Mrs Xie did in helping her child learn Chinese literacy was more than using the language per se. She helped her daughter apply her Chinese reading and writing skills to solve real-life problems.

Using games for heritage language literacy learning

Playing games is an engaging way to help your children develop heritage language literacy skills. You can often find ready-made games in your heritage language on the internet or from other sources such as bookstores. Marian who lives in Australia said that her 7-year-old son loves playing French magnetic word games after dinner. They use magnetic words and phrases to make all kinds of silly and funny sentences.

You can also create your own language games to help your children become more interested in heritage language reading and writing. For example, after reading a book or a text in your heritage language, you can create a game to help your child review what he/she just read by playing bingo, musical chairs, vocabulary games, recollection games, grammatical pattern games, role-playing games, card games or solving a puzzle.[86]

Making reading and writing an integral part of your family experience

Home reading and writing experiences can make children aware that reading and writing are a part of real-world experiences and can provide them with a richer variety of literacy experiences than they might find in school.[87] In addition, reading and writing together with other family members can promote family communication and unity. There are many ways that you can make heritage language reading and writing a family event.

For example, reading heritage language newspapers together in the morning while having breakfast, reading an interesting novel together after dinner, reading advertisements before shopping in a heritage grocery store and reading heritage language film descriptions before renting a movie. It is likely that when all family members are involved in these activities, children see the meaning and relevance of reading.

You can also make heritage language writing a family event. Linda Lamme[88] suggests some very useful home writing ideas, which I believe will help heritage language learning children as well. According to Lamme, home writing typically falls into three classifications: writing that is mailed or delivered (nowadays also via the internet[89]) such as greeting cards, letters, invitations and thank-you notes; writing that communicates within the family such as diaries, scrapbooks, notes, lists and messages; and writing that is essentially play (signs, labels, tickets and coupons).

Greeting cards

Greeting cards are excellent writing experiences. It takes imagination to condense a message into a short space and provide humour, rhythm or any other clever writing technique. They may require many rough drafts and modifications. Mrs Schneider shared that her family often sit together to write and rewrite greeting cards for their relatives in Israel before major Jewish holidays. Mrs Schneider said that her two children were always enthusiastic in writing these greeting cards.

Letters

Letter writing in the heritage language is another activity that all family members can participate in. For example, Polina asks her children to write to her mother in Moscow every month. With the wide use of the internet, such letters can be received instantly and answered quickly. Besides writing letters or e-mails, you can also encourage your children to write to their favourite authors and sports or film icons in their heritage countries.

Invitation and thank-you notes

You can use all occasions to encourage your children to write invitations and thank-you notes in your heritage language. Depending on your children's ages, invitation and thank-you notes can be simple or sophisticated.

Notes to family members

Writing notes and messages to family members not only enhances family communication, promotes affection and eases tension, but it is also a good opportunity for heritage language learning. One parent, for example, found that the notes she put in her children's lunch box had served the following functions:[90]

- Reminders.
- Jokes.
- Riddles.
- Word games.
- Word scrambles.
- Codes.
- Reading cursive script.
- Giving praise.
- Suggestions.
- Computer notes.
- Happy thoughts.
- Poems.
- Song lyrics.

There are many other occasions and opportunities when your family can work together to write in the heritage language: making family scrapbooks, family calendars and homemade books. In addition, you can write stories and short articles to submit to heritage language newspapers. For example, I have read many interesting stories and prose written by heritage language learning children in an overseas Chinese newspaper (侨报). When parents make reading and writing an enjoyable family routine, it is likely that children will read and write enthusiastically.

Balancing home language literacy learning and extracurricular activities

During middle childhood, children spend more time involved in school-related learning and extracurricular activities such as sports and hobbies. The time spent on these activities will definitely compete with home language literacy learning. Therefore, it is necessary to find ways to balance between the two.

The following are two suggestions. First, you may want to ask yourself whether you want to keep all the extracurricular activities in your child's life or give up some activities to devote more time to heritage language literacy learning. Giving up some extracurricular activities will leave space for heritage language learning and reduce stress in your life and your child's life. Alternatively, you can shorten some extracurricular activities or rotate different activities (e.g. Monday afternoon for music lessons, Tuesday evening for heritage language lessons, Wednesday afternoon for sports practice).

Second, you can incorporate your child's extracurricular activities into heritage language learning. For example, if your child is interested in sports, you can use sports as a major attraction to help your child learn heritage language literacy. You can download sports news in the heritage language for your child to read. You can encourage your child to write about sports news with relatives in your heritage country. You can talk about sports in your heritage language when you take your child to practice.

Considering home and school collaboration

During middle childhood, children spend increasingly significant amounts of time in the school environment. The dominant influence of the mainstream language appears to be threatening the very existence of the home language. However, it does not have to be. It is possible that home language literacy can develop simultaneously with school language literacy.

One way to make this simultaneous development happen is by not treating heritage language reading and writing as an isolated activity. Instead, it should be related to your children's school learning activities. Another way to make children's heritage writing relevant to their school work is to take advantage of your children's school reading and writing assignments as a crutch to help them with heritage language reading and writing[91] and vice versa. Take Mrs Yamamoto's practice as an example: three times a week, Mrs Yamamoto asks her 11-year-old daughter to write a paragraph in Japanese on her German homework or read a text in Japanese on a school subject. Mrs Yamamoto reported that her child benefited from these activities.[92]

Mrs Yamamoto's practice is interesting in that she does not separate her child's heritage language writing from her school learning activities and integrates her child's school subject learning into heritage language writing. In doing so, Mrs Yamamoto makes heritage writing more relevant to the child.

Communicating with your children's teachers can help promote your children's home language literacy development. For example, Mrs Cho writes letters to her daughter's teachers at the beginning of every school year to let them know that her child is also learning Korean literacy at home. Once in a while, she sends her daughter's Korean writing samples to the teachers. Some teachers share her daughter's Korean writing in class. Mrs Cho believes that her daughter's teachers' reactions have helped her daughter make progress in Korean literacy. When teachers take advantage of children's home language knowledge, children tend to learn better in their mainstream literacy. Similarly, if parents take advantage of school literacy, their children's heritage language development will also benefit.

Networking with other parents

Networking with other parents who are raising multilingual and multiliterate children can help you in several ways. It can help you share teaching strategies and compare notes, as well as help you vent your frustrations when you encounter challenges. It can also help you find friends for your children and help your kids see that they are not alone in learning more than one language and one literacy. Communicating online requires your children to read and write, which is a form of learning in action. With the advances in communication technology, such as the internet and Skype, it has become increasingly easy to connect with parents and children around the globe.

Your Turn

Before you move to the section on assessment, you may want to reflect on what you have read so far and look at the activities suggested in the box below.

Activities and Reflective Questions

- Ask your child to read a heritage language text. Observe what kinds of strategies he is using when encountering new words. Is he able to figure out these new words on his own? Ask him to read another heritage language text; this time you use the strategies suggested in this chapter to help him decode when he encounters new words. Do you observe any differences in these two activities?

- Based on the information discussed in this chapter, identify 100–500 tier-two words in your heritage language by searching through several heritage language newspapers or magazines. Make a list of these words and use them as a base to teach your child heritage language vocabulary.
- Look for a grammar book in your heritage language. Make a list of difficult features in your heritage language. Then find some heritage language texts and see whether these grammatical features are prevalent. If so, make a plan on how you can teach these rules to your child through the various activities introduced in this chapter.
- Select an appropriate heritage language text for your child. Develop a list of questions based on Example 5.1. Try these questions with your child while she is reading the chosen text. Do you think these questions help your child understand the text better? Did you find any other advantages associated with this type of interaction?
- Try to use the language experience approach (LEA) with your child. Do you notice any advantage of this method compared with the other methods you have tried in the past? Do you think that your child tends to read and write better?
- Dictate some words to your child and let him know that it does not matter whether they make mistakes. Analyse your child's spelling. Do you find your child's invented spellings are rule driven? Use your child's invented spellings as a basis for talking about conventional spelling. Do you find that your child tends to learn better this way? If so, how do you explain it?
- Provide a blank card for your child; ask her to make a greeting card for a relative in your heritage country or your family. Brainstorm with your child what to put on the card. Ask your child to read the card to other people in the family and then revise the card based on the comments.
- Based on your child's personality, think about strategies that will make reading and writing his heritage language a more pleasant experience. Try these strategies and observe how your child reacts.
- Keep a reflective journal about your experience in helping your child develop her heritage language literacy skills. Periodically, re-read your observations of your child and your thoughts in your journal. What have you discovered when you re-read them?

Assessing Home Language Literacy Progress

Assessment focus

During middle childhood, you may want to focus on assessing your children's heritage language literacy development in two major areas: heritage language reading comprehension (that is, whether your children understand what they read and make meaning of what they read) and their heritage language writing application (that is, whether your children can actively use heritage language in reality).

Assessing reading comprehension

There are many ways to assess reading comprehension. In this section, I will introduce how to use graphic organisers[93] to check your children's reading comprehension (alongside the six assessment methods described in Chapter 3). If your children are not able to fill in the information in the graphs with words, they can also use pictures. The goal is to find out whether they understand a text.

Character map

A character map is a kind of graphic organiser that is used to analyse a character's traits with the support of his/her behaviours. Its purpose is to assess whether your children are able to understand a character by gathering information from the actions of the character and to infer his/her traits. A character map is suitable for assessing comprehension of reading materials, such as fiction, non-fiction or comic books. For example, after your child reads a book or text, you can ask him/her to put the information about the main character into a character map, as illustrated in Figure 5.2. If your child can supply the information either in verbal or written form, he/she understands the text.

Main idea map

A main idea map is a visual analysis of the relationships between the main ideas of a text and supporting details. This assessment is suitable for checking the

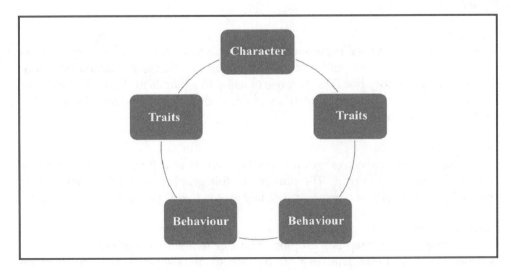

Figure 5.2 Character map

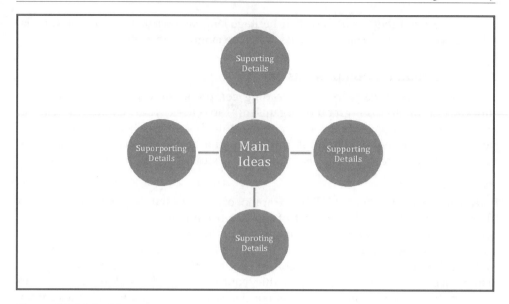

Figure 5.3 Main idea map

comprehension of information or non-fiction text. The purpose of this assessment is to see whether your children are able to identify the explicit and implicit central ideas of the text with the support of the details or facts in a text. For example, after reading a text or a book, you can ask your child to fill in a chart, as shown in Figure 5.3.

Story map

A story map is a visual representation of the critical features of a story (such as characters, setting, events and ending). This map is suitable for fiction and non-fiction text with a story line. The purpose of using this map is to check whether your children understand the critical features of a fiction or non-fiction text. Figure 5.4 is an illustration of the map.

Pyramid summary

A pyramid summary arranges a text's key words in a pyramid. This graph is suitable for all kinds of texts. The purpose of this graph is to check whether your children grasp the gist of a text by using key words (see Figure 5.5 for an example).

Cause-and-effect map

A cause-and-effect map is a graphic organiser that shows a critical relationship between events in a text. This map can be used to check whether your children are able to draw conclusions from a text by understanding the cause and effect relationship. This map can be used for both fiction and non-fiction texts. Figure 5.6 is an example.

Before you use the aforementioned graphic organisers to assess your children's reading comprehension, please make sure that you demonstrate to your children how to use these graphics.

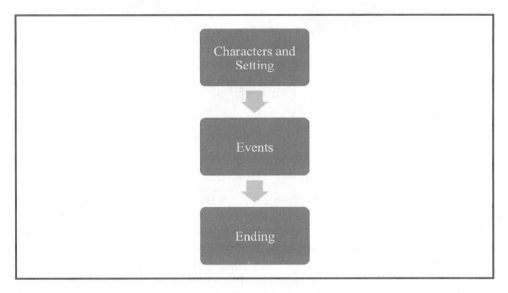

Figure 5.4 Story map

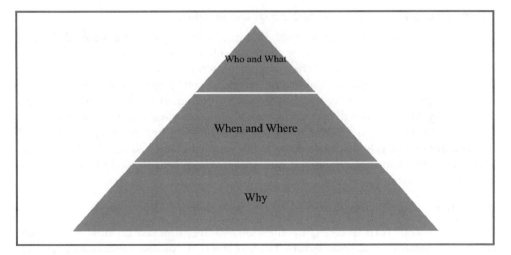

Figure 5.5 Pyramid summary

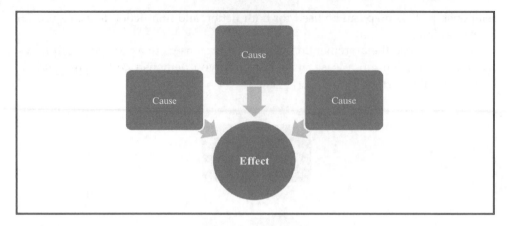

Figure 5.6 Cause-effect map

Assessing writing application

There are also many different ways to assess your children's writing abilities in your heritage language. However, the best and most natural way to assess your children's writing competence is to use real-life and relevant writing samples that your children have produced over a period of time (a week, a month, a quarter or a year) on varied topics and styles, such as diaries, e-mails, letters, notes and birthday party invitations. Compare and analyse the different writing samples and determine whether your children are making progress in the areas of organising thoughts and writing conventions.

Using assessment as an occasion of celebration

The most important thing to bear in mind when evaluating your children's literacy achievement is that you should be celebrating their progress. You can evaluate reading and writing achievements together with your children. Display their work and discuss with them how far they have come along. Showing their progress is often the best way to motivate your children. Since her daughter Jessie's 4th birthday, Mrs Cho has displayed Jessie's writing samples in the living room. Year after year, the family guests and Jessie's peers attending her birthday parties have had the opportunity to celebrate Jessie's heritage language (Korean) achievement. Mrs Cho found that this has helped motivate her daughter to continue her Korean literacy development.

Your Turn

Now it is your turn to reflect on the suggestions proposed on how to evaluate children's literacy progress. Before reading further, please take a look at the following activities and questions.

Activities and Reflective Questions

- Even though the graphic maps are introduced in this chapter as methods of assessing children's reading comprehension, you can also use them to teach children strategies to understand texts. Try to use these graphic maps as a way to help your child grasp the meaning of a given text. Did you find that using graphic maps facilitated your child's reading comprehension?
- Evaluate a sample of your child's writing. Focus on creativity, conventionality (e.g. grammar) and confidence (using writing as a means of self-expression). What have you found about your child? Suppose your child is strong in the creativity and confidence aspects of writing and weak on spelling or grammar, should you encourage your child to write more? Why or why not?
- Plan a party for your child and exhibit her heritage literacy work. Observe your child's reaction to other people's comments.

Summary

The goal for home language literacy development during middle childhood is to help children transition from their emergent heritage language literacy skills to conventional skills, to assist them in using their school (mainstream) language literacy skills to benefit their home language literacy development and vice versa, and to guide them through the demands of regular school work, extracurricular activities and home language literacy activities. To achieve this goal, selecting the right kinds of heritage language literacy materials for your children is important. You may want to consider choosing reading materials with different topics and genres, balancing intensive and extensive reading materials, matching school and home reading materials and taking advantage of reading materials about everyday and real-life occasions (situational readings). Moreover, to facilitate your children's heritage language literacy development, you may want to expose them to good quality and developmentally suitable children's literature. Furthermore, to increase children's motivation to read, you may want to consider using materials created by your children, exploring multimedia reading and popular culture materials.

When guiding your children to develop their heritage language reading skills, you may want to help them develop decoding skills, build vocabulary and understand grammatical rules including difficult language features. To help your children develop heritage language reading comprehension, you can engage them in shared reading and provide more opportunities for reading.

When conducting writing activities with your children, you can help them develop handwriting fluency and understand the process of writing by valuing their invented spelling. You can model writing through shared writing. To help your children develop a love for writing, you can provide more opportunities for them to practise writing. To encourage your children to develop heritage language literacy skills, you may want to consider doing activities, such as story retelling, literacy talk, real-life literacy practices, language games, and making it a family event. In addition, networking with other parents and children and considering home and school collaboration will be beneficial to your children's heritage language literacy development.

Finally, when assessing your children's heritage language reading progress, focus on reading comprehension and employing different graphic maps. When assessing your children's writing progress, focus on everyday writing samples. Most importantly, celebrate your children's progress and motivate them to continue their heritage language literacy development in the next stage – adolescence.

Notes and References

1. Middle childhood covers the developmental period from ages 6 to 11. This period corresponds approximately to the third cognitive development stage proposed by Swiss Psychologist Jean Piaget (concrete operational stage – 6/7 years to 11/12 years of age).
2. Dehart, G.B., Sroufe, L.A. and Cooper, R.G. (2004) *Child Development: Its Nature and Course*. Boston, MA: McGraw-Hill Higher Education.
3. DeHart, C.B., Sroufe, L.A., and Cooper, R.G. (2004) *Child Development: Its Nature and Course*. Boston, MA: McGraw Hill.
4. Brice, A.E. and Brice, R.G. (2009) *Language Development: Monolingual and Bilingual Acquisition*. Boston, MA: Allyn & Bacon.
5. Rogoff, B. (1990) *Apprenticeship in Thinking: Cognitive Development in Social Context*. Oxford: Oxford University Press.
   Lave, J. and Wenger, E. (1991) *Situated Learning: Legitimate Peripheral Participation*. Cambridge: Cambridge University Press.
6. Roggoff, B., Turkanis, C.G. and Bartlett, L. (2001) *Learning Together: Children and Adults in a School Community*. Oxford: Oxford University Press.
7. Conventional literacy skills means the literacy skills exhibited by mature adults in any given language.
8. Lamme, L.L. (1984) *Growing Up Writing: Sharing with Your Children the Joys of Good Writing*. Washington, DC: Acropolis Books.
9. Au, K.H., Mason, J.M. and Scheu, J.A. (1995) *Literacy Instruction for Today*. New York: Pearson.
10. If you want further information on how to measure text difficulty, please see Nuttall, C. (1996) *Teaching Reading Skills in a Foreign Language* (p. 26). London: Heinemann Educational Books.
11. 红楼梦 is one of the four most famous Chinese classical novels. It was written by 曹雪芹 in the Qing Dynasty (清朝).
12. Example provided by Mrs Zhang on 23 July 2007 via e-mail.
13. Nuttall, C. (1982) *Teaching Reading Skills in a Foreign Language* (pp. 30–32). London: Heinemann Educational Books. Although the author was refereeing children who are learning a foreign language, I believe that this applies to children who are learning heritage language literacy as well.
14. Nuttall, C. (1996) *Teaching Reading Skills in a Foreign Language* (p. 32). London: Heinemann Educational Books.
15. Example provided by Mrs Cho on 12 December 2009 via e-mail.
16. On WWW at http://www.amityfoundation.org/page.php?page = 1435.

17. Nuttall, C. (1996) *Teaching Reading Skills in a Foreign Language*. London: Heinemann Educational Books.
18. McQuillan, J. (1998) The use of self-selected and free voluntary reading in heritage language program: A review of research. In S.D. Krashen and J. McQuillan (eds) *Heritage Language Development* (pp. 73–87). Culver City, CA: Language Education Associates.
19. Nuttall, C. (1982) *Teaching Reading Skills in a Foreign Language*. London: Heinemann Educational Books.
20. Example provided by Diya's mother on 3 July 2005.
21. Lewin, T. (2010) If your children are awake, then they're probably online. *The New York Times* (January 20).
22. Wang, X-L. (2010) A comparative study of how moral values are conveyed in Chinese, American English, and French children's comic literature. Paper presented at the 5th Conference of the Asia Pacific Network for Moral Education, Nagasaki, Japan, 13 June.
23. Fleet, A. and Lockwood, V. (2002) Authentic literacy assessment. In L. Makin and C.J. Diaz (eds) *Literacies in Early Childhood: Changing Views, Challenging Practices* (pp. 135–153). Sydney: MacLennan & Petty.
24. Ranker, J. (2007) Using comic books as read-aloud: Insights on reading instruction from an English as a second language classroom. *The Reading Teacher* 6 (4), 296–305.
25. Kinney, J. (2007) *Diary of a Wimpy Kid*. New York: Amulet Books.
    Kinney, J. (2008) *Diary of a Wimpy Kid: Rodrick Rules*. New York: Amulet Books.
    Kinney, J. (2009) *Diary of a Wimpy Kid: The Last Straw*. New York: Amulet Books.
    Kinney, J. (2009) *Diary of a Wimpy Kid: Dog Days*. New York: Amulet Books.
26. Barratt-Pugh, C. and Rohl, M. (eds) (2000) *Literacy Learning in the Early Years*. Buckingham: Open University Press.
27. Miller, D. (2009) *The Book Whisperer: Awakening the Inner Reader in Every Child*. San Francisco, CA: Jossey-Bass.
28. McQuillan, J. (1998) The use of self-selected and free vocabulary reading in heritage language programs: A review of research. In S.D. Krashen, L. Tse and J. McQuillan (eds) *Heritage Language Development* 73–87. Culver City, CA: Language Education Associates.
29. Beck, I.L., McKeown, M.G. and Kucan, L. (2002) *Bring Words to Life: Robust Vocabulary Instruction* (pp. 27–28). New York: Guilford Press.
30. Example provided by Merissa on 3 February 2008.
    If you want to explore further the kinds of books that are suitable for children, please use the following book as a guide. Gunning, T.G. (1989) *Best Books for Beginning Readers*. Boston, MA: Allyn and Bacon.
31. Example provided by Karl in May 2009 through a visit to Karl's apartment in Shanghai.
32. E-mail communication on 12 February 2005.
33. Bissex, G.L. (1980) *CNTS At Work: A Child Learns to Write and Read*. Cambridge: Harvard University Press.
    Edwards, S.A., Maloy, R.W. and Verock-O'Loughlin, R.-E. (2003) *Ways of Writing with Young Kids: Teaching Creativity and Conventions Unconventionally*. Boston, MA: Allyn Bacon.
34. Brice, A.E. and Brice, R.G. (2009) *Language Development: Monolingual and Bilingual Acquisition* (p. 11). Boston, MA: Allyn & Bacon.
35. Wang, M., Yang, C. and Cheng, C.-X. (2009) The contributions of phonology, orthography, and morphology in Chinese-English biliteracy acquisition. *Applied Psycholinguistics* 30, 291–314.
36. Keung, Y.-C. and Ho, C.S-H. (2009) Transfer of reading-related cognitive skills in learning to read Chinese (L1) and English (L2) among Chinese elementary school children. *Contemporary Educational Psychology* 34, 103–112.

37. Fitzgerald, J. (2003) Multilingual reading theory. *Reading Research Quarterly* 38 (1), 118–122.
38. Pajoohesh, P. (2007) A probe into lexical depth: What is the direction of transfer for L1 literacy and L2 development. *Heritage Language Journal* 5 (1), 117–146.
39. Edwards, V. (2009) *Learning to be Literate: Multilingual Perspective* (p. 70). Bristol: Multilingual Matters.
40. Pressley, M. (2006) *Reading Instruction that Works: The Case for Balanced Teaching.* New York: Guilford Press.
    Pressley, M. (2001) *Learning to Read: Lessons from Exemplary First-Grade Classrooms.* New York: Guilford Press.
41. Koralek, D. and Collins, R. (1997) Tutoring strategies for the primary grades. On WWW at http://www.readingrockets.org/article/113.
42. Beck, I.L., McKeown, M.G. and Kucan, L. (2002) *Bring Words to Life: Robust Vocabulary Instruction.* New York: Guilford Press.
43. Bear, D.R., Invernizzi, M., Templeton, S. and Johnson, F. (2008) *Words Their Way: Word Study for Phonics, Vocabulary, and Spelling Instruction.* Upper Saddle River, NJ: Pearson.
44. Beck, I.L., McKeown, M.G. and Kucan, L. (2002) *Bring Words to Life: Robust Vocabulary Instruction.* New York: Guilford Press.
45. This example is taken from: Beck, I.L., McKeown, M.G. and Kucan, L. (2002) *Bring Words to Life: Robust Vocabulary Instruction.* New York: Guilford Press.
46. Beck, I.L., McKeown, M.G. and Kucan, L. (2002) *Bring Words to Life: Robust Vocabulary Instruction.* New York: Guilford Press.
47. White, N.L., Anderson, N.L. and Carrico, H. (2009) *Linking Assessment to Reading Comprehension Instruction: A Framework for Actively Engaging Literacy Learners, K-8.* Boston, MA: Pearson.
48. Brice, A.E. and Brice, R.G. (2009) *Language Development: Monolingual and Bilingual Acquisition.* Boston, MA: Allyn & Bacon.
49. Ruddell, R.B. (2009) *How to Teach Reading to Elementary and Middle School Students: Practical Ideas from Highly Effective Teachers.* Boston, MA: Allyn & Bacon.
50. Beck, I.L., McKeown, M.G. and Kucan, L. (2002) *Bring Words to Life: Robust Vocabulary Instruction* (p. 19). New York: Guilford Press.
51. Beck, I.L., McKeown, M.G. and Kucan, L. (2002) *Bring Words to Life: Robust Vocabulary Instruction* (pp. 33–35). New York: Guilford Press.
52. Beck, I.L., McKeown, M.G. and Kucan, L. (2002) *Bring Words to Life: Robust Vocabulary Instruction.* New York: Guilford Press.
    Beck, I.L. and McKeown, M.G. (2001) Text talk: Capturing the benefits of reading aloud experiences for young children. *The Reading Teacher* 55 (1), 10–20.
53. Morrow, L.M. (2001) *Literacy Development in the Early Years: Helping Children Read and Write* (p. 205). Boston, MA: Allyn & Bacon.
54. These ideas are developed based on Pressley, M. and Afflerbach, P. (1995) *Verbal Protocols of Reading: The Nature of Constructively Responsive Reading.* Hillsdale, NJ: Erlbaum.
55. Alfassi, M. (1998) Reading for meaning: The efficacy of reciprocal teaching in fostering reading comprehension in high school students in remedial reading classes. *American Educational Research Journal* 35, 309–332.
    Brown, A.L. and Palincsar, A.S. (1987) Reciprocal teaching of comprehension strategies: A natural history of one program for enhancing learning. In J. Borkowski and L.D. Day (eds) *Cognition in Special Education: Comparative Approaches to Retardation, Learning Disabilities, and Giftness* (pp. 81–132). Norwood, NJ: Ablex.
    Palincsar, A.S. and Brown, A.L. (1984) Reciprocal teaching of comprehension-fostering and comprehension-monitoring activities. *Cognition and Instruction* 1, 117–175.

56. Ideas in this paragraph are developed based on McDevitt, T.M. and Ormrod, J.E. (2010) *Child Development and Education* (pp. 219–221). Upper Saddle River, NJ: Merrill.
57. Ideas suggested in this section are based on Tompkins, G.E. (2009) *50 Literacy Strategies: Step by Step* (pp. 109–110). Boston, MA: Allyn & Bacon.
58. Gambrell, L.B. (2009) Forward for morrow. In L.M., *Literacy Development in the Early Years: Helping Children Read and Write*. Boston, MA: Pearson.
59. Connelly, V., Gee, D. and Walsh, E. (2007) A comparison of keyboarded and hand written compositions and the relationship with transcription speed. *British Journal of Educational Psychology* 77, 479–492.
60. Graham, S. (2009–2010) Want to improve children's writing? *American Educator* 33 (4), 20–40.
    Graham S, and Weintraub N. (1996) A Review of Handwriting Research: Progress and Prospects from 1980 to 1994. *Educational Psychology Review* 8, 7–87.
61. Graham, S. (2009–2010) Want to improve children's writing? *American Educator* 33 (4), 20–40.
62. Chinese characters are called Hanzi, which are used in China, Japan and Korea.
63. Cook, V. and Bassetti, B. (eds) (2005) *Second Language Writing System*. Clevedon: Multilingual Matters.
64. Peck, M., Askov, E.N. and Fairchild, S.H. (1980) Another decade of research in handwriting: Progress and prospect in the 1970s. *Journal of Educational Research* 73, 282–298.
65. Graham, S. (2009–2010) Want to improve children's writing? *American Educator* 33 (4), 20–40.
66. See endnote 70 in Chapter 2 and endnote 1 in Chapter 4.
67. Equivalent to Years 2–4 in Australia, New Zealand, and parts of the UK. Also see endnote 1 in Chapter 4.
68. Graham, S. (2009–2010) Want to improve children's writing? *American Educator* 33 (4), 20–40.
69. If you want to explore this further, please visit www.peabody.vanderbilt.edu/casl.xml for more information and ideas.
70. Connelly, V., Gee, D. and Walsh, E. (2007) A comparison of keyboarded and hand written compositions and the relationship with transcription speed. *British Journal of Educational Psychology* 77, 479–492.
71. Shanker, J.L. and Cockrum, W.A. (2009) *Locating and Correcting Reading Difficulties*. Boston, MA: Allyn & Bacon.
    Gregary, E. (2008) *Learning to Read in a New Language* (pp. 166–167). Los Angeles, CA: Sage.
72. Observation took place in Mrs Edwards' home on 19 May 2009.
73. Tompkins, G.E. (2009) *50 Literacy Strategies: Step by Step* (pp. 60–62). Boston, MA: Allyn & Bacon.
74. Some of the ideas included in this section are based on Lamme, L.L. (1984) *Growing Up Writing: Sharing with your Children the Joys of Good Writing* (pp. 16–17). Washington, DC: Acropolis Books Ltd.
75. Ouellette, G. and Sénéchal, M. (2008) Pathway to literacy: A study of invented spelling and its role in learning to read. *Child Development* 79 (4), 899–913.
76. Sipe, L.R. (2001) Invention, conventions, and intervention: The teachers' role. *The Reading Teacher* 55 (3), 264–273.
77. Bissex, G.L. (1980) *GNTS at Work: A Child Learns to Write and Read*. Cambridge: Harvard University Press.
78. He, T-H. and Wang, W-L. (2009) Invented spelling of EFL young beginning writers and its relation with phonological awareness and grapheme-phoneme principle. *Journal of Second Language Writing* 18 (1), 44–56.

79. Richgels, D.J. (1995) Invented spelling ability and printed word learning in kindergarten. *Reading Research Quarterly* 30, 96–109.
80. Martins, M.A. and Silva, C. (2006) The impact of invented spelling on phonemic awareness. *Learning and Instruction* 16, 41–56.
81. Ouellette, G. and Sénéchal, M. (2008) Pathways to literacy: A study of invented spelling and its role in learning to read. *Child Development* 79 (4), 899–913.
82. Martins, M.A. and Silva, C. (2006) The impact of invented spelling on phonemic awareness. *Learning and Instruction* 16, 41–56.
83. Brown, H. and Cambournes, B. (1990) *Read and Retell*. Portsmouth, NH: Heinemann.
84. This term was coined by Hazel Brown and Brian Cambournes to describe the reappearance of certain linguistic forms, structures, concepts and conventions that have been read or heard by children in the retelling sessions. See Brown, H. and Cambournes, B. (1990) *Read and Retell*. Portsmouth, NH: Heinemann
85. Examples provided in 3 March 2009 parents workshop.
86. Most game ideas suggested here are based on Yao, T.-C. and McGinnis, S. (2002) *Let's Pay Games in Chinese*. Boston, MA: Cheng & Tsui Company.
87. Lamme, L.L. (1984) *Growing Up Writing: Sharing with Your Children the Joys of Good Writing* (p. 196). Washington, DC: Acropolis Books.
88. Lamme, L.L. (1984) *Growing Up Writing: Sharing with Your Children the Joys of Good Writing* (p. 196). Washington, DC: Acropolis Books.
89. This example was added by the author of this book.
90. Lamme, L.L. (1984) *Growing Up Writing: Sharing with Your Children the Joys of Good Writing* (p. 196). Washington, DC: Acropolis Books.
91. Vihman, M.M. (1998) Later phonological development. In J.E. Bernthal and N.W. Bankson (eds) *Articulation and Phonological Disorders* (pp. 113–147). Boston, MA: Allyn & Bacon.
92. Example provided by Mrs Yamamoto on 24 July 2007.
93. Many ideas developed in this section are inspired by White, N.L., Anderson, N.L. and Carrico, H. (2009) *Linking Assessment to Reading Comprehension Instruction: A Framework for Actively Engaging Literacy Learners, K-8*. Boston, MA: Pearson.

Chapter 6
Adolescence (12–18 Years)[1]

This chapter identifies the learning characteristics of adolescence and notes the major focus in heritage language development during this period. Effective strategies are suggested on how to select materials and conduct activities to help your children develop self-motivated learning habits and keep them interested in furthering their multiliteracy development throughout their lives. Developmentally responsive assessment methods are discussed to help you ensure your children's progress. Activities and questions are provided to help you relate the recommended strategies to your own practice.

Typical Learning Characteristics

The typical cognitive characteristics of adolescence can be described as an increased ability for hypothetical (scientific) and logical thinking. Adolescents 'no longer require concrete things and events as objects of thought but can come up with new, more general logical rules through internal reflection'.[2] Unlike children in the previous developmental stages (early childhood and middle childhood), adolescents can solve problems by beginning to think about possibilities and then proceeding to reality (they begin to reason more as a scientist by devising ways to solve problems and test solutions systematically).[3]

Adolescents also begin to demonstrate the abstract quality of thought at the formal operational level, that is, they can make logical inferences merely through verbal representation. For example, children in the earlier developmental stages would need to see the concrete relationship in A, B and C to be able to make the logical inference that if $A > B$ and $B > C$, then $A > C$. Adolescents can reach the logical conclusion $A > C$ without having to rely on concrete steps.[4]

Adolescents' developing power of thought opens up new cognitive and social horizons, and drives them to idealism. They begin to engage in extended speculation about ideas – a quality they desire in themselves and others. Such thoughts often lead adolescents to compare themselves to others.[5] They tend to be self-conscious and self-focusing (with an exaggerated sense of personal uniqueness). As a result, they are sensitive to public criticism and prone to taking risks.

In addition, peer influence plays a vital role during this period. Adolescents tend to engage in behaviours that are condoned by their peers either in reality or in the media.

Thus, in order to help your teenage children continue to develop home language literacy, employing effective strategies is essential. The following suggestions are proposed for your consideration:

- Refrain from criticising your children in home language learning activities, particularly in front of others. Try to be as positive and supportive as possible. Using humour to replace criticism tends to achieve better results.
- Value your children's opinions and allow choices and freedom when carrying out heritage language learning activities.
- Provide opportunities for your children to take risks in home language literacy learning and encourage self-exploration.
- Motivate your children to be self-regulated[6] learners.
- Encourage your children to network with other peers who are learning heritage languages or who are living in your heritage language country/ region.
- Help your children develop critical thinking abilities while reading and writing their heritage language.
- Use innovative methods to engage your children in heritage language learning.
- Be positive when you encounter resistance from your adolescent children (even though it may be hard at times). Trust that they will ultimately find their own way through if you are willing to provide constant support.

Heritage Language Literacy Development Focus

Given the learning characteristics of adolescents, the focus of heritage language literacy learning should be on helping children become critical, independent heritage language readers and writers, develop self-monitoring learning habits and strive to be life-long learners.

Selecting Literacy Materials

When selecting heritage language reading materials for your adolescents, using the following strategies may help you achieve a positive outcome.

Choosing developmentally appropriate reading materials

Many multilingual children do not read as well in their heritage language as in their school/mainstream language. As a result, parents often choose heritage language reading materials written for younger children to compensate for their adolescents' low heritage language reading level. However, for adolescents, reading materials written for younger children will be considered insulting. For example, I once asked my teenage sons to read a Chinese text for young children. The text contained words and phrases such as 小朋友 (little friends), 小树 (little trees) and 小动物 (little animals). They felt that I had insulted their intelligence (My older son Léandre commented, '你就这么小看我们?' (You reduced us to this level?). They vehemently rejected material for 'babies'. One way to avoid such a situation is to choose materials that are simple in vocabulary and grammar, but more sophisticated in content. Revisiting the technique on how to simplify texts discussed in Chapter 5 may be helpful.

When choosing heritage language texts for adolescents, you may also want to take into consideration their psychological needs and provide them with a variety of reading materials, such as adventure, science fiction, biographies, mysteries, fantasy, romance, comedy, tragedy and horror, to help them find their place in the world and encourage self-discovery (e.g. identity issues), build self-esteem and a healthy sense of self. For instance, Aaleigha, who lives in Minnesota, read her 17-year-old son the German classics of her own adolescent favourites, such as *Tonio Kröger* and *Der Tod in Venedig* (*Death in Venice*) by Thomas Mann and *Die Leiden des jungen Werther* (*The Sorrows of Young Werther*) by Johann Wolfgang Von Goethe. She said that her son found that the adolescent issues in these German classics transcend time and history. Through reading these classics, Aaleigha's son became more motivated to read German. Recently, Aaleigha reported that her son has been admitted to college and planned to major in German language and literature.[7]

Thus, trying to find materials in your heritage language that address adolescents issues may keep your children motivated.

Promoting high-order thinking through multiple literacy materials

High-order literacy is unlikely to be achieved merely by more story reading or by limiting reading to narrow field of interests.[8] Instead, it can be developed by reading a wide range of materials on topics as diverse as finance, math, sports, television, film[9] and history. Becoming more informed in different fields and topics will help adolescents develop high-order thinking.

For example, when watching a film, high-order thinking involves the ability to understand the message or meaning through visual or auditory effects such as camera zooms, panoramic views, fade-outs and split screens and to figure out the content of a message by integrating scenes, character behaviours and dialogue into an accurate story line.[10] Similarly, critically evaluating messages such as aggression, ethnic and gender stereotypes and consumerism is a form of high-order thinking.

Therefore, it is important to help your children use multiple heritage language literacy sources to develop their thinking skills. Christina from Sydney often forwards news on Polish politics as well as her thoughts to her 16-year-old son via e-mails. Her husband Feliks often uses hypermedia technology to create multimedia reading materials for their son (with links to videos and websites) or hypermedia versions of reading materials by videotaping an event of interest to him with Polish captions or narratives. Father and son discuss the connections to their life in Australia. Both Christina and her husband believe that their son has become more sophisticated in his thinking and reasoning through reading multiple literacy materials.[11]

Research shows that teenagers take an active role in technology-mediated literacy in their home environment.[12] If you can encourage your teenage children to build on what they have already been doing by expanding their heritage language reading and writing topics, your children will not only develop critical thinking abilities, but also heritage literacy skills.

Using inferential reading materials

Good readers can often uncover implicit information in a text by filling in the missing pieces. This ability is called inferencing. To help adolescents develop this ability in relation to heritage language materials, you may want to choose texts that are rich in inferences so that they have to search for clues in the text. The third Harry Potter book, *Harry Potter and the Prisoner of Azkaban*, by J.K. Rowling[13] is a good example of an inferential text (see Example 6.1).

Example 6.1

'Harry Potter was a highly unusual boy in many ways. For one thing, he hated the summer holidays more than any other time of the year. For another, he really wanted to do his homework but was forced to do it in secret, in the dead of night...' (p. 1)

In this book, readers have to figure out who Harry Potter is by looking for information and clues as to why he is unusual and infer that he is a 13-year-old boy, who also happens to be a wizard. He doesn't do anything like regular 13-year olds.[14] Inferential texts such as this can help a reader fill in the missing information, thereby developing inferential abilities in reading. Moreover, adolescents often enjoy reading inferential texts because it makes them think and guess.[15]

Allowing gender preferred reading materials

The arrival of adolescence is typically accompanied by gender intensification, that is, adolescents exhibit increasing gendered attitudes and behaviours and move towards a more traditional gender identity.[16] You may have noticed that boys and girls begin to have different reading interests in late elementary and middle school.[17] Boys show a stronger preference for topics related to mystery and non-fiction; while girls prefer animal stories, fairy tales and realistic fiction.[18] By adolescence, such gender reading preferences become even more pronounced. Suzanna reported that her 14-year-old son refused to read his older sister's books and found them 'girly'; likewise, her 16-year-old daughter regarded her brother's books as uninteresting. Suzanna tries to be sensitive to her children's reading preferences and find materials that are suitable to her children's interests. Suzanna feels that if parents force their children to read something that they dislike, children will not be motivated to read.[19]

Even though helping children overcome gender stereotypes is important, respecting their reading preferences during adolescence can help them sustain their heritage language reading. If you are concerned with the gender stereotype issues, find a way to discuss your concerns with your children without intruding into their personal reading preferences.

Exploring poetry, metaphor, proverbs and sayings

Although poetry, metaphors, proverbs and sayings in a heritage language can be introduced to children at a younger age, introducing them during adolescence may be more effective. This is because adolescents, with their increased abstract and hypothetical thinking abilities, can better appreciate these linguistic features. For example, the word *blue* in English can mean the colour as well as the mood (depressed); the word *red* can mean the colour as well as other things. For example, if you *see red*, you are getting angry. The word *red* can also be associated with a particular political orientation (e.g. communism). Not only can adolescents appreciate the basic meaning of these colour words, but also their extended meanings.

More importantly, metaphors, proverbs and sayings tend to contain cultural wisdom. Understanding and knowing how to use them will help move adolescents' heritage language development to a more advanced level.

Watching television programmes or movies with subtitles

It has been reported that Finland has higher reading scores in international education achievement tests, such as PISA,[20] compared to children from other developed countries. One of the reasons suggested for Finnish children's success is the fact that they read subtitles, because Finland imports a lot of foreign language television programmes and movies. Thus, Finnish children are more accustomed to reading Finnish subtitles when watching foreign television and films. Though research needs to confirm this speculation, it is likely that reading subtitles can promote literacy development.

In addition, typical adolescents have developed the ability to coordinate information through visual and auditory modalities. Watching television and reading simultaneously may even stimulate multi-sensory information processing.

Valuing popular culture

As mentioned in the previous chapter, popular culture may be a way to get children interested in their heritage languages. During adolescence, using these reading materials can help you understand how your children construct meaning based on their personal interests and provide you with a window into how they form their identities. Moreover, popular culture can help adolescents develop critical literacy abilities when reading heritage language materials.

Jeremy, who lives in Osaka, Japan, frequently uses his British English heritage language popular culture materials as a springboard to help his 15-year-old twins think about their bilingual, bi-racial and twin identity. Because these materials are so relevant to their lives, Jeremy's twin daughters appreciate reading English more than ever.[21]

Considering texts about traditional holidays

Using reading materials about traditional cultural holidays can help adolescents deepen their cultural knowledge and appreciate their traditions. Although you can introduce these materials at a younger age, your children tend to appreciate the symbolic meanings embedded in cultural holidays better during adolescence. For example, the food items served during the Chinese New Year's celebration have symbolic meanings: rice cakes (年糕) symbolise that a person will have a better year than the last; dumplings (饺子) symbolise that a person's fortune will be wrapped and will not disappear; fish (鱼) symbolises that a person will have surplus (e.g. extra money in the bank); and almonds (杏仁) symbolise that a person will be happy in the new year.[22]

Benefiting school subjects with heritage language reading materials

In Chapter 5, I discussed how to incorporate children's home language reading materials into their school reading materials. During the adolescent period, you can continue with this practice. However, you can now transfer responsibility to your children and begin asking them to locate heritage language reading materials that are relevant to their interests and school subjects. Taking the responsibility to locate heritage language materials to help them learn school subjects might motivate your children to develop skills that will be useful for their future independent heritage language reading.

Semahat, who lives in the Netherlands, encouraged her 16-year-old daughter to complete her Dutch world history homework by looking for information on Turkish websites. Her daughter enjoyed doing such research in Turkish and learned more information as a result.[23]

Your Turn

Activities and Reflective Questions

- Review the home literacy teaching framework in Chapter 2 and the four-step home literacy planning process in Chapter 3. On a piece of paper, write down the connection of the strategies introduced in this chapter to the framework and the planning process.
- Recall your own adolescent years. What books did you like to read? Did these books help you deal with your adolescent issues or understand the world? Would you consider introducing these books to your child? Alternatively, look for contemporary books written for adolescents in your heritage language and introduce them to your child. If your child cannot

read them independently, consider reading to them or simplifying the books. How did your child react to these books? Did you find any evidence that your child connects with them?

- Look through some heritage language texts. Analyse the texts and see which ones are inferential by using the information introduced in this chapter. Let your child read the text and ask him to supply the implicit information such as:
  ○ Who is performing the action (agent)?
  ○ To whom is it done (object)?
  ○ What is used to do it (instrument)?
  ○ Who experiences the feeling or thought (experiencer)?
  ○ Where does it comes from (source)?
  ○ What is the result or goal (goal)?
- Reflect on your child's experience. Do you think the inferential text helped your child's reading comprehension or encouraged him to read further?
- Look for some heritage language texts that contain metaphors and proverbs. Circle them and ask your child to interpret them in their own term (vocabulary). Observe what strategies they use to find out the meanings of these metaphors and proverbs. Are you pleasantly surprised that your child has grown intellectually in their problem-solving strategies?
- Look for a text regarding a cultural holiday in your tradition. Circle the places you think indicate underlying cultural meanings or concepts. Introduce the text to your child and ask him to infer the symbolic meaning. What have you found?
- Explore some heritage language websites that contain information relevant to your child's academic subjects in school. Introduce these sites to your child and encourage her to continue searching. Did your child begin to use these sites? If so, what should you do to help her take advantage of these sites for her school learning or expand her interests?

Conducting Literacy Activities

Reading

Using reflective reading response logs

A reflective reading response log is a type of journal in which readers write their reactions and opinions about the materials they read. The purpose is to help adolescents reflect on what they read and seek deeper understanding of the texts. In addition, reflective reading response logs can help children develop writing fluency.[24]

Initially, you can provide your children with a model chart to orient what they need to include in the reflective response log. The following is a template (you can add additional information based on your needs).

Identify the main points/ideas/issues in the text	
Enter your response or opinion on these points/ideas/issues	
Connect these points/ideas/issues to other texts you read in the past	
Connect these points/ideas/issues to your experience	
Identify words, phrases, information or aspects that you do not understand	
Other thoughts or comments about the text	

If your children cannot finish the chart in complete sentences, you can encourage them to put in whatever they can manage. Alternatively, you can fill in the log with them (modelling). In fact, many adolescents have already engaged in this kind of activity in school. Therefore, the skill transfer from mainstream language to home language should be doable. Moreover, engaging in activities like this in their home language will facilitate their school learning. A graduate student of mine tried this with her 14-year-old daughter and found it very helpful for her child's Spanish (home language) and English (school language) reading comprehension. She also commented that her daughter became more thoughtful when discussing the books she read.[25]

Reading beyond texts

Helping adolescents read beyond the text will help them become independent readers and active users of their heritage language. When reading heritage language texts, you can help your children move from reading the lines to reading between the lines, to eventually reading beyond the lines. In other words, the goal is to prepare your children to make the transition from reading to inform (knowledge taking) to reading to transform (knowledge making). The benefit associated with this practice is that it may help your children take personal responsibility for their own meaning construction and become life-long readers in their heritage languages. The following are some suggestions for you to consider:[26]

- Ask for creative responses and questions, support your children's interpretation of a text and avoid preaching and imposing your own ideas.
- Invite and welcome expressions of curiosity.
- Encourage children to consider issues from alternate perspectives by using the Devil's advocate approach.
- Teach how to give as well as receive creative critiques.
- Appreciate contrary or opposing views (ward off the 'halo' effects, that is, just because it is in print and by an authoritative figure, one cannot challenge).
- Provide critical-constructive feedback.

It is likely that your children are taught to respond in this way in school. If so, it will be easier for you to ask your children to do the same in reading their heritage language and to encourage them to read beyond the lines and seek deeper meaning.

Attending to non-textual information

Helping your adolescent children become conscious about non-textual information[27] can also help them become independent readers in their heritage language. Much of this kind of information may need to be consciously taught, particularly when the heritage language print conventions are different from your children's mainstream language. You may wish to try the following.[28]

Type style. You can deliberately point out the differences in type style to your children and indicate that the type styles may contain important information to help them understand a text. For example, headlines and footnotes often have a different typeface from the body of a text. Frequently, bold and italic styles may be used to indicate different kinds of prominence. In addition, the function of different typefaces is often to make words easier to locate, define a technical term, emphasise something or refer to something that is different from the rest. The conventions used in your children's mainstream language may be different from those used in their heritage language.

Punctuation marks. There are different ways to use punctuation marks in different languages and understanding their functions in a heritage language is important. For example, in English a period is ' . ', whereas in Chinese it is ' 。'. In English, to quote someone, " " or ' ' are used and in German „ " or ‚ ' are used. Consciously teaching your children information such as the functions of punctuation marks will aid their heritage language comprehension.

Symbols. The symbols used in text have different functions in different languages. For example, the symbol « » in French is used as a quotation mark, whereas the same symbol in Chinese is called 书名号, which is used for a book title. It is useful if you explain the conventions used in your heritage language to your children.

Reference aids[29]. You can also draw your adolescent children's attention to reference aids such as titles, blurbs, author's biographic information, summaries and tables of contents. Doing the following exercises may be helpful.

- Ask your children to match items in a list of titles with a selection of blurbs, arranged in random order.
- Ask your children to match extracts from texts with a selection of blurbs and titles.
- Ask your children to read one author's information and match it to a list of selected book titles, tables of contents or summaries.

Diagrams. Diagrams such as illustrations, graphs and tables can provide important information for comprehending and interpreting texts. You may be surprised that many children actually skip diagrams when reading texts. You can help your children pay attention to the information contained in diagrams by choosing one, supplying several statements and asking children to match the statement with it. You can also provide several statements and ask your children to match them with one of several unlabelled diagrams. Alternatively, you can develop several questions and ask your children to answer them with the information provided in the diagrams.

Index. Using an index to locate the information in the text is an important skill that will aid your children's reading comprehension. Many children do not automatically use the index. You may want to purposefully point out the functions of the index as well as features such as abbreviations, definitions and glossaries.

Employing strategies that promote academic literacy development

Academic literacy is the reading and writing skills used to understand and analyse school subjects. Traditionally, academic literacy proficiency is the domain of schools. However, promoting academic literacy-related skills in the home environment can support children's academic success. Older children still need assistance in developing academic literacy skills. You may want to consider the following approaches when your children are reading heritage language texts.

Recognising and interpreting different types of texts. Different types of heritage language texts are characterised by different organisational structures depending on their purpose and focus. Helping your children recognise these different types of texts and know how to interpret them will not only increase their reading comprehension, but also promote their academic literacy development. There are seven types of academic texts:[30]

- Descriptive texts (to describe what something is).
- Enumerative texts (to provide a list related to a topic).
- Sequential or procedural texts (to provide an overview of how to do something or a sequence of events that have occurred).
- Comparison and contrast texts (to provide a comparison of how two or more things are the same or different).
- Problem-solution texts (to state a problem and offer solutions).
- Persuasive texts (to take a position on a certain issue and justify it).
- Cause and effect texts (to give reasons why something happened).

You can introduce these kinds of texts in your heritage language to your children and help them recognise the differences by looking for the clues that lead them to the type of structure being used and the cohesive ties that link structures to ideas both within and across sentences.[31]

Integrating various strategies when reading texts. The ability to analyse a text by using good strategies is important for academic reading comprehension. A good reader should be able to:[32]

- activate prior knowledge and relate it to a given text;
- predict what will be addressed within a text given that knowledge;

- ask important questions about the text;
- use visual imagery to enhance comprehension;
- paraphrase as well as summarise what has just been read;
- monitor and repair breakdowns in comprehension;
- integrate the use of these various strategies.

You can help your children develop these strategies when reading heritage language texts.

Reading aloud

Reading aloud has traditionally been an activity for young children. However, teachers who teach older children have recently found that reading aloud is still a favourite activity for adolescents.[33] There are many positive benefits associated with reading aloud for heritage language learning adolescents.

First, reading aloud can help children gain access to difficult heritage language texts that they cannot yet read independently. For example, Mrs Gong's daughter, at age 16, is not able to read classical Chinese poems by herself. Mrs Gong reads these poems to her. Without Mrs Gong's help, her daughter would not be able to enjoy these beautiful and profound poems in her heritage language.[34]

Second, reading aloud to adolescents can help motivate them to read their heritage language. If children enjoy what their parents read to them, they may be motivated to read. Recall the example used earlier in this chapter, Aaleigha's readings of the German classics inspired her son to major in German language and literature in college.

Third, reading aloud can help your children gain background information for both their school and heritage language literacy development. It is likely that your children will have an easier time in comprehending written texts if they have heard them before. For example, my husband read many literary classics in French to my children. When my older son Léandre had to read some of them in his high school English class, he found his prior knowledge made reading the English literature easier for him.

Fourth, reading aloud can model reading fluency in your heritage language and show your children what reading in a heritage language should sound like (e.g. what are the appropriate pauses and what are inappropriate breaks).

Finally, reading aloud to your children can help them increase their heritage language vocabulary.

When reading to your adolescent children, please pay attention to the following:[35]

- Select a heritage language text that is exemplary in language use, content and style.
- Lead your children into the text by setting the scene and generating interest in the context. Explain difficult vocabulary and background knowledge while not letting go of the enjoyment.

- Pay attention to how you use your voice. Exude enthusiasm to attract your children and use clear enunciation. You can listen to professional recordings of read aloud sessions to improve your own reading skills.

Finally, use frequent eye contact to engage your children during reading. This is also a good way for you to measure your children's level of interest in the text and their comprehension through observing their facial expressions.

Making heritage language reading an everyday practice

To ensure that your children read their heritage language as a life-long practice, it is important to read it frequently. You may want to consider subscribing to heritage language newspapers and magazines for your children (online versions are encouraged). Making reading materials accessible to children is helpful. I noticed that putting newspapers in the middle of the dining table encourages my children to read. Every morning, when my kids are having breakfast, they habitually look for their favourite parts of the papers. Initially, they were only interested in advertisements. Gradually, they began to read articles that caught their eye.

Writing

Promoting peer networks through informal register

During adolescence, children tend to listen to their peers more than their parents or teachers. Taking advantage of peer influence can help adolescents in their heritage language literacy development. With the availability of social network sites, such as MySpace, Facebook and Twitter, adolescents have more opportunities to socialise with other peers. You can take advantage of what they are doing in these online social networks and communication platforms and encourage them to network with adolescents in your heritage country or your heritage community.

Using Silvija's case as an example: she was originally from Croatia and now lives in New Jersey. Silvija helped her 13-year-old daughter get connected with a Croatian girl who lives in Zagreb, Croatia. The two girls have been in contact for almost two years. They often post photos of their various activities, share their school experiences and life stories.[36] If your child can find a pal like Silvija's daughter, it is likely your teens will enjoy using their heritage language. However, you may want to monitor what they do in these social networks to avoid cyber bullies and other related issues.

Moreover, you can also take advantage of your teens' favourite communication forms to encourage them to write in their heritage language. For example, instant text messaging is a popular communication means among many teenagers. Despite the debate on whether text messaging prevents children from writing formally, many literacy experts now believe that it can promote overall literacy development.[37] Moreover, communicating through instant text messages can support friendship, intimacy and social networking, which are vital for adolescent development. Furthermore, text-messaging vocabulary in different languages is linguistically interesting, and it provides opportunities for children to study the features of difference languages. For instance, lol (laugh out loud), brb (be right back), gg (gotta go), mwah (kiss), yt (your there), pos (parents over shoulder), Gr8 (great) and Db8 (debate) in English, 电我 (给我打电话/call me), 短我 (请给我回短信/text me) and 88 (再见/good-bye) in Chinese and PTDR (pété de rire/laugh out loud), ab1to (à bientôt/see you soon) in French are rule governed. You can discuss with your children about the interesting features in these abbreviated words and let them tell you the rules of these words in their heritage language and mainstream language. More importantly, by treating text messaging as a legitimate means of communication, you can help your children understand that the informal registers (such as texting) and formal registers (conventional writing) serve different purposes.

You can also use texting and twittering in your heritage language as a means of exchanging information between you and your teenage children (e.g. sending reminders to your children, asking questions or simply checking on them). You may have noticed that if you don't try to find out what your teenagers are doing and feeling, you may have missed many events in their lives, big or small.

Finally, you can encourage your teenage children to develop a web page in their heritage language. If they already have one in their mainstream language, you can encourage them to make it multilingual. Research on bilingual English and Bengali teens in London shows that producing web pages helped adolescents extend and improve their writing in both English and Bengali.[38]

Writing based on family photographs

Using family photographs is an innovative way to engage adolescents in writing their heritage language.[39] Writing about family photographs is a good opportunity for multilingual children to explore their identities. Children can use family photos (including photos from older generations) to write in different genres, such as a commentary about a historical event, a memoir, an autobiography, a short story or an essay. It is likely that adolescents will be interested in this kind of writing if you offer them the opportunity. Of course, initially, it may be difficult. Your children can begin by labelling the photos in the heritage language and then writing first a sentence, then a paragraph and eventually a narrative or an essay.

Fourteen-year-old Mitra found it fascinating to arrange his photos chronologically from infancy to recent years. He wrote a very thoughtful essay in Persian to describe his changes both physically and psychologically. He proudly sent it to his grandparents in Iran. Mitra's mother commented that family photographs were the impetus for him to write in Persian.[40]

Writing through watching or making films

A couple of summers ago, I was reading a book titled *The Film Club* by a Canadian author, David Gilmore.[41] I was impressed by the author's method of turning his teenage son's life around by having him watch three movies a week (the movies were selected by the father). This book sheds light on how to reach out to adolescents, understand their interior life and motivate them to learn (in our case, develop their heritage language).

You can select heritage language films that are relevant to adolescents and discuss the issues and messages embedded in these films. When children become interested, they will naturally want to talk about them. Seize the moment and ask them to talk or write about their thoughts on issues of concern to them. You will be surprised to find that your children may actually use the phrases and vocabulary they heard in a film to communicate. Thus, using films may be a powerful tool for heritage language literacy learning.

You can also encourage your children to make their own movies by providing them with a camcorder or a flip video camera if they have not already done so. They can videotape an event of their own choice and then edit it with their heritage language (e.g. write the subtitles). You can work together with your children on these movie projects. Your children can put the final product online for their friends and your family to enjoy.

Teaching communication and writing styles

The adolescent period is perhaps the best time for parents to discuss stylistic differences between the heritage and mainstream languages because, at this point, children have already developed logical and analytical abilities.

Research has confirmed that there are different ways to communicate in different cultures. For example, there is more indirectness in high-context cultures such as the Confucian heritage cultures: the Chinese, Korean and Japanese cultures (where people rely on a broad array of social clues) than in low-context cultures such as North American and European cultures (where people rely on few social clues to communicate).[42] As a result, people from high-context cultures tend to interpret indirect messages better than people from low-context cultures.[43] You may want to draw your children's attention to the different communication styles in writing. For example, Chinese older people offer 'lucky money' (压岁钱) to children during Chinese New Year celebrations. Knowing this custom, 15-year-old Jinjin (Jim) wrote to his Chinese grandparents in a Chinese New Year greeting card, '今年过年你们要给我多少压岁钱?' (How much lucky money are you going to give me this New Year?). Mrs Wei pointed out to her son that it was too direct to write to Chinese elders in this way, and he should only drop subtle hints.[44]

In addition, different cultures tend to have different writing styles. For example, research suggests that Greek engineering students and Anglo-American students tend to exhibit different writing styles regarding politeness strategies despite the fact that they are in the same field of engineering. The Anglo-American students tend to avoid imposing their ideas whereas the Greek students tend to be more authoritative and empathetic, controlling readers' inferences by seeking their agreement.[45]

It is likely that your children will be influenced by mainstream writing styles through attending school in their country of residency. Thus, it is important to discuss with your children the differences between the heritage culture writing styles and the mainstream language writing styles. There is no reason why a child cannot develop two or more writing styles in different languages. Deliberate comparison of cultural differences can help your children become more skilful in code switching (shift writing style from one language to another).

Beyond reading and writing

Cultivating motivation by creating a real reason for reading and writing

All things considered, motivation is the foremost fact in ensuring that adolescents will continue to read and write their heritage languages throughout their lives. Research consistently suggests that motivation is essential for sustained learning. It leads to an increase in effort and energy, and it also increases initiative and improves performance.[46] Thus, creating a need for your children to read and write their heritage languages can help them discover the power of print and become avid heritage language users.

Parents can help their children realise that heritage language writing can be used as an effective tool or channel for self-expression (e.g. to express emotions, thoughts, concerns and anxieties). Forming the habit of keeping journals and diaries in their heritage language may be a good way for adolescents to find a safe place to express themselves. Writing responses to an issue of their choice may be another way for adolescents to express themselves. You can help your children by providing them with a sample (a model).

Julie, who lives in Sweden, shared that, initially, her 16-year-old daughter Catherine did not want to write in French at all. Persuading her to put pen to paper was painstaking. Occasionally when Catherine tried, she could barely write a paragraph. Julie began to motivate her daughter by showing her what writing could do for a person. For example, once when her daughter was extremely upset by her boyfriend's betrayal, Julie encouraged Catherine to write down her feelings of hurt in French. This seemed to help Catherine a great deal in coping with her personal situation. Since then, Catherine has been writing almost every day. According to Julie, her daughter's entries in her French journal can now exceed two or three pages in length. Despite grammatical and spelling mistakes and mixed Swedish words and expressions, Catherine enjoys writing in French and understands how reading and writing French can open up new possibilities for expressing herself.[47]

Using reading and writing to identify and label emotions

Adolescents experience many changes and many emotions. As Nancy De Vries Guth and Tamie Pratt-Fartro[48] commented:

> Adolescents are a strange and wonderful mix of mature and child-like qualities, manifested in no particular order. They shift from serious, concerned citizens to teasing children with one comment and can be reduced to silence or tears with a look from a peer or teacher. It is very important to understand the variability of

the adolescent years and enjoy the challenges if one is to be successful working with these demanding, yet giving' children.

Using the heritage language learning experience as a channel to help them understand and express their feelings may be beneficial to their development. It has been suggested that children need to be helped to use language to recognise and express their feelings and learn how to identify and label them.[49] Thus, you may want to intentionally help your children identify their emotions and label them with their heritage language. For example, when your children express frustrations, joyfulness or anger, you can ask them to write their feelings down and think about the accuracy of the words they use to label how they feel. If your children don't know how to use the exact words to label their feelings in their heritage language, you can help them. When preparing heritage language reading materials for your children, you can intentionally draw your children's attention to places where words and phrases are used to express emotions. You can also ask your children why they feel the way they feel and write their thoughts down and then discuss them.

When children feel the power of words, they will use them to express emotions more accurately (e.g. *moody* is not necessarily *depressed*). Identifying emotion through language use can help both children and parents understand their emotions, which is important during adolescence.

Encouraging sibling teaching

If your adolescent children have younger siblings, you may want to offer them opportunities to teach their younger siblings heritage language literacy. Initially, your adolescents may not be skilful teachers. You can be a model. The benefits of letting adolescents take the responsibility for teaching is that they can further develop both their heritage language literacy skills and teaching strategies. Most importantly, they will develop self-confidence through teaching their younger siblings.

Fostering critical literacy abilities

In an earlier part of this chapter, we discussed how to use popular culture materials and films to help adolescents develop heritage language literacy. To continue the discussion, in this section I will address how to use these materials to help your children develop critical literacy abilities in their heritage language.

Critical literacy means that a reader is actively questioning the stance (position and attitude) found within, behind and among texts. Critical literacy is an emancipatory endeavour that encourages children to ask questions about the representation, benefits, marginalisation and interests of texts.[50] Because heritage language learners read different languages associated with different cultural ideologies, it is important for them to develop critical literacy abilities.

Helping children analyse heritage language texts, such as moral dilemmas, can prompt children to ask questions and to think about the complex messages embedded in the texts. Mohamed, who lives in London, shared how he helped his two teenage sons develop critical literacy abilities in Arabic. When reading Arabic religious texts, Mohamed often encourages his children to read beyond the surface of the print and find their own interpretations. According to Mohamed, in his household, the children's questions are never regarded as silly or stupid. He thinks that every question raised by his children deserves a serious response.[51]

Being involved in heritage cultural community

In order to help adolescents develop sustained interest in their heritage language, it is very important for them to be involved in their heritage culture either in person or online. When children are learning heritage language literacy as an isolated endeavour, they are unlikely to continue once their parents are not 'on their back'.

Mrs Lee from New Jersey has encouraged her 16-year-old son to involve himself in the local Korean community's activities, such as organising community baking sales, community picnics, writing community newsletters and participating in church choir practice. These community activities gave Mrs Lee's son ample opportunities to use his heritage language in meaningful ways.[52]

Strengthening school and home collaboration

In Chapter 5, I discussed the importance of the school–home connection when helping children develop their home language literacy. In this section, I will share some ideas on how to make this connection happen during adolescence.

For example, you can ask your children to retell and rewrite mainstream language texts in their heritage language.[53] Your children can be encouraged to retell or rewrite the same story or the same topic in their mainstream language by changing the genre or style in their heritage language (such as changing a drama or play to an essay). Or they can be encouraged to write new stories in their heritage language based on their school texts. Similarly, you can encourage your children to retell or rewrite a school/mainstream text from a heritage cultural perspective.

There are at least two benefits in doing so. First, this practice encourages the connection between home and school literacy. Second, it helps children take into consideration the cultural perspective when developing literacy.

Becoming life-long heritage language users

Ultimately, the most sustainable way to keep adolescents wanting to continue with their heritage language development is to help them self-monitor. Self-monitoring is also called self-regulation. It is a process of setting standards and goals for oneself and engaging in self-motivated learning. Self-regulation may not be achieved immediately. However, if you can incorporate this goal into your heritage language literacy teaching plan, your children may become life-long heritage language users.

You can begin by helping your children determine their own heritage language literacy learning goals through providing them with options. By doing so, children will feel empowered in their own learning. For example, my older son Léandre often refuses to do Chinese language assignments. Instead of pestering him, I ask him what alternatives he would suggest. He often proposes several options (amazingly, most of them are quite reasonable). I usually try to respect his choice. Once I asked him to do the assignment given by his Chinese School teacher. He proposed that instead of doing the assignment, he could start to make sentences with the words he had learned that semester. I agreed with his choice and he was quite cooperative in completing the assignment. In this case, the goals Léandre set were lower than those his teachers had set for him, but it was his choice. He thus felt obligated to follow through with it.[54]

Once children decide their learning goals, you may also need to help them self-monitor (self-observe) their progress. Research suggests that self-monitoring brings about changes in learning.[55] Using Léandre's example again, when he decided that he wanted to make sentences with the Chinese words he learned, he needed to monitor whether he could indeed fulfil his own learning goals. Obviously, children are not necessarily competent in observing their learning behaviours, and they may not necessarily know whether they make mistakes or not. What you can do is help them reflect on what they have done and ask questions to help them observe their own learning behaviours. In the aforementioned example, I suggested to Léandre that he might want to check the punctuation in his sentences and the correct use of adjectives. With my guidance, he gradually understood what self-monitoring entailed.

To help children become self-monitoring, you may also want to help them develop self-instruction skills in heritage language learning. This process requires you to demonstrate heritage language learning strategies. You can model self-instruction by showing (through thinking aloud or speaking your thoughts) what you would do in a given heritage language learning task. In the above example, I showed Léandre that when making a Chinese sentence, I needed to pay attention to word order and logic when putting words together. Developing self-instruction can also be in the form of reinforcing correct strategies. In this case, I described to Léandre what he was doing right: 'Yes, you are right to insert a comma in the phrase attached to 因为 (because) ... Great, I see you are thinking about using different words with the same meaning 立刻, 敢紧, 连忙 (immediately) in this sentence... It's really good that you remembered to put a stop at the end of the sentence this time...'.

To help children develop self-monitoring in heritage language learning, you may also want to help them self-evaluate their work. Questions such as these can help: Do you think you have put enough effort into this assignment? If you were to grade yourself, what grade do you think you would give yourself and why? Do you think that you have fulfilled the learning goals you set for yourself?

Encouraging self-reinforcement is a good way to encourage self-regulation. For example, if Léandre has completed his Chinese homework with great effort, he should be encouraged to treat himself to something he enjoys doing, such as playing computer games. If he has not completed his Chinese homework because of lack of effort, he should be encouraged to spend less time playing computer games. When children begin to self-reinforce, their learning behaviours tend to improve.

Moreover, to help your children become life-long heritage language users, you may want to teach them some specific reading and writing strategies. I introduced intensive and extensive reading strategies in Chapter 5. In order to continue to help your children know how to select reading materials for intensive and extensive reading, you may want to deliberately look for heritage language reading materials and ask them which ones should be used as intensive reading texts and which ones should be used as extensive reading texts.

Furthermore, you may want to teach your children the skills to prioritise reading materials and know that not every text deserves equal attention. For some texts, scanning and skimming is good enough to get the gist. For others, reading the headlines is sufficient to know what they are about. For still others, going over the whole text carefully is important. Learning how to prioritise reading materials can help children avoid feeling discouraged about never finishing. When my husband was a child, he could never start a new book without finishing the previous one. This prevented him from reading more. Children need to be shown that reading can be used to find information or for personal enjoyment. If a book does not serve these functions, they can abandon it and look for a new one.

It is also a good idea to help your children develop research and reference skills and know where to find help when encountering learning difficulties. You can encourage your children to use different internet search engines, reference materials such as thesauri and dictionaries. You can also help them understand the different purposes of reference tools. For example, a dictionary is used to look up a word to find out its meaning, spelling or pronunciation. A thesaurus is frequently used to look for different ways to express an idea.[56] In non-alphabetic languages such as Chinese, teaching children how to use reference tools is necessary because the layout of Chinese dictionaries is different from an alphabetical language dictionary. In addition, children need to know when to use a dictionary and when to gather meaning from context. To check every word in the dictionary will seriously slow down reading and take away all the joy.

Finally, teaching children how to a use multilingual dictionary is also helpful. I remember when I was learning English, my teachers forbade us to use a Chinese dictionary. They insisted that we use only English dictionaries. The rationale was that if we used the Chinese dictionary, we would never learn English well. We now know that such practice is not sound. In fact, we have evidence to suggest that using the dictionary in a child's stronger language can help them understand the meaning in a weaker language (often the heritage language).

Your Turn

Activities and Reflective Questions

- Read a heritage language text with your child. Help her become aware of the non-text information in the text. Carry out this activity for a while. Have you noticed any progress that your child is making in her reading comprehension by paying attention to the non-text information?
- Select an interesting heritage language text that is above your child's current reading level. Read the text to your child when he is relaxed. Use an engaging voice (you may want to practise before reading) and pause to check your child's comprehension by asking questions. How does your child feel about this activity? Do you feel that this might be an interesting way to engage your child in heritage language literacy learning? Do you find other advantages in carrying out this activity during the adolescent period?
- If reading or writing his heritage language has not become part of your child's daily routines, would you like to make this happen? If so, how can you begin? (Hint: Think of what would be the most natural thing for your child to do in his daily routines. For example, leave a note, read relevant news or read an instruction to solve a computer problem).
- Can you find a way to motivate your child to write a reflective response after reading a heritage language text by using the template introduced in this chapter? Initially, this may be difficult for your child. You can help your child by asking her to start with her school reading assignments. The goal is to get familiar and comfortable with the structure. Then, you can suggest that your child do it in the heritage language. Alternatively, you can model how to write the reflective response. At the beginning, your child can just write down the key words. She can later put these key words into sentences and paragraphs. It is important not to make this task too difficult, and do it gradually. In particular, you may want to point out the benefits of writing a reflection after reading a text.
- Can you find a way to help your child keep her feelings, thoughts and reactions to life events by helping him to keep a personal diary? Find a way to ask questions. You may be surprised that your teenage child sometimes does need your advice and opinion.
- There are many ways you can help your child master the skills of looking for clues to comprehend a text. Try the following activities:[57]
  - Provide a specific topic and five summaries. Ask your child to tell you which of the summaries are likely to be relevant to the given topic.
  - Give your child the table of contents of a book and provide a list of questions. Ask your child in which chapter would he expect to find the answer to each of the questions?

- o   Show your child a chapter heading with its subtitles and then provide him with a list of questions. Ask your child which of the questions he thinks the chapter deals with.
- o   Write down a topic and ask your child which parts in the book are about the topic and which parts are likely to contain information relevant to the topic.
- Research and introduce text-messaging vocabulary in your heritage country to your child. You can begin to text message your child daily by asking, for example, how she is doing, what she wants for dinner and what she wants to do this weekend.
- Besides trying the suggestions on how to help children develop critical literacy abilities, can you find your own innovative ways? Do you see the relevance of helping children develop critical literacy abilities and their heritage language learning as well as their overall critical thinking abilities?
- This chapter has introduced several strategies for motivating children to become life-long heritage language users. Try some of them in your own situation. Can you find ways to help your child in this direction?
- If you have a chance to visit your heritage country, take your child to a library or bookstore. Show him different kinds of dictionaries and reference books. Alternatively, you can also do online searches with your child. Explain to your child the different uses of these dictionaries or reference books. Depending on your child's response to this activity, you can also ask him to tell you whether he can figure out the different functions of the reference tools by looking up some words and comparing the definitions in different dictionaries. The purpose is to help your child understand that some reference books are more useful than others, and sometimes he has to consult more than one dictionary.[58]

Assessing Home Language Literacy Progress

Assessment focus

The major assessment focus during the adolescent period is threefold:

- To assess whether children are able to actively use their heritage language to construct meaning and solve real-life problems.
- To assess whether children demonstrate high-order thinking abilities when reading and writing their heritage language.
- To assess whether children are able to self-monitor their heritage language learning behaviours.

Thus, when evaluating your children's heritage language progress, you may want to look for evidence in the following areas:

- Can your children communicate their thoughts and feelings effectively in reading and writing their heritage language? (Construct meaning)
- Do your children know where to find resources when they don't understand their heritage language texts? (Solve problems)
- Can your children demonstrate critical thinking abilities when using their heritage language? (High-order thinking)
- Can your children self-monitor their heritage language progress by identifying the gaps in their knowledge, abilities and skills and find appropriate sources to fill in the gaps? Do your children usually correct their own mistakes in their heritage language? (Self-regulation)

It is important that your children's heritage language progress should be measured against themselves and not other children, in particularly, with peers in the heritage countries.

Using innovative assessment methods

You can continue to use the six assessment methods introduced in Chapter 3 and the graphic organiser assessment method introduced in Chapter 5 to assess and evaluate your children's heritage language literacy progress during adolescence. In addition, you can look for evidence of progress (such as meaning construction, problems solving, high-order thinking and self-regulation) by using the following innovative methods.

Music

Many adolescents develop an interest in pop music. Boys tend to be interested in playing electric musical instruments and girls tend to be more interested in listening to it. Overall, adolescents tend to identify with pop music because they enjoy the freedom to express themselves. Therefore, you can incorporate their interests by asking them to compose the lyrics to a song in their heritage language (in lieu of writing a formal essay). Sometimes, children show exceptional talent, which may not otherwise be revealed in a conventional assessment situation. For example, if you ask my younger son Dominique to write an essay in French, he is unlikely to do a good job. However, if you encourage him to write lyrics in French for him to sing while playing his electric guitar, he will show his great French expressive skills. When assessing your children's heritage language progress, you may want to ask them to show you what they can do in an area that interests them or collect samples of their work over a period of time to see whether they have made progress.

Children's interests

In the same vein, when assessing your children's heritage language progress, you can either ask them to write or read something that interests them or use what they have written. Again, I use Dominique as an example: if you ask him to read or write about football, the motivation is strong and he is likely to do better a better job than writing on a topic he has no interest in.

Real-life writing samples

Real-life writing, such as e-mails or letters, reflects your children's real ability to use their heritage language. You can ask your children to share some samples from their real-life writings with you. This is a more reliable way for you to assess their heritage language progress. For example, you can read the samples with them, give them your positive comments and circle the places that have mistakes. However, the samples must be voluntarily provided to you by your children. At no time should you violate their privacy and read their spontaneous writing, such as e-mails, without their permission.

Self-assessment

In Chapter 3, I briefly introduced the idea of self-assessment. You can use the self-assessment template demonstrated in that chapter to help your children monitor their own heritage language progress. If your children get into the habit of self-assessing each time they complete a task, they are likely to find their strength and weakness. Most importantly, your children will feel empowered in the evaluation of their progress, which will encourage them to continue with their heritage language learning.

Your Turn

Activities and Reflective Questions

- When assessing your child's heritage language progress, what should you look for as a measure of her growth in heritage language literacy development? Make a list of the possible assessment areas before you teach a certain area of literacy skills. Use these areas first as a guide to your teaching and then as a measure to check her heritage language progress.
- How do you use the results of an assessment to inform you about your next teaching activities?
- List your child's hobbies and interests. Is it possible for you to draw on these to encourage your child to write or read his heritage language and use those samples to measure his heritage language progress?
- Review the self-assessment template in Chapter 3. Try to replace the questions in this template with questions that will assess your child's writing progress.
- Keep a reflective journal of your own assessment process. Were you successful? If not, what could be the reason?

Summary

This chapter has introduced various strategies to help your children develop heritage language literacy during life's most challenging period – adolescence. The focus is on how to help adolescents continue and commit to being life-long avid users of their heritage language.

When selecting heritage language reading materials and conducting heritage language literacy activities, it is important to attend to the developmental and psychological needs of adolescents by including pop-culture reading materials and by encouraging peer networking and self-reflection. In addition, offering opportunities for adolescents to teach younger siblings will help them develop self-confidence. To facilitate adolescents' high-order thinking abilities, select texts that are inferential, that contain a variety of topics and that help develop their critical and academic literacy. To attract adolescents to good literature, read aloud to them. To help develop heritage language comprehension, show them how to write reflective reading responses and look for clues beyond the texts, attending to non-textual information. To help increase cultural knowledge and understanding, consider reading materials about traditional holidays and teach heritage cultural communication styles. Moreover, linking their school/mainstream language reading to home language reading and motivating them by developing self-regulated learning behaviours are also important.

Finally, use writing for real purposes (such as music, children's interests and real-life writings) to measure progress. Empower adolescents to develop abilities to assess their own development and ensure sustained heritage language learning behaviour.

If you attend to the needs of your children, use the right strategies and be supportive, they are likely to become life-long heritage language users.

Notes and References

1. There are different ways to identify the age range of adolescence. Recently, developmental psychologists have tended to extend the adolescent period to early 20s. The adolescent period covered in this chapter is from ages 12 to 18 (see Berk, L.E. (2009) *Child Development*. Boston, MA: Allyn & Bacon). The reason to cap the adolescent age at 18 in this chapter is because most children before 18 are living with their parents at home. Thus, the home environment (in particular, parenting) has an important impact on children's multilingual and multiliteracy development.
2. Berk, L.E. (2009) *Child Development*. Boston, MA: Allyn & Bacon.
3. Santrock, J.W. (2007) *Adolescence*. Boston, MA: McGraw Hill.
4. Santrock, J.W. (2007) *Adolescence*. Boston, MA: McGraw Hill.
5. Santrock, J.W. (2007) *Adolescence*. Boston, MA: McGraw Hill.
6. Self-regulation is a term used in psychology (especially in educational psychology). It is a form of self-control or self-monitoring in the learning process, which consists of strategies such as setting standards and goals for oneself and engaging in self-motivated learning.
7. E-mail communication on 12 January 2010.

8. Manzo, A.V., Manzo, U.C. and Estes, T.H. (2001) *Context Area Literacy: Interactive Teaching for Active Learning*. New York: John Wiley & Sons.
9. Television or film has its own specialised code of conveying information. Researchers liken the task of cracking this code to that of learning to read and call it television literacy. Berk, L.E. (2006) *Child Development*. Boston, MA: Allyn & Bacon.
10. Berk, L.E. (2006) *Child Development*. Boston, MA: Allyn & Bacon.
11. E-mail communication on 20 February 2008.
12. Cruickshank, K. (2004) Literacy in multilingual contexts: Change in teenagers' reading and writing. *Language and Education* 18 (6), 459–473.
13. Rowling, J.K. (1999) *Harry Potter and the Prisoner of Azkaban*. New York: Scholastic Inc.
14. Herrell, A. and Jordan, M. (2002) *50 Active Learning Strategies for Improving Reading Comprehension*. Upper Saddle River, NJ: Merrill.
15. Herrell, A. and Jordan, M. (2002) *50 Active Learning Strategies for Improving Reading Comprehension*. Upper Saddle River, NJ: Merrill.
16. Galambod, N.L., Almeida, D.M. and Petersen, A.C. (1990) Masculinity, femininity, and sex role attitude in early adolescence: Exploring gender intensification. *Child Development* 61, 1904–1914.
17. See endnote 1 in Chapter 4 for the equivalent educational systems in 31 countries.
18. Galda, L., Ash, G.E. and Culllina, B.E. (2000) Children's literature. In M.L. Kamil, P.B. Monsenthal, P.D. Pearso and R. Barr (eds) *Handbook of Reading Research: Volume III* (pp. 361–379). Mahwah, NJ: Lawrence Erlbaum.
19. E-mail communication on 11 March 2009.
20. The Programme for International Student Assessment (PISA) is a worldwide evaluation of 15-year-old school children's scholastic performance, performed first in 2000 and repeated every three years. The purpose is to see whether schools are effectively preparing students for the workforce. It is coordinated by the Organisation for Economic Co-operation and Development (OECD). The goal is to improve educational policies and outcomes.
21. E-mail communication on 8 November 2009.
22. Wang, X-L. (2005) *Exploring the Meaning of Chinese New Year: Some Ideas for Teachers*. Cheshire: Trafford Publishing.
23. E-mail communication on 27 August 2009.
24. Tompkins, G.E. (2009) *50 Literacy Strategies: Step by Step*. Boston, MA: Allyn & Bacon.
25. Personal communication on 7 September 2009.
26. Note that many of the ideas in this section are developed based on Manzo, A.V., Manzo, U.C. and Estes, T.H. (2001) *Context Area Literacy: Interactive Teaching for Active Learning*. New York: John Wiley & Sons.
27. Nuttall, C. (1982) *Teaching Reading Skills in a Foreign Language*. London: Heinemann Educational Books.
28. Ideas introduced in this section are based on Nuttall, C. (1982) *Teaching Reading Skills in a Foreign Language*. London: Heinemann Educational Books.
29. Some people refer to these reference aids as reference apparatus. See Nuttall, C. (1982) *Teaching Reading Skills in a Foreign Language*. London: Heinemann Educational Books.
30. Westby, C.E. (1994) The effects of culture on genre, structure, style of oral and written texts. In G. Wallach and K. Butler (eds) *Language Learning Disabilities in School-Age Children and Adolescents* (pp. 180–218) New York: Macmillan. Note: the ideas were from Brice, A.E. and Brice, R.C. (2009) *Language Development: Monolingual and Bilingual Acquisition*. Boston, MA: Allyn & Bacon.
31. Brice, A.E. and Brice, R.C. (2009) *Language Development: Monolingual and Bilingual Acquisition*. Boston, MA: Allyn & Bacon.

32. Ehren, B.J. (2005) Looking for evidence-based practice in reading comprehension instruction. *Topics in Language Disorders* 25 (4), 310–321.
33. Zehr, M.A. (2010) Reading aloud to teens gains favor among teachers. *Education Week*: edweek.org, 4 January.
34. Personal communication 15 March 2009.
35. Ideas suggested in this section are based on Dwyer, E.J. and Isbell, R. (1990) Reading aloud to students. *Educational Digest* 56 (1), 70–71.
36. E-mail communication 4 February 2010.
37. On WWW at http://www.eurekalert.org/pub_releases/2009-12/uoia-tto121009.php.
38. Anderson, J. (2001) Web publishing in non-Roman scripts: Effects on the writing process. *Language and Education* 15 (4), 229–249.
39. The ideas suggested in this section are based on Van Horn, L. (2008) *Reading Photographs to Write with Meaning and Purpose, Grade 4–12*. Newark, DE: International Reading Association.
40. E-mail communication on 2 February 2010.
41. Gilmore, D. (2008) *The Film Club*. New York: Hachette Book Group USA.
42. Hall, E. (1983) *The Dance of Life*. New York: Anchor Press.
43. Sanchez-Burk, J., Lee, F., Choi, I., Nisbett, R. and Zhao, S.-M. (2003) Conversing across cultures: East-West communication styles in work and nonwork contexts. *Journal of Personality and Social Psychology* 85 (2), 363–372.
44. E-mail communication on 3 March 2009.
45. Koutsantoni, D. (2004) Relations of power and solidarity in scientific community: A cross-cultural comparison of politeness strategies in the writing of native English speaking and Greek engineers. *Multilingua* 23, 111–143.
46. Wang, X-L. (2009) Ensuring sustained trilingual development through motivation. *Bilingual Family Newsletter* 26 (1), 1–7.
47. E-mail interview conducted on 23 September 2009.
48. De Vries Guth, N. and Pratt-Fartro, T. (2010) *Literacy Coaching to Build Adolescent Learning: Five Pillars of Practice* (p. 13). Thousand Oaks, CA: Corwin.
49. Greenspan, S.I. (2007) *Great Kids: Helping Your Babies and Children Develop the Ten Essential Qualities for a Healthy, Happy Life*. Philadelphia, PA: Da Capo Press.
50. Stevens, L.P. and Bean, T.W. (2007) *Critical Literacy: Context, Research, and Practice in the K-12 Classrooms*. Thousand Oaks, CA: Sage.
51. E-mail communication on 27 September 2007.
52. E-mail exchange in January 2008.
53. Most ideas suggested in this section are inspired by Ada, A.F. (2003) *A Magical Encounter: Latino Children's Literature in the Classroom*. Boston, MA: Allyn & Bacon.
54. Example cited from Wang, X.-L. (2009) Ensuring sustained trilingual development through motivation. *The Bilingual Family Newsletter*.
55. McCombs, B.L. and Marzano, R.J. (1990) Putting the self in self-regulated learning: The self as agent in integrating skill and will. *Educational Psychologist* 25, 51–70.
56. Johnson, D.D. (2001) *Vocabulary in the Elementary and Middle School* (pp. 75–93). Boston, MA: Allyn & Bacon.
57. Ideas suggested are based on Nuttall, C. (1982) *Teaching Reading Skills in a Foreign Language*. London: Heinemann Educational Books.
58. Ideas are based on Johnson, D.D. (2001) *Vocabulary in the Elementary and Middle School* (pp. 75–93). Boston, MA: Allyn & Bacon.

Chapter 7
Parents' Practices, Voices and Concluding Remarks

This chapter revisits some multilingual literacy home teaching practices demonstrated by the parents featured in this book. Through analysing the strategies and reflections of these parents, the key areas of their successes and distinct differences are discussed. The chapter concludes by briefly recapitulating the main points conveyed throughout the book, leaving you with a positive message: Although multilingual literacy development in the home environment is challenging, it is possible with support, dedication and effective strategies.

Parental Practices and Voices

Throughout this book, you have met many parents and read bits and pieces about their multilingual home literacy practices. Although these parents varied in their cultural and linguistic backgrounds as well as in their educational and socioeconomic status, they all held the same conviction: they were determined to bring up their children in more than one language and culture. Despite the various challenges that these parents encountered, for the most part they were successful in their multilingual childrearing. Below, I will revisit some of their home literacy teaching strategies and share their thoughts on multilingual and multiliterate home teaching. Through these parents' practices and voices, you may reaffirm your own practices or gain further insights into your own multilingual childrearing.

Home Literacy Teaching Strategies

Multilingual childrearing plan

As discussed in Chapter 3, unlike school literacy instruction, home literacy teaching, including heritage literacy home teaching, is usually regarded as casual and informal. The process of home literacy teaching planning is rarely mentioned in the literature as an important step for success. Ms Andersson, whom you met in Chapter 3, has clearly realised the importance of planning based on her own unsuccessful multilingual childrearing experience. In my interviews with the parents featured in this book, they all agreed that planning was vital in effectively teaching heritage language literacy to their children. For example, Mrs Cho (mentioned in Chapters 2 and 5) commented:

> I had no plan when I first started to teach Jessie how to read and write Korean. In those early years, I acted like a headless fly, bumping around without a

direction. I gradually realised the necessity of planning through working with my daughter. I did notice that if I planned what I wanted to do with Jessie, I was more organised and more successful ... I began to develop a monthly plan for I wanted to do for Jessie's Korean language learning and marked the important steps on my calendar and then followed through.

Time and frequency

All the parents featured in this book agreed that the amount of time that parents spend helping their children with their heritage language learning and how often they work with them could affect their learning quality and progress. As Mrs Yamamoto (Chapter 5) put it,

> there is no question about it: it's work! I have worked diligently with my daughter everyday on her reading and writing since she was 5-years-old. Sometimes, the job is daunting and lonely. Looking at the bright side, what I have invested in my daughter's Japanese language learning does pay off. My daughter is doing well and I am confident that she will be able to function, if she ever has to work and live in Japan.

Support

The families featured in this book were all very supportive of their children's multilingual development. You have probably noticed that many fathers in these families were actively involved in multilingual childrearing. For example, Kabil's father (Chapter 4) frequently read Turkish children's books to him. Mr Belinsky (Chapter 5) helped his daughter learn to read Russian through the internet. Karl (Chapter 5) helped his son make German heritage language books from German magazines. Jeremy (Chapter 6) frequently used English pop-culture materials to help his Japanese twin daughters read their heritage language English. Feliks (Chapter 6) created multimedia reading materials for his son and discussed these materials with him. Mohamed (Chapter 6) helped his children to read Arabic language texts and materials with a critical lens.

We also witnessed support from extended family members in some of the featured families. For example, Ashley's grandmother (Chapter 2) took an active role in helping Ashley with her Chinese learning on a daily basis.

We observed the support from the heritage community as well. For example, the Korean community in which Mrs Kim (Chapter 2) lived provided all kinds of opportunities for her daughter in terms of her culture and language learning: Korean Bible study group, Korean language school and daily opportunities to play with Korean-speaking children.

Opportunities to use heritage language

All parents featured in this book believed that it was critical to provide opportunities for their children to practise their heritage language literacy skills in various real-life activities and events. For example, Isha (Chapter 5) gave her 10-year-old son many practical opportunities to read and write in Panjabi: writing notes and birthday party invitations and exchanging e-mails with relatives in Pakistan. Mrs Xie (Chapter 5) took her daughter to the local Chinese community bank to get first-hand experience of doing financial transactions in the Chinese language. Silvija (Chapter 6) encouraged her daughter to connect with a Croatian peer online. The girls have opportunities to exchange e-mails and share their life experiences. Mrs Schneider (Chapter 5) made writing greeting cards in Hebrew to her relatives in Israel a family routine. Polina (Chapter 5) encouraged her children to write to their grandmother in Russia every month.

Attention to children's needs

Most of the parents featured in this book tried to attend to the needs of their children during their different developmental stages. For example, Aaleigha (Chapter 6) read German classic works related to adolescent issues to her son and helped him think about adolescent issues. Suzanna (Chapter 6) selected different books for her son and daughter to respect their different reading needs. As Aaleigha commented,

> Like everything else in a child's life, parents need to consider their children's emotional, psychological and developmental needs when helping them with their multilingual development. Children are like tender grass, if we take care of their growing needs and give them the right amount of fertilizer and water, they tend to grow better.

Motivation

Many parents featured in the book found different ways to motivate their children in their multilingual development. Take Julie (Chapter 6) as an example, she cleverly motivated her daughter Catherine to write down her feelings in her diary and helped her realise how words can help express complex emotions. As Julie explained,

> I knew that if I just asked Catherine to write French, she would never do it but once when she was upset (her boyfriend betrayed her), I suggested to her that she write down her feelings in French. I persuaded her that none of her Swedish friends would be able to read it and she would have a lot more freedom to express her emotions privately.

Julie believes that children often need a reason or purpose to write, particularly in the languages of which they have less command. If parents know how to seize the moment and find reasons to motivate children, children will be more willing to cooperate with their parents.

Creativity in heritage language reading materials and activities

We also noticed that some of the featured parents were quite creative and innovative in their home language literacy activities. For example, Karen (Chapter 5) wrote her own Swahili books with her three children, using her family photos and her children's illustrations. Marita's mother (Chapter 6) encouraged Marita to write in Persian, using his family photos. Mrs Lek (Chapter 4) asked her child to match her Thai shopping lists to items that she put in the shopping cart in a Thai grocery store. Mrs Shokhirev (Chapter 4) glued Russian words onto cereal boxes to provide a print-rich environment for her infant son.

Incorporation of heritage culture and heritage language teaching

Many parents featured in this book were also mindful of teaching their heritage cultural knowledge simultaneously with their heritage language literacy. For example, Mrs Wei (Chapter 6) taught her son the culturally proper way to write to his grandparents. Mrs Lee (Chapter 6) encouraged her 16-year-old son to participate in local Korean community activities (baking sales, church choir practices, community newsletter writing and community picnics) and helped him learn his Korean in the community context.

Connection between home literacy and school literacy

Several parents featured in the book made efforts to connect their children's heritage language literacy learning with their school learning. For example, Semahat (Chapter 6) encouraged her teenage daughter to complete her Dutch world history homework by looking for information on Turkish websites. Mrs Cho (Chapter 5) wrote letters to her daughter's teachers about Jessie's Korean learning at home. As a result, Jessie's teachers were able to offer support for her heritage language learning. For example, Jessie's teachers sometimes shared her Korean writing in class. Mrs Cho also helped her daughter to understand her English school subjects by reading Korean language materials. Mrs Yamamoto (Chapter 5) did the same by helping her daughter write German schoolwork in Japanese and vice versa.

Assessment

Many of the parents featured in this book used some form of assessment to monitor their children's progress, and they also used assessment as a way of celebrating their children's achievements. For example, Mrs Cho (Chapter 5) displayed her daughter's Korean writing at her birthday parties as a way of celebrating her achievement.

Reflection on practice

Quite a few parents included in this book kept diaries or reflective notes on their observations of their children's heritage language literacy learning process.

In their observations, some parents also wrote about their experiences and thoughts. Sonja (Chapter 4) revealed:

> I try to keep brief notes on my son's Dutch language development milestones as well as mistakes. I also record my thoughts on my own teaching. I think about what I did well and what I didn't do well. Keeping a journal makes me more conscious about what I do. I would recommend it to other parents.

Maintaining a positive attitude and persevering

Despite the challenges and frustrations and despite the lack of societal support, one thing common to the featured parents was that they were positive and determined. None would ever have given up. Silvija (Chapter 6) summed it up well:

> I have to be positive. I always believe that if I don't do anything or give up in the middle of it, nothing will happen. So, if I want my daughter to develop her Croatian reading and writing abilities, I have to help her work on it. I cannot just do nothing and hope things will happen to her.

Differences among parents

Although all the parents featured in this book shared the common goal of raising multilingual and multiliterate children, they did not hold the same beliefs about the purpose of literacy. In addition, we also noticed that not all the parents used the same methods to teach their children.

Differences in parental beliefs

It is interesting to see that some of the parents from the Confucian traditional cultures, such as Mrs Kim (Chapter 2), Mrs Xu (Chapter 4), Mrs Lee (Chapter 6), Mrs Wei (Chapter 6), Mrs Xie (Chapter 5), Mrs Gong (Chapter 6), Mrs Minami (Chapter 4), Mrs Yamamoto (Chapter 5), Mrs Zhang (Chapter 4) and Mrs Cho (Chapters 2 and 5) all believed that the main purpose of heritage language literacy learning (in their separate cases, Chinese, Japanese and Korean) was to help children build skills for future academic and professional success in addition to maintaining their heritage culture. They all believed that reading and writing should be taught systematically and explicitly. They all shared the same view as Tony's grandfather (see Chapter 2: Eve Gregory's study[1]) that reading or writing was a form of serious work. They all regarded the explicit teaching of heritage language reading and writing skills as the key to success. They all believed that heritage language learning would bring their children academic and economic success in their future. For example, Mrs Wei said:

> If my child wants to become fluent in his Chinese, he needs to work hard on it. I have told him many stories about how ancient Chinese scholars pushed

themselves to achieve the best results. Success in anything needs dedication and diligence. I think there will be no gain if there is no pain.

By contrast, the parents of European and North American cultural backgrounds, such as Julie (Chapter 6), Sonia (Chapter 4), Karl (Chapter 5), Mrs Edwards (Chapter 5), Aaleigha (Chapter 6), Marian (Chapter 5), Hanna (Chapter 4) and Jeremy (Chapter 6) believed that their children's home language literacy learning should be based on children's needs and wants. Home language reading and writing should be fun and interesting. Parents should not force their children to read or write if the children resisted. All these parents agreed that heritage language learning would be beneficial to their children, intellectually and culturally. As Sonia commented, 'I try to make my son's Dutch development an enjoyable activity. I talk to him, I read interesting books to him and I play with him'.

Other parents featured in the book, such as Mohamed (Chapter 6), Isha (Chapter 5), Ommar's father (Chapter 4), Semahat (Chapter 6), Mitra's mother (Chapter 6), Eddie's mother (Chapter 4) and Ayati's mother (Chapter 4) believed that the most important purpose of teaching their children their heritage language reading and writing skills was to help their children study and understand their religion. Many of them believed that repetition and memorisation was a good method to learn religious texts. For example, Ommar's father revealed that 'I want my son to know Arabic so that he can read religious texts. To remember what he learned, he has to repeat, repeat and repeat until he knows the texts by heart... Repetition is a form of learning'.

Finally, parents such as Christina (Chapter 6), Silvija (Chapter 6), Polina (Chapter 5), Mrs Shokhirev (Chapter 4) and Mrs Belinsky (Chapter 5) stood between the parents mentioned above with regard to their beliefs on home language literacy teaching and learning. On the one hand, they agreed with the idea that literacy was work, but on the other hand, they also believed children should enjoy what they read and write. Mrs Belinsky commented, 'It's really a matter of balance. I think both hard work and enjoyment should be considered'.

Differences in literacy teaching methods

Many parents featured in the book were creative and innovative in their teaching. They used different methods to help their children learn heritage language literacy. There seems to be no one method that was more effective than another. Instead, what worked for their children was the best method in their situation. For example, Eddie's mother (Chapter 4) read books to her son in English and discussed them in Arabic. Mrs Cho (Chapter 5) asked her daughter to read a variety of genres weekly. Diya's parents (Chapter 5) provided wedding and greeting cards for their daughter, who, for example, learned and recited beautiful verses and poems from a wedding invitation card in Hindi. Marian (Chapter 5) played magnetic word games after dinner with her son, making silly and funny sentences. Jeremy (Chapter 6) used pop-culture materials to help his twin daughters read in their heritage language English. Mrs Gong (Chapter 6) read classical Chinese poems to her daughter. Mrs Xu (Chapter 4) labelled household objects in Chinese. Mrs Minami (Chapter 4) asked her 5-year-old daughter to help shelve groceries with Japanese labels after each trip back from the Japanese supermarket. Hanna (Chapter 4) intentionally read her German newspaper aloud and drew her 3-year-old son's attention to the interesting photos and captions. Ommar's father (Chapter 4) asked him to fetch his Arabic and English newspapers.

We also noticed that some parents' home literacy teaching resembled school teaching. For example, Mrs Edwards (Chapter 5) used the language experience approach (LEA) to teach her son how to write. Other parents' teaching was casual. For example, Mrs Lek (Chapter 4) used everyday circumstances to teach her daughter heritage language literacy by asking her child to match her Thai shopping lists to the labels of items when shopping in the Thai grocery store.

Moreover, we found that parents conducted their heritage language literacy activities with different emphases. For example, Mrs Cho and Mrs Yamamoto incorporated their children's heritage language learning into academic learning. Mohamed cultivated his children's heritage learning focusing on religious observance. Aaleigha helped her child's heritage language learning by attending to his psychological needs. Mrs Gong concentrated on helping her child's literacy development by reading classical literature. Christina and her husband Feliks (Chapter 6) paid attention to their son's critical thinking ability by discussing news from Polish politics and multimedia reading materials.

Concluding Remarks

Having revisited the various home teaching strategies of the parents featured in this book and heard their thoughts regarding teaching in the home environment, I would like to restate some important points conveyed throughout the book about raising multilingual and multiliterate children.

It is important to start with a home teaching plan and schedule

Research has suggested that deliberate planning in multilingual childrearing will help facilitate success.[2] All the parents featured in this book confirmed, based on their multilingual childrearing experiences, that to have a plan is better than not. Even though not all the parents started their journey with a clear plan, many realised the importance of it along the way. I can affirm this point in my own multilingual childrearing practice. I clearly see the effects of planning on my own children's Chinese literacy learning. The planning process provides me with a road map, which makes me feel more confident to carry out my teaching activities.

However, it does not mean that I cannot change my plan. In fact, I often modify my plan based on specific situations. For example, before this year's Chinese New Year, I planned to introduce my children to 25 Chinese characters (字) and phrases (词) by asking them to read a short article that I had composed. While I was executing my plan, I noticed that they were more interested in food names on the packages of the Chinese goodies I offered them. Instead of insisting on my planned words and phrases, I rewrote my article by replacing them with some of the words and phrases from the Chinese food packages. Even though I did not exactly teach all the words and phrases I had planned, the original plan still helped; I taught my children the words and phrases that are associated with the Chinese New Year celebration.

In addition, I noticed that having a consistent time for heritage language literacy activities is better than a random time and schedule. For example, in my home, five o'clock in the afternoon rings a bell for my kids. They know that this is the time when we work on Chinese reading or writing (three days a week during the regular school year). Establishing this schedule was not easy. It actually took a quite a few years to 'condition' my children with this habit.

Assessing children's home literacy progress can help plan for the next cycle of teaching

Assessing children's home literacy learning process can help you determine whether your teaching is successful and help you plan for the next cycle of teaching. Thus, when planning a teaching activity, always think about what you want to see your children achieve (the areas to evaluate and assess) and when finishing the activity, always check whether your children are able to accomplish what you have planned. Use the various strategies discussed in Chapters 3–6 to measure your children's progress and use their learning outcomes to determine what you need to do when planning the next cycle of teaching.

Having a realistic expectation will help you remain optimistic

Given the specific situation of heritage language learners (e.g. time constraints and non-heritage language learning environment), the expectation for their development needs to be realistic. It is not fair for us to use other children (in particular, children from the heritage language environment) as a yardstick to measure children who learn heritage language reading and writing in a non-heritage language environment. It is not even fair for us to compare one child with another.

Because the learning environment and needs of heritage language learning children are unique, the expectation for their achievements needs to be based on their specific learning environments. We need to feel encouraged by even the smallest progress made by our children. Having a realistic expectation can keep us optimistic. However, this does not mean that we cannot aim high. For example, Mrs Cho's daughter and Mrs Yamamoto's daughter will probably function better than many of our children in terms of their heritage language literacy proficiency. In their specific conditions, these two families are able to help their children achieve high literacy levels. On the other hand, we should be equally happy for Mrs Lek's daughter, Tamarine, who can read and write Thai at a first grade level, even though she is now in middle school. In her situation, Tamarine and her parents did their best.

Children's needs are paramount

Children at different developmental levels and with different abilities have different needs. Many of the parents featured in the book have endorsed the importance of recognising children's needs.

Children have several kinds of needs that we as parents need to attend to. First, we need to take care of their physical needs. After a long day in school, children need time to relax and have fun. You need to find a way to balance their free time with time dedicated to learning their heritage language. Second, we need to pay attention to our children's emotional needs and provide them with opportunities to talk about their joy of achievement as well as venting their frustration in learning. Additionally, we need to create opportunities for them to find their emotional connections with their heritage culture. It is clear that if a child does not have an emotional bond with a heritage culture, it is hard to motivate them to read or write in that heritage language. Finally, we need to attend to children's developmental needs for home literacy learning activities that are suitable to their age and cognitive levels. Only when our children's needs are taken care of, can they learn effectively.

Providing unconditional support

Your support is crucial for your children's heritage language literacy development. They rely on you to help them through the challenging journey. You need to provide them with unconditional support, which means that your children need to feel that you are always there for them, no matter what. Children are willing to take risks when they feel secure. Parental unconditional support will provide that kind of security. Risk taking is necessary in language and literacy learning.

Cultivating motivation is essential for life-long heritage literacy development

The research literature and parents' testimonies have shown that motivation plays an essential role in home language literacy learning. To be motivated to learn, children need to see the meaning and relevance of learning to read and write in home languages. Thus, you may want to consider motivating your children as an important task on your multilingual and multiliterate agenda. Each time you plan a home literacy teaching activity, you may want to ask yourself, 'How can I make this activity more attractive to my children'? The motivation strategies introduced in Chapter 6 may help you.

In addition, you may want to help your children develop the growth mindset,[3] that is, their multiliteracy abilities can be developed over time with effort. For more information on how to motivate your children, I recommend a good book written by

Carol Dweck (the leading expert in motivation), *Mindset: The New Psychology of Success*.[4] This book will give you new insights on how to motivate your children to discover their talents (in this case, their multilingual and multiliterate talents).

Taking an eclectic teaching approach works better than one approach

Throughout this book, you have been introduced to many strategies and approaches in home heritage language literacy teaching in addition to the home literacy teaching framework discussed in Chapter 2. When looking at the practices of parents featured in this book, we can see that these parents used different approaches and methods to achieve their different purposes. Thus, it is perhaps more effective to take an eclectic approach, namely, to take a bit from different approaches and combine them to fit the needs of your children. The best teaching method is what best fits your children.

Negotiating between your cultural beliefs and your children's mainstream culture

In Chapter 2, we discussed that different cultures have different beliefs about the purpose of literacy. In this book, you also observed that the featured parents practised home literacy teaching differently. Although it is important to stand firm on your cultural ground, it is equally important to consider your children's unique position (influenced by both your heritage culture and the mainstream culture in which they live[5]). It is important to negotiate between your cultural beliefs and the beliefs in your children's culture. Take Mrs Cho's example again. For the most part, she practised a very Asian style of teaching. Yet, she also incorporated the mainstream cultural style by communicating with her daughter's schoolteachers. Mrs Cho firmly believes that parental negotiation between cultures benefits multilingual children.

Reflection helps improve home literacy teaching

In Chapter 3, the importance of reflection was discussed. As you have seen, some parents featured in the book also find it useful. Keeping a reflective journal is an active and deliberate cognitive (thinking) process. It provides you with the opportunity to step back and look at your teaching from a distance. I think Mrs Wei's analogy illustrates the point, 'When you are busy doing what you are doing, you often get lost. Just like when you walk in the forest, you tend to only see the path near you, but, if you stand on the top of a mountain, you have a greater view; you see many more paths'.

Reflection can help you identify your strengths and the improvements needed in your interactions with your children so that you do not repeat your mistakes and continue with your successful strategies. Effective teachers (parent teachers included) never just forge ahead with teaching; they always think before and after their teaching. In addition, reflective journals also help you see, over a period of time, what you have done, how you have done it and what your children have achieved.

Reflection does not have to be long or even written in complete sentences. Sonja, for instance, kept only brief notes. She believed that these notes kept her more conscious of what she was doing.

Networking with other parents can keep you going

As Mrs Yamamoto stated, raising multilingual and multiliterate children can sometimes be daunting and lonely. Thus, it is important to network with other parents in a similar situation. Nowadays, with the internet, it is easier to form such networks. In fact, I was able to get connected with many of the parents featured in this book through the internet. The advantage of networking with other parents is that you are not doing things alone. When you are frustrated, you can find help from other parents, who can provide moral support.

Having confidence in your children

Anyone who has experience in raising multilingual children will occasionally (for some may be frequently) encounter resistance from their children, especially during the adolescent period. This situation can be frustrating and discouraging. However, if we maintain a positive attitude, we may be able to turn our children's negativity to positivity. To be able to do this, we need to have confidence in our children and believe that they are capable of learning their heritage language as long as we, the parents, are willing to find that switch (motivation) to turn them on.

Being an advocate for multilingual children

As the African proverb states, it takes a village to raise a child. It certainly takes more than just parents to raise a multilingual and multiliterate child. It takes the whole society to support the needs of multilingual children (including financial and educational opportunities). Even though many parents are right now taking the major responsibility to raise multilateral and multiliterate children, it is not enough. With the increasing globalisation trend, it is in humanity's best interest that we work together to advocate for multilingualism and multiliteracies. You can begin from a local level by making your voice heard in your child's school parent and teacher association and community organisations, concerning the issues of multilingual children. You can later move your advocacy for multilingual children to a national and international arena. Only when everyone joins together to provide support for multilingual children, can their needs be met appropriately.

It is an Advantage to Know More

As now you are finishing this book, it is always positive to think about what you have invested or will invest in your children's learning. As the bilingual expert Ellen Bialystok put it, 'Knowing more has never been a disadvantage when compared to knowing less'.[6] Ultimately, the children who are immersed in multilingual and multiliterate worlds will learn to call on a greater wealth of metacognitive and metalinguistic strategies.[7]

I have heard so many laments from people who have missed the opportunity to become multilingual and multiliterate. They genuinely wished their parents had helped them. So, do not let your children say this about you!

Summary

This chapter recapitulated the home language literacy practices of the parents featured in this book. The wide range of effective strategies used by these parents is well worth our consideration. For example, design a plan for home literacy teaching, pay attention to children's various needs and provide them with support, use different innovative strategies to engage and motivate children, provide opportunities to practise home language literacy in the everyday context, make efforts to connect school learning to heritage language learning, use developmentally responsive assessment methods to monitor progress and reflect on teaching strategies for further improvement.

This chapter also discussed the differences among the featured parents, such as their different beliefs about the purpose of literacy and their different teaching emphases.

It concluded with some important take-home messages regarding home literacy teaching:

- It is important to set up a home literacy teaching plan and schedule.
- Assessing children's literacy progress can help improve the next cycle of teaching.
- Having realistic expectations of your children's achievements can help you become optimistic.
- Attending to children's needs is paramount.
- Providing unconditional support for your children can ensure success.
- Cultivating motivation is essential for life-long heritage language literacy development.
- Taking an eclectic teaching approach is better than only one approach.
- Negotiating between your cultural beliefs and your children's mainstream culture will benefit your children.
- Reflecting on what you do will help you improve your teaching.
- Networking with other parents can keep you going.
- Having confidence in your children.
- Being an advocate for multilingual children will benefit globalisation.

It is an advantage to know more than one language and literacy. Even though multilingual childrearing is challenging and occasionally frustrating, it is exciting and rewarding. With support, dedication and the right strategies, the time that you invested in it will be well worthwhile.

Best wishes for your multilingual and multiliterate childrearing!

Notes and References

1. Gregory, E. (2008) *Learning to Read in a New Language.* Los Angeles, CA: Sage.
2. Cuero, K. and Romo, H. (2007) Raising a multilingual child. Paper presented at the Annual Meeting of the American Sociological Association, 10 August, New York.
   Wang, X-L. (2008) *Growing Up with Three Language: Birth to Eleven* (pp. 40–55). Bristol: Multilingual Matters.
3. Dweck, C.S. (2006) *Mindset: The New Psychology of Success.* New York: Random House.
4. Dweck, C.S. (2006) *Mindset: The New Psychology of Success.* New York: Random House.
5. Cruickshank, K. (2004) Literacy in multilingual context: Change in teenagers' reading and writing. *Language and Education* 18 (6), 459–473.
6. Bialystok, E. (2002) Acquisition of literacy in bilingual children: A framework for research. *Language Learning* 52 (1), 159–199.
7. Gregory, E. (2008) *Learning to Read in a New Language: Making Sense of Words and Worlds* (p. 25). Los Angeles, CA: Sage.

Appendix A: Useful References on Children with Cognitive and Language Learning Disabilities

Armon-Lotem, S. (2010) Instructive bilingualism: Can bilingual children with specific language impairment rely on one language in learning a second one? *Applied Psycholinguistics* 31 (2), 253–260.

Beukelman, D.R. and Mirenda, P. (2005) *Augmentative and Alternative Communication: Supporting Children and Adults with Complex Communication Needs*. Baltimore, MD: Brooks Publishing Co.

Bird, E.K.-R., Cleave, P., Trudeau, N., Thordardottir, E., Sutton, A. and Thorpe, A. (2005) The language abilities of bilingual children with Down Syndrome. *American Journal of Speech-Language Pathology* 14 (3), 187–199.

Cheuk, D.K.L., Wong, V. and Leung, G.M. (2005) Multilingual home environment and specific language impairment: A case-control study in Chinese children. *Paediatric & Perinatal Epidemiology* 19 (4), 303–314.

Communication Disorders Quarterly: A Journal of the Hammill Institute on Disabilities. New York: Sage.

Gebesee, F., Paradis, J. and Crago, M.B. (2004) *Dual Language Development and Disorders: A Handbook on Bilingualism and Second Language Learning*. Baltimore, MD: Brookes.

Girbau, D. and Schwartz, R.G. (2008) Phonological working memory in Spanish–English bilingual children with and without specific language impairment. *Journal of Communication Disorders* 41 (2), 124–145.

Greenspan, S.I. (2005) Working with the bilingual child who has a language delay. *Early Childhood Today* 20 (3), 27–28.

Guendouzi, J., Loncke, F. and Williams, M.J. (2010) *The Handbook of Psycholinguistic and Cognitive Processes: Perspectives in Communication Disorders*. London: Psychology Press.

Guiberson, M.M. (2005) Children with cochlear implants from bilingual families: Considerations for intervention and a case study. *Volta Review* 105 (1), 29–39.

Gutiérrez-Clellen, V.F., Simon-Cereijido, G. and Wagner, C. (2008) Bilingual children with language impairment: A comparison with monolinguals and second language learners. *Applied Psycholinguistics* 29 (1), 3–19.

Gutiérrez-Clellen, V.F., Simon-Cereijido, G. and Leone, A.E. (2009) Code-switching in bilingual children with specific language impairment. *International Journal of Bilingualism* 13 (1), 91–109.

Jacobson, P. and Livert, D. (2010) English past tense use as a clinical marker in older bilingual children with language impairment. *Clinical Linguistics & Phonetics* 24 (2), 101–121.

Lee, S-Y. and Gorman, B.K. (2009) Production of Korean case particles in a Korean-English bilingual child with specific language impairment: A preliminary study. *Communication Disorders Quarterly* 30 (3), 167–177.

McCauley, R.J. and Fey, M.E. (eds) (2006) *Treatment of Language Disorders in Children*. New York: Brookes.

Nickels, L. and Croot, K. (2009) *Progressive Language Impairments: Intervention and Management.* London: Psychology Press.

Norbury, C.F., Tomblin, J.B., Dorothy, V.M. and Bishop, D.V.M. (eds) (2008) *Understanding Developmental Language Disorders: From Theory to Practice.* New York: Psychology Press.

Paradis, J. (2010) The interface between bilingual development and specific language impairment. *Applied Psycholinguistics* 31 (2), 227–252.

Paradis, J. Crago, M. and Genesee, F. (2005/2006) Domain-general versus domain-specific accounts of specific language impairment: Evidence from bilingual children's acquisition of object pronouns. *Language Acquisition* 13 (1), 33–62.

Paradis, J., Crago, M. and Genesee, F. (2010) *Dual Language Development and Disorder.* Baltimore, MD: Brookes.

Paul, R. (2006) *Language Disorders from Infancy through Adolescence: Assessment and Intervention.* New York: Mosby.

Raman, I. and Weekes, B.S. (2005) Acquired dyslexia in a Turkish-English speaker. *Annals of Dyslexia* 55 (1), 79–104.

Rinaldi, C. and Péez, M. (2008) Preschool matters: Predicting reading difficulties for Spanish-speaking bilingual students in first grade. *Learning Disabilities – A Contemporary Journal* 6 (1), 71–86.

Salameh, E.K., Nettelbladt, U. and Gullberg, B. (2002) Risk factors for language impairment in Swedish bilingual and monolingual children relative to severity. *Acta Paediatrica* 91 (12), 1379–1384.

Schwartz, R.G. (2008) *Handbook of Child Language Disorders.* New York: Psychology Press.

Swanson, H.L, Sáez, L. and Gerber, M. (2006) Growth in literacy and cognition in bilingual children at risk or not at risk for reading disabilities. *Journal of Educational Psychology* 98 (2), 247–264.

Toppelberg, C.O., Munir, K. and Nieto-Castañon, A. (2006) Spanish-English bilingual children with psychopathology: Language deficits and academic language proficiency. *Child & Adolescent Mental Health* 11 (3), 156–163.

Westman, M., Korkman, M., Mickos, A. and Byring, R. (2008) Language profiles of monolingual and bilingual Finnish preschool children at risk for language impairment. International *Journal of Language & Communication Disorders* 43 (6), 699–711.

William, A.L., McLeod, S. and McCauley, R.J. (2010) *Interventions for Speech Sound Disorders in Children.* Baltimore, MD: Brookes.

Wydell, T.N. and Kondo, T. (2003) Phonological deficit and the reliance on orthographic approximation for reading: A follow-up study on an English–Japanese bilingual with monolingual dyslexia. *Journal of Research in Reading* 26 (1), 33–48.

Appendix B: Sample English Books for Infants and Young Children

These books are listed for you as a reference when you look for books for your infants and young children in your heritage language or for you to create dual-language books or you can replace the English words with your heritage language.

Aliki (1986) *Feelings*. New York: Greenwillow Books.
Aylesworkth, J. (1995) *Old Black Fly*. New York: Henry Hold.
Berenstain, S. and Berenstain, J. (1971) *Berenstain's B Book (Bright and Early Books for Beginning Beginners)*. New York: Random House Books for Young Readers.
Boynton, S. (1997) *Snoozers*. New York: Little Simon.
Bridwell, N. (1985) *Clifford and the Grouchy Neighbors*. Logan, IA: Perfection Learning.
Bridwell, N. (2010) *Clifford the Big Red Dog*. New York: Cartwheel Books.
Carle, E. (1989) *The Very Busy Spider*. New York: Philomel Books.
Carle, E. (1996) *The Grouchy Ladybug*. New York: HarperCollins.
Carle, E. (2009) *The Very Hungry Caterpillar*. New York: Philomel Books.
Cousins, L. (1999) *Maisy's Colors*. Somerville, MA: Candlewick Press.
Ehlert, L. (1989) *Color Zoo*. New York: HarperCollins.
Gilman, P. (1993) *Something from Nothing*. New York: Scholastic Press.
Hill, E. (1994) *Spot Goes to a Party*. New York: Puffin Books.
Hill, E. (2003) *Spot Goes to the Farm*. New York: Puffin Books.
Hill, E. (2003) *Spot's Birthday Party*. New York: Puffin Books.
Hill, E. (2003) *Where's Spot*. New York: Puffin Books.
Marzollo, J. (1998) *Do You Know Now?* New York: Harper Festival.
McGrath, B.B. (1999) *Pepperidge Farm Goldfish Fun Book*. New York: Harper Festival.
McGrath, B.B. (2000) *Kellogg's Fruit Loops! Counting Fun Book*. New York: Harper Festival.
Pieńknoski, J. (1995) *Animals*. New York: Little Simon.
Potter, B. (2009) *The Tale of Benjamin Bunny*. Mankato: Child's World.
Prater, J. (1997) *Oh Where, Oh Where?* New York: Scholastic.
Rešček, S. (2006) *Hickory, Dickery Dock: And Other Favorite Nursery Rhymes*. Wilton: Tiger Tales.
Seeger, V. (2006) *Black? White? Day? Night? A Book of Opposites*. New York: Roaring Brook Press.
Dr. Seuss (1957) *The Cat in the Hat*. New York: Random House Books for Young Readers.
Dr. Seuss (1960) *Green Eggs and Ham*. New York: Random House Books for Young Readers.
Dr. Seuss (1954) *Horton Hears A Who*. New York: Random House Books for Young Readers.
Stanley, M. (1998) *Baby*. New York: Barron's Educational Series.
Taback, S. (1999) *Joseph had a Little Overcoat*. New York: Viking Children's Books.
Tucker, S. (1994) *Toot Toot*. New York: Little Simon.
Tucker, S. (1994) *Quack Quack*. New York: Little Simon.
Tucker, S. (1994) *Rat-A-Tat-Tat*. New York: Little Simon.
Tucker, S. (1994) *Yum Yum*. New York: Little Simon.
Wade, L. (1998) *The Cheerios Play Book*. New York: Simon & Schuster.

Index

Authors

Ada, A.F., 147, 156
Adams, M.J., 25, 29, 40, 42
Afflerbach, P., 85, 128
Aldridge, J., 7, 18
Alfassi, M., ,106, 128
Aliki, 172
Almeida, D.M., 134, 155
An, R., 79, 101
Anderson, J., 2, 16, 26, 34, 41, 45, 143, 156
Anderson, N.L., 102, 121, 128, 130
Anthony, J.L., 27, 41
Armon-Lotem, S., 170
Arther, L., 12, 20
Ash, G.E., 134, 155
Askov, E.N., 108, 129
Au, K.H., 90, 126
Aylesworkth, J., 172
Azuara, P., 64, 65, 83

Baker, L., 6, 17
Baker, S.A., 30, 43
Banai, K., 29, 43
Barker, S., 107, 128
Barnitz, J.G., 28, 42
Bar-Shalom, E.G., 9, 19
Barradas, O., 8,18
Barrat-Pugh, C., 11, 13, 20, 27, 43, 55, 62, 73, 86
Bartlett, L., 89, 126
Bassetti, B., 108, 129
Bates, E., 25, 41
Bean, T.W., 12, 20, 146, 156
Bear, D.R., 101, 128
Beck, I.L., 97, 101, 102, 103, 104, 127, 128
Beecher, B., 12, 20
Belsky, J., 31, 44
Benbow, C., 30, 43
Bennett, K.K 6, 17
Bentin, S. 27, 42
Berenstain, J., 172
Berenstain, S., 172
Bergin, C., 31, 44
Bergin, D., 31, 44
Berk, L.E., 131, 133, 154
Bermel, N., 4, 17

Bernas, R., 29, 43, 68, 84
Bettelheim, B., 71, 85
Beukelman, D.R., 170
Bialystok, E., 8, 18, 28, 42, 168, 169
Bird, E.K.-R, 170
Bishop, D.V.M., 171
Bissex, G.L, 99, 112, 127, 129
Black, J.K., 64, 83
Bodrova, E., 74, 86
Bourdieu, P., 11, 20
Boyton, S., 172
Bracken, S.S., 25, 41
Braxton, B., 68, 84
Brecht, R.D., 2, 16
Brice, A.E., 88, 100, 102, 126, 127, 128, 140, 155
Brice, R.G., 188, 100, 102, 126, 127, 128, 140, 155
Bridwell, N., 172
Broadhurst, D., 11, 20
Brooks-Gunn, J., 25, 40
Brown, A.L., 106, 128
Brown, H., 114, 115, 130
Bruner, J.S., 79, 87
Burchinal, M., 6, 18
Burrill, L.E., 57, 62
Bus, A.G., 31, 42
Butler, S., 6, 17
Byring, R., 171

Cambournes, B., 114, 115, 130
Campbell, J., 74, 86
Campbell, T.F., 25, 41
Carle, E., 103, 106, 127, 128, 172
Carrico, H., 102, 121, 128, 130
Caspi, T., 29, 43
Cazden, C., 9, 19, 37, 46
Chang, M.C. 28, 42
Chao, S., 2, 16
Chen, Y.G., 3, 16
Cheng, C.X., 28, 29, 42, 100, 127
Cheuk, D.K.L., 170
Chevalier, J.F., 12, 20, 35, 45
Cho, G., 2, 16
Cho, K.S, 2, 16
Choi, I., 144, 156

Subjects